Sacred Aia

Sacred Aid

Faith and Humanitarianism

MICHAEL BARNETT

JANICE GROSS STEIN

OXFORD
UNIVERSITY PRESS

OXFORD
UNIVERSITY PRESS

Oxford University Press, Inc., publishes works that further
Oxford University's objective of excellence
in research, scholarship, and education.

Oxford   New York
Auckland   Cape Town   Dar es Salaam   Hong Kong   Karachi
Kuala Lumpur   Madrid   Melbourne   Mexico City   Nairobi
New Delhi   Shanghai   Taipei   Toronto
With offices in
Argentina   Austria   Brazil   Chile   Czech Republic   France   Greece
Guatemala   Hungary   Italy   Japan   Poland   Portugal   Singapore
South Korea   Switzerland   Thailand   Turkey   Ukraine   Vietnam

Published by Oxford University Press, Inc.
198 Madison Avenue, New York, NY 10016

www.oup.com

Oxford is a registered trademark of Oxford University Press

Library of Congress Cataloging-in-Publication Data
Sacred aid : faith and humanitarianism / edited by Michael Barnett, Janice Stein.
p.   cm.
Includes bibliographical references (p.   ) and index.
ISBN 978-0-19-991602-3 (hardback : alk. paper) — ISBN 978-0-19-991609-2 (pbk. : alk. paper)
1. Humanitarian assistance. 2. Church work with disaster victims. I. Barnett,
Michael N., 1960– II. Stein, Janice Gross.
HV554.4.S23   2012
363.34'8—dc23   2011047127

1 3 5 7 9 8 6 4 2

Printed in the United States of America
on acid-free paper

Contents

Acknowledgments

THIS VOLUME WOULD not have been possible without the financial, intellectual, and emotional support of many, along with the occasional moment of divine intervention. First and foremost, we are indebted to the Luce Foundation. Several years ago they began funding professional schools of international affairs to undertake projects in the area of religion and world affairs, and we were among the early recipients. The very generous grant allowed us to explore the relationship of religion and humanitarianism in world affairs, but perhaps equally impressive was the intellectual support and encouragement we received from the Luce Foundation and its officers, notably Terry Lautz and Toby Volkman. It is rare to have been given the autonomy to try different ways to address an important issue, and we certainly needed it. We very much appreciate the trust they showed, and we hope that they look back without regret.

The Luce grant gave us the opportunity to run several events, most importantly for this volume a series of workshops in Cairo and Geneva. Our first meeting in Cairo in June 2008 brought together several of the contributors and included practitioners from many Cairo-based aid agencies (secular and religious alike). We thank the American University in Cairo, particularly the Center for Migration and Refugee Studies and the John D. Gerhart Center for Philanthropy and Civic Engagement, and Craig Calhoun for their financial and intellectual assistance. In October 2009, working with the Humanitarian Forum (London), the International Council of Voluntary Agencies (Geneva), and the Centre on Conflict, Peacebuilding and Democracy at the Graduate Institute of International Affairs and Development (Geneva), we brought together most of the contributors to this volume and more than twenty practitioners from faith-based agencies from around the world. For helping us organize and hold this event, we give special thanks to James Shaw-Hamilton, Dr. Hany El-Banna, Ed Schenkeberg, Sandra Reisman, Oliver Richmond, and Keith Krause. Importantly, most of the contributors to this volume had the opportunity to present short memos and get feedback on their observations from the ensuing discussions. Working from the reaction to their memos, the contributors met in Geneva in July 2010 and presented full drafts. In addition to benefiting from the comments of the other authors, we also were fortunate to get feedback from Timothy Shah, Raymond Duvall, Ruth Marshall, Antonio Donini, Kevin Hartigan, Gilles Carbonnier, Caroline Abu-Sadah, Annette Jansen, and Rosemary Hicks. Janice Gross Stein would like to thank the Munk School of Global Affairs for its support. Michael Barnett would like to thank the Humphrey School of Public Affairs, which oversaw the Luce grant and provided considerable institutional support (namely Keith Vargo, Leanne Mfalingundi, and Jeremy Gordon); Amir Stepak; and George Washington University.

We are fortunate to work with Oxford University Press. David McBride has been incredibly supportive, even in our darkest moments. Two anonymous reviewers provided critical but constructive feedback, for which we are quite grateful. Rachel McLeary also gave us a lot to think about. Lastly, we benefited from the opportunity to present our findings at several venues, among them the World Conference on Humanitarian Studies in 2011.

August 15, 2011
Michael Barnett,
Washington, D.C.
Janice Gross Stein
Toronto, Ontario

Sacred Aid

I

Introduction

THE SECULARIZATION AND SANCTIFICATION
OF HUMANITARIANISM

Michael Barnett and Janice Gross Stein

THE RELATIONSHIP BETWEEN the religious and secular worlds is an enduring global mystery. Several decades ago, many in the West thought the puzzle had been solved; they concluded that modern life is characterized by the ascendance of secularism at the expense of religion in public and private life. What forces were having this corrosive effect? The destruction of traditional society, urbanization, and new opportunities opened up by the modern world were encouraging people to abandon those beliefs that ceased to be functional for their current circumstances. Science, with its insistence on empirical evidence and naturalistic explanations, was dislodging the acceptability of religion's reliance on God's laws to explain the workings of the world. Modern notions of progress were leading people to find their just rewards in the here and now and not in the afterlife. The rise of liberalism and democracy was shifting authority toward people who recognized humanly made laws and away from clergy who revered heavenly decrees.[1] God might not be dead, as Nietzsche flamboyantly claimed, but she was no longer master of the universe.

Unfortunately for proponents of this secularization thesis, no one bothered to tell the religious.[2] Modernizing societies did not abandon their religion, as is evident in such diverse countries as India, Iran, and Israel. Many of the most popular and powerful political movements in the world had religious agendas, used religious imagery, and called for reintroducing religious law into public life. Domestic tensions and conflicts that once seemed to have a primarily ethnic, national, or tribal character now began to show the markings of religion.

Note: For this Introduction to the volume, in addition to the people identified in the Acknowledgments we also want to thank Elizabeth Ferris.

Perhaps most upsetting to the secularization thesis, the regions that were most confidently secular, prominently the West, showed signs of a religious revival. Americans, for instance, were not abandoning religion; rather, they were attending church in record numbers and reporting that religion was an increasingly important part of their lives. The setbacks to secularization also were evident in international politics. No sooner had the world healed from the wounds inflicted by the Cold War than new battle lines were imagined between contending civilizations, which were defined by competing religious traditions that had as much tolerance for each other as the Soviets and Americans had during the Cold War.[3] Ideological battles between capitalism and communism were now superseded by religious battles that pitted one sect against another; religiously based conflicts seemed bloodier, more enduring, and nastier. Although religion tended to make news when it was associated with violence, religious organizations convened intersectarian and interfaith dialogues, engaged in peacemaking, and put debt relief for deeply impoverished countries on the international agenda. Even the avowedly secular United Nations system, which defines authority according to state sovereignty and a secularized international community, began to recognize the importance of religion as it initiated projects on such issues as faith and development. In fact, one rather surprising UN reform proposal imagined a new "Spirituality Council" to exist alongside the Security Council and the position of chaplain for the UN General Assembly. Religion was making itself felt in every dimension of a world once imagined as solidly secular.[4]

Although students of humanitarianism never quite caught secularization fever, without too much contrivance a similar story of religion's rise, decline, and rise can be told within the history of humanitarianism. Religious discourses and organizations helped to establish humanitarianism in the early nineteenth century, and it is only a slight exaggeration to say "no religion, no humanitarianism." Over the course of the nineteenth century, however, many religious organizations began to downplay their interest in conversion in favor of improving the lives of the local peoples; they became less reliant on the "good book" and more reliant on the public health manual. By the early twentieth century, many religious organizations were beginning to work with secular agencies and use secularized international legal principles and international institutions to further their goals. Missionaries, for instance, were quite involved in the campaign to establish international human rights conventions during the interwar years. Then, after World War Two, Western governments became the chief funders of humanitarian action and increasingly favored secular agencies such as CARE. Once-avowedly religious organizations such as World Vision

International and Catholic Relief Services downplayed their religious identity. Much like the rest of the world, it seemed as if humanitarianism was succumbing to the pull and power of secularism. Religion might have been instrumental in the establishment of humanitarianism, but it passed the torch to secularism.

Yet this storyline, much like the secularization thesis itself, overlooks the enduring power and presence of religion. Just because religion increasingly shared the stage with secularism did not mean that religion was about to exit the stage; on the contrary, it remained very much front and center. In fact, religious-secular relations appeared to enter a new chapter in which religion was gaining in strength and influence within humanitarianism. Although the figures and trends should not be taken as hard evidence—what little we know tends to be limited to Christian agencies in the West—religious agencies entered a period of very healthy expansion. Between World War Two and the 1980s, while the size of the private voluntary sector grew significantly, nearly all of the growth was accounted for by secular agencies. Since the 1990s, though, a significant percentage of the growth is the result of a surge in faith-based action.[5] More impressively, the number of new agencies that are faith-based has risen dramatically over the last two decades. Not all denominations are growing at a similar rate; the Evangelical agencies dominate, accounting for almost 80 percent of all faith-based agencies at present and the bulk of the new population of faith-based agencies over the last three decades.[6] Further evidence comes from trend lines in global Christianity. Although religiously based transnational activism has changed over time, there is little record of a drop; instead, there have been occasional dips in an otherwise steady and upward climb.[7] American churches have increased their giving to overseas ministries by almost 50 percent over the past decade and, according to recent figures, gave nearly $3.7 billion; the Southern Baptist Convention spends nearly $300 million a year on international ministries, while spending by the Assemblies of God is almost $200 million annually.[8] According to Robert Wuthnow, the "number of full-time missionaries serving abroad has increased steadily over the same period and is significantly larger than a half century ago."[9] More than forty-two thousand U.S. citizens were working full-time as missionaries, an increase of 16 percent over the last decade and significantly over the high-water mark of the 1950s. The Assemblies of God support more than 2,500 missionaries. And perhaps most impressive, as many as 350,000 Americans have spent between two weeks and a year abroad serving as short-term mission volunteers, while an estimated one million have served for less than two weeks.[10]

What explains this spectacular growth? American Christians are more affluent than ever before, local communities that once were poverty-ridden

have now become middle-class, and more-affluent congregations can afford
to give more to foreign populations. Globalization has deepened their interest
in finding ways to engage worldwide. There are new lands of opportunity for
activism and missionary work. And the growing number of megachurches can
directly establish global ministries rather than work through intermediaries.[11]
Of course, not all of this overseas work can be categorized as humanitarian,
but it is likely that just as Christianity is globalizing, so too is Christian-based
humanitarianism.

Although it is difficult to know if there has been a comparable change in
the Islamic world, there is evidence that transnational aid is not only growing
but also becoming more institutionalized and formalized. Although modern
"humanitarianism" arose in early nineteenth-century Europe, there were
organized charitable societies in the Muslim world centuries before then,
though nearly all were immediately associated with religious institutions and
were not quasi-independent agencies.[12] Islamic Relief is probably the best
known of the new group of agencies, in part because it was established in
England. Created in 1984 in response to the humanitarian crises in Ethiopia
and the Sudan, Islamic Relief started from rather modest beginnings (and
very modest ambitions) and became a leading aid agency, perhaps the most
recognizable Islamic aid agency in the West. As of 2007, it operated with a
budget of approximately $109 million (a figure that does not include money
raised by local branches), with dozens of missions around the world. Explanations of growth in the Islamic aid sector mimic those in the Christian aid
sector, but with the added urgency that many of the world's disaster zones are,
in fact, located in Islamic societies.[13]

Although Christian and Islamic aid agencies probably account for the vast
majority of private religious giving, if only because these religions surpass others
in population and organizational reach, they certainly are not alone. Jewish
organizations such as Ahavta and the American Jewish World Service have
become increasingly active, closely associated with the growing popularity of
"tikkun olam," that is, a desire to use good acts to "repair the world" that, according to Jewish Kabbalah tradition, was shattered at the point of creation.[14] In this
volume, Erica Bornstein draws attention to Hindu giving. Although there are
relatively few Buddhist aid organizations, the Taiwanese-based Tzu Chi was
among the few international aid organizations allowed access to the earthquake
victims in China in 2009 and the Burmese flood victims in 2008.[15]

Another reason religious-based action is getting more attention is because
humanitarianism is undergoing its third wave of globalization. In the first
wave, Western aid agencies began spreading to the far corners of the world,

leading to new kinds of cross-cultural encounters. In the second wave, there was an explosion of agencies, largely coming from the West and frequently working in conflict zones in the global South, triggering an attempt by aid agencies to identify common standards and vocabularies. During this wave, secular agencies had a decided advantage in the race for funding because most major donor states and faith-based organizations were equally wary of each other. The third wave has been fueled by growth in both transnational religious activism and humanitarian agencies from outside the West. In the last two decades, a globalizing Christianity and Islam have created new kinds of networks and associations that are designed to deepen and extend their place in the world. At times, Christian and increasingly Islamic agencies work in countries in which the other religious community represents the majority population. And, during this period as well, both donor governments and faith-based agencies developed warmer relations, leading to a rise in official assistance headed to religious organizations.

Lastly, the humanitarian sector is also wondering what association, if any, exists between religion and violence. Religion and aid delivery can be a highly combustible mix. Most Western aid is now directed to societies in which the majority population or the single largest religious group is Muslim: Somalia, Bosnia and Herzegovina, Sudan, Palestine, Iraq, Afghanistan, Pakistan. Although most local populations are likely grateful for the assistance, humanitarian relief nevertheless arrives against the backdrop of a long history of mistrust between Christianity and Islam, caused in part by a legacy of Christian missionary work in Muslim societies, Western intervention, and episodes of acute violence that are conventionally interpreted as caused by religion.[16] Aid agencies often acknowledge that they want to save not only lives but societies, which means exposing local populations to human rights and other values associated with the West and Christianity.

Christian aid agencies are not the only ones growing in their reach. In response to emergencies and the desire to help their fellow Muslim in faraway lands, Arab and Islamic societies have been developing new institutions to deliver relief and address what they believe are the "root causes" of chronic poverty and despair. In the same way Muslim societies worry that Western powers are using aid agencies as a Trojan horse, Western governments worry that Muslim governments are using aid to radicalize societies. These concerns were already in place prior to September 11, 2001, but since then Islamic agencies have been under especially vigilant scrutiny.

Recognition that aid agencies coming from different religious and cultural traditions might have contrasting views on the purpose of aid and the principles that should guide its delivery, and that many aid agencies are treated as foot soldiers of broader cultural and rival communities, has led to several initiatives designed to promote greater mutual understanding and lower the chances of violence and conflict. Perhaps the best known are the Humanitarian Forum, currently run by the founder of Islamic Relief, Dr. Hany El-Banna, and the Islamic Charities Project (formerly the Montreux Initiative), launched by the Swiss government in 2005 to help remove unjustified obstacles from Islamic charities that can demonstrate their bona fides and accountability. The International Committee of the Red Cross, which outside of Europe is often seen as a religious agency, has led an effort to bring together international humanitarian law and Islamic law.[17] In part because there is growing animosity, in part because there is much at stake, and in part because many in the humanitarian sector hope to draw on the common human desire to relieve unnecessary suffering and forge a more hopeful and cosmopolitan future, there has been a surge of interest in cross-cultural dialogue and collaboration. We have no evidence of the impact of these initiatives, but the strong interest in their continuation suggests that the humanitarian community recognizes there is considerable need for interfaith understanding.

Much like the wider world, the secular and the religious in the world of humanitarianism are exhibiting the countervailing trends of creating and maintaining difference, building and barricading bridges, and emulating and rebelling against one another. This volume explores these contradictory and complementary tendencies through examination of the secularization and sanctification of humanitarianism. By secularization of humanitarianism we mean the process by which elements of the everyday and the profane insinuate themselves and become integrated into humanitarianism, thus challenging its sacred standing. Secularization is evident in the growing role of states and commercial enterprises, the centrality of fundraising, encroachment of earthly matters such as governance, processes of bureaucratization and professionalization, and the kinds of evidence that are required to demonstrate effectiveness. By sanctification of humanitarianism, we mean creation of the sacred, establishment and protection of a space that is viewed as pure and separate from the profane. Sanctification is evident in the insistence on a space free of politics, and in the calling of a humanitarian ethic that acts first and asks questions later, insists that motives must be innocent and altruistic, and guards against a world in which interests and instruments trump values and ethics. Secularization and sanctification are enduring aspects of humanitarianism, evolving in historically dynamic ways, shaping its trends, practices, and tensions.

This volume explores several aspects of the secularization and sanctification of humanitarianism. It examines their dynamic relationship and codification. One popular view is that they are linked at each other's expense, that is, an increase in sanctification means, by definition, a retreat of the secular, and vice versa. This version of the subtraction thesis—where an increasingly secular world diminishes the role of religion or the growing role of religion diminishes the secular—appeals intuitively because (despite scattered evidence) it seems easy to keep score. This subtraction thesis is evident in comparisons carried out by scholars of the resources and numbers of religious and secular agencies to determine whether religion is in retreat or growing.[18] Yet not all relationships are zero-sum, competitive, or gladiatorial. Another possibility is that sanctification processes can alter the character of the secular, and secularization processes can alter the character of the religious.

We can see how secularization and sanctification shape one another by treating each as multilayered, multidimensional, and nonlinear. Secularization proceeds in distinctive ways in public and private life and in changing forms and scope of authority relations; it creates functional differentiation in society and alters patterns of religious practice, belief, and worship, as it advances and retreats.[19] Sanctification is also multilayered, multidimensional, and nonlinear, and leaves its mark in many ways. Rather than reducing the religious or the secular to a single dimension, such as organizational identity, we are interested in the multiple and multilevel processes that are responsible for producing secularization and sanctification in different areas of humanitarian action. Secularization and sanctification processes are messy, involved in a constant process of trespassing and policing, and they are changing as they engage the "other."

Secularization and sanctification can be understood as process, strategy, and outcome. As indicated by the suffix, these are structural forces that are in motion, propelled and arrested by broader political, cultural, economic, and sociological trends. There is nothing natural about the religious or the secular worlds; they are social constructs and produced through human imagination and practice. This volume explores the structures and everyday acts of aid agencies and other actors that create, sustain, and dissolve these differences. In this way, it follows in the footsteps of much contemporary scholarship that is interested in the mutual constitution of the religious and the secular. But we also examine the strategic reasons agencies that are classified as either religious or secular might want to simultaneously associate with those in the other camp while also keeping their distance. Secularism is not just a process; it also is a strategy used by elites to advance their agendas and restrain the authority and power of religious actors. Sanctification too is not just a process but also a strategy that is used by actors to invest their activities with moral significance and generate autonomy from rival actors. We are less interested in secularization and sanctification as outcomes in large part because they tend to invite scorekeeping—who is up, who is down?—and more interested in their processes of mutual creation.

We treat both secularization and sanctification as rich with a multiplicity of meanings that are being constantly debated, fixed, and reimagined. It is widely accepted that religion and religious interpretation are constantly evolving, with the presumption that the meaning of religious practice and experience can change with the times and historical circumstances. We see these features in humanitarianism, particularly in the debate among the devout regarding what sort of charitable practices are desirable and allowed. Although no one would dispute that religion is a source of meaning, the possibility that secularism might also be a source is largely neglected and even dismissed.[20] Yet secularism can be a source of meaning, representing its own kind of faith. In other words, religious faith is one kind of faith, but it is not the only kind that exists. This observation is hardly controversial but, instead, overlaps with a fair bit of scholarship that has difficulty putting neat brackets around the religious and the secular and, furthermore, often finds the religious in what are frequently considered to be secular institutions. Although the chapters demonstrate several ways to approach the many meanings of faith, Émile Durkheim's legacy and the category of the sacred proved most attractive. For Durkheim, and for many of us in the volume, the sacred transcends what traditionally passes for the religious. Drawing on his work and our research in the humanitarian sector, we suggest that the sacred can have meanings with varying effects and consequences.

It is not easy to capture processes of secularization and sanctification. To begin, indicators for virtually every aspect are thin, at best. The humanitarian sector is data-poor, frustrating any attempt to talk about trends, patterns, and dynamics. The data that exist, moreover, offer only a limited view. For instance, a census of the humanitarian sector based on the number of religious and secular organizations can tell us about relative growth, but it is probably as myopic as is counting regular churchgoers for capturing religious revival or decline. Although we try to bring numbers to bear where we can, many of the chapters also present detailed political ethnographies, attempting to capture secularization and sanctification through interpretive methods, historically rich discourses, and institutional configurations.

The theme of secularization and sanctification offers a novel lens for examining humanitarianism—and the study of contemporary world politics. It encourages us to add to the subtraction thesis—to consider the kinds of relationships that exist between the religious and the secular. It warns against treating secularization and sanctification as unidimensional and emphasizes their varying dimensions, layerings, and run-offs. It joins with other scholars who insist on seeing secularization and sanctification not only as historical processes but also as strategies deployed by actors to further their agendas. And, perhaps most provocatively, it argues against the dominant line in international relations theory—that the only kind of faith is religious faith—as it posits a transcendental in the secular.

The rest of this introductory chapter is organized into three sections. Section one introduces the foundational concepts of humanitarianism, religion, the sacred, and secularism. Each is a highly contested concept; they are not just analytical categories but also categories of practice, concepts whose meaning changes depending on context and history, and concepts that are highly dependent on each other. It is impossible to propose a lexicon of these terms that will correspond to any particular historical moment. Instead of trying to settle what will be forever contested, we offer definitions that build on current scholarship and the understandings used by many in the humanitarian community. Section two explores various themes in the secularization and sanctification of humanitarianism. We begin by examining whether and how religion and secularism matter. After we suggest the possibility that the religious and the secular are distinct spheres, we immediately complicate our argument by acknowledging the blurriness of the boundaries and investigating the implications of this "gray" zone of secularization and sanctification.

Section One: Humanitarianism, the Religious, the Secular, and the Sacred

We have no idea whether there is more debate among aid workers regarding the definition of humanitarianism or theologians regarding the definition of religion, but we can report that both debates are quite spirited. We situate these concepts within their contemporary context, fully aware of how contingent are these understandings.

Humanitarianism

Many favor the International Committee of the Red Cross's definition of humanitarianism: impartial, independent, and neutral provision of life-saving relief in emergency settings. Others, however, find this too restrictive because it omits the multiple ways in which people attempt to relieve the suffering of others. In this view, humanitarianism is as old as human history, evident in religious, spiritual, and philosophical commitments that have inspired acts of compassion.[21] Others reject the ICRC's definition on the grounds that it is unnecessarily limited to life-saving relief and treats the symptoms rather than the underlying and long-term causes of suffering. In this view, humanitarianism includes not just medical relief but also human rights, development, public health and other kinds of social interventions. In general, humanitarianism, much like religion, can have an omnipresent quality.

However, if we decide to limit the history of humanitarianism to when individuals started using the concept to characterize their actions and those of others, then it is roughly two centuries old and includes both life-saving relief and attention to underlying causes of suffering. Specifically, around the turn of the nineteenth century humanitarianism slowly entered into everyday vocabulary. Although there is no bright line to clearly distinguish humanitarianism from previous and current forms of charity, compassion, and philanthropy, three characteristics arose in the early nineteenth century and have been present ever since that are marks of distinction.[22]

It slowly became associated with compassion across boundaries. In the beginning, humanitarianism included both international and domestic action; it could refer to abolitionists and to advocates for child labor reform. Precisely when and why the concept of humanitarianism became reserved for cross-border action is unclear, through the creation of the ICRC in 1863 as the world's first official international humanitarian organization probably was a tipping point. The association with compassion across boundaries is related to the assumption that humanitarianism goes beyond the call of duty. Who has duties to whom? People, organizations, and governments provide assistance every day, and most of the time we consider these kinds of actions as the fulfillment of obligations and do not describe their actions as "humanitarian." Parents give their children food, clothing, and shelter, and it would sound odd to describe such action as humanitarian. A police officer responding to a crime is not a Good Samaritan; she is doing her job. Villages often have a moral economy that materializes when famine, destitution, and hardship strike; members of the community are doing their duty. We expect citizens and the government to act when another part of the country is stricken by a natural disaster. It is only when such assistance crosses a boundary that we tend to call it humanitarian. What duties do we have to each other? It is impossible to identify them in advance precisely because they are formed in and around changing material forces and moral sentiments, and they can vary with the moral boundaries of the community. In general, we are mainly interested in acts of intervention that cross a border; but as Erica Bornstein chapter demonstrates, we have much to learn from activities of relief, charity, and philanthropy that stay close to home.

Humanitarianism's vow to help strangers in distant lands is related to a second defining characteristic: its transcendental significance. Although this is not a feature that is normally associated with humanitarianism, it figures so prominently in histories of humanitarianism, and certainly in this volume, that we feel justified in including it as a defining characteristic. By transcendental we mean, quite simply, the belief that there is something larger than us, and in this respect it has characteristics of the religious experience but should not be restricted to what is commonly understood as religion. For instance, Paras and Stein's chapter identifies how the notion of "humanitarian space" has a transcendental quality for both faith-based and secular humanitarian organizations.

Although humanitarianism has this other-worldly quality, it also is very much of this world. Humanitarianism is imprinted by modernity, the Enlightenment, and the belief that it is possible to engineer progress. In this way, humanitarianism is connected to governance; a stunning development of the last two centuries is the deepening and growing governance of humanitarianism. For much of human history, acts of compassion were a largely private affair, the domain of the privileged, the pious, and the philanthropic. When individuals were in need, because of their everyday circumstances or exigencies, they had to rely on the kindness of others. Beginning in the nineteenth century, and especially pronounced in the twentieth century, there was a growing zeal for creating institutions and other standing bodies, increasingly and self-consciously organized around principles of rationality that are the hallmark of the modern organization. Also, the humanitarian movements of the nineteenth century, including those that were devoutly religious, were nevertheless confident that modern scientific techniques and public interventions would improve the human condition. They imagined perfecting society, though, through markets and not with the heavy hand of the state. And, as Bornstein demonstrates in this volume, the British state extended this market ideology to colonial India. The nineteenth-century laissez-faire ideology slowly receded in the early twentieth century, as the state accepted more responsibilities for its citizens. Many of the same factors that led to expansion of the welfare state also contributed to growing willingness on the part of Western states to expand various kinds of aid and assistance to vulnerable populations. Since World War One, organization of humanitarian action has largely followed the tremendous internationalization, institutionalization, and rationalization of global affairs. In general, what distinguishes humanitarianism from previous acts of compassion is that it is organized and part of governance, connects the immanent to the transcendent, and is directed at those in other countries.

Religion

Religion is defined in multiple ways, but for our analysis of humanitarianism Peter Berger's definition works well. Religion is "establishment, through human activity, of an all-embracing sacred order, that is, of a sacred cosmos that will be capable of maintaining itself in the ever-present face of chaos."[23] Berger's definition has four implications that are critical to our discussion of religion and humanitarianism. By focusing on religion as an effect of human action, he emphasizes the human processes behind its creation as opposed to the supernatural processes of discovery and revelation. By omitting God from the definition, he allows the possibility that religion need not depend on a deity of any sort. By treating the sacred as a product of human activity that is intended to be set off from the rest of the world, he follows closely in the tradition established by Durkheim, whose definition of religion distinguished between the sacred and the profane. A critical difference between Berger and Durkheim, though, is that Berger emphasizes the function of the sacred in relationship to chaos. In this respect, religion is about the search for meaning, but a meaning that is intended to help humans avoid a sense of existential dread. Although religion can serve many functions, Berger's emphasis on the relationship between the sacred and chaos is particularly provocative given our interest in the relationship between religion and humanitarian action; these are responses to moments that suggest life is random and capricious, an attempt to make sense of unbearable suffering. Religion, according to Berger, helps humans escape the terror.[24] Humanitarianism serves a similar function.

The centrality of the sacred to the definition of religion derives from Durkheim's arguments in *The Elementary Forms of Religious Life*.[25] Durkheim is generally concerned with how shared social ideas, beliefs, and practices form the basis of society. In contrast to those scholars who claim that individual self-interest can be the glue for human connection and sense of community, Durkheim argued that societies, even liberal and market-driven societies that celebrate individualism, are bound together by common values and a shared culture. Here is where religion enters. For Durkheim, religion is "a unified system of beliefs and practices relative to sacred things, that is to say, things set apart and surrounded by prohibitions—beliefs and practices that unite its adherents in a single moral community called a church."[26]

Importantly for our purposes, Durkheim does not treat religion as dependent on a belief in God or any other transcendental deity. Instead, it depends on the existence of the categories of the sacred and the profane: "The distinctive character of religious beliefs and practices, in Durkheim's view, is that they form a shared socio-linguistic framework that divides the furniture of the universe into two mutually exclusive categories, the sacred and the profane." What is the sacred? Durkheim and others following in this tradition lean on a rather straightforward but powerful understanding: the sacred includes those things that are regarded as "superior in dignity and power to profane things."[27] Because the profane can be understood as the "everyday," the sacred exists outside of the everyday. The sacred, according to Peter Berger, is invested with a quality of "mysterious and awesome power, other than man and related to him." Humans have a tendency to construct orders that are beyond themselves, more powerful sources than "the historical efforts of human beings," but they remain nevertheless human creations even as they are invested with transcendental reverence.[28]

This transcendental quality may be attributed to natural or artificial objects, to animals, or to men—or to objectifications of human culture. There are sacred rocks, sacred tools, and sacred cows.[29] The Sabbath is sacred in the Abrahamic religions because it represents a day of the week unlike the other six; there are special rituals, habits, and practices that keep it sacred and separate from everything else.[30] As the example of the Sabbath suggests, the sacred can be understood as the realm of collective practices that help to maintain the moral community, in contrast to the profane, which consists of the "utilitarian activities of individuals pursuing self interest."[31] The profane need not be evil; it need be merely quotidian and everyday. Or, even more simply put, the profane is everything that "does not stick out." For Durkheim, then, human society and human beings exist in two realms: one that is moral and collective and another that is self-regarding and private. Religion and the sacred allow individuals to become more morally and community-minded than they otherwise might be.

Secularism

Thus far we have focused on religion in isolation from the secular. Many scholars of religion insist that separation of the two is impossible because religion and the secular developed in relationship to one another. Not surprisingly, there are many definitions of secularism. In fact, scholars do not speak of secularism but rather of secularisms.[32] What these definitions have in common, though, is the presumption that whereas once God and a sense of the divine infused self, society, and the state, now self, society, and the state no longer refer to God to make sense of themselves, to organize, to resolve conflict, to choose between alternatives, or to legitimate action.[33] Because most scholars are interested in the process of secularization, they tend to treat secularization as an uneven, unsteady, and unstable process, This has important implications: what counts as the religious and the secular in one historical context might be different in another; the religious and secular can coexist, mingle, and mutually constitute one another; we become immediately suspicious of the subtraction thesis, the idea that secularization comes at the cost of religion, perhaps best captured by Marx and Engels's famous aphorism: "All that is solid melts into air, all that is holy is profaned, and man is at least compelled to face with sober senses his real conditions of life and relations with his kind."[34] Many of the chapters in this volume, and particularly those by Bornstein and Taithe, demonstrate in interesting and significant ways how the religious and the secular spring from one another.

The Blurred Boundary Between Religion and Secularism

By adopting a definition of religion that does not pivot around God but instead leans heavily on the sacred, we blur the boundaries between the secular and the religious in the humanitarian world, and beyond.[35] In this respect, we are working within the more recent tradition in religious studies that concerns "family resemblances," directing scholars to identify a set of beliefs, commitments, and institutionalized practices that combine to produce an entity that can be defined as more or less religious.[36] Religions have various characteristics—an appeal to supernatural entities, conversion experiences, doctrines, rituals, understandings of the meaning of suffering, distinctions between the sacred and profane, and so on—but not all these characteristics need be present in order to count as a religion. This ecumenical solution to the essentially contested concept of religion has much to recommend it. It permits identification of the grays in a world otherwise defined in black and white. It invites comparison between organized beliefs that are conventionally defined as religious and those that are typically dismissed as having nothing to do with religion.[37]

Yet for those interested in labeling, coding, and precision, it leaves much to be desired. Ideally, we would identify a priori the necessary elements of religion. The sacred is clearly such a necessary condition, but what else? We also would want to know whether there is some threshold that must be crossed, a tipping point of sorts. On this possibility, Durkheim says: "When a certain number of sacred things sustain relations of coordination and subordination between them, forming a system that has a certain unity but does not enter into any other system of the same kind, this set of beliefs and corresponding rites constitutes a religion."[38] A "certain number"? Neither he nor anyone else has identified that magical number.

The difficulty of restricting religion to God is also evident when discussing religious experience. Drawing on the work of William James, John Dewey insisted that we not confuse religion with religious experience; people can develop a belief in the divine that does not depend on the existence of a God.[39] Religion, according to Dewey, constitutes a special body of beliefs and practices that recognizes there is an unseen higher power controlling human destiny and deserving obedience, reverence, and worship. Religion usually has some kind of institutional organization.[40] Religious experience, on the other hand, is when the "self is . . . directed toward something beyond itself and so its own unification depends upon the idea of shifting scenes of the world into that imaginative totality we call the Universe."[41] Individuals can have religious experiences without belonging to a religion or associating the experience with what typically passes for institutionalized religion.

This claim parallels the general observation that humans are engaged in a search for meaning. Although for Berger the urgency to find meaning is generated by a desire to avoid a sense of chaos, for others, including Charles Taylor, it is to find "something beyond or transcendent to their lives."[42] The search for meaning, understood in these terms, broadens the definition of religion beyond God. Processes associated with the Enlightenment, modernity, and secularization have led to considerable disenchantment, but humans nevertheless demonstrate a remarkable ability to discover enchantment in their daily lives and maintain faith in the divine. Dewey and Taylor are capturing the fundamental need of people to find meaning in their lives and to anchor that meaning in something bigger than themselves.[43]

There is, lastly, a fine line between the religious and the secular—because both have a sense of the sacred. Durkheim argued that secular beliefs can be "indistinguishable from religious beliefs proper." If the religious is constituted by the distinction between the sacred and the profane, then it is possible to imagine that aspects of what constitutes our secular world might, in fact, have a religious element. In his view, seemingly secular institutions such as civic republicanism have a religious dimension because they distinguish between the sacred and the profane; republicanism contains symbols, rituals, and practices that separate it from the everyday world of politics. Human rights, he suggested, allow individuals to become "the object of a sort of religion . . . a common faith." The process of individualization and secularization noted by so many of his contemporaries and subsequent students of modern society did not remove the individual from society. Instead, it potentially sanctified the individual and imbued individual rights with elements of religious belief. After all, Durkheim argued, "It possesses robust, sacred symbols and institutions that express collective sentiments; it reaffirms and protects itself by means of both positive and negative rites, for example, public celebrations of defenders of individual rights or the prosecution of those who would violate such rights."[44] Durkheim would not be surprised to find how the church of human rights has expanded over the last century. In general, we should not reduce the sacred to religion; instead, we should recognize the extent to which the sacred can exist within secularism itself.

Section Two: No Bright Lines or Heavenly Lights

We arrived at the theme of the secularization of religion and the sanctification of the secular in humanitarianism after a journey from a much more conventional beginning. We started with a rather simple, straightforward, neat, and utterly traditional question: What effect, if any, does religion have on humanitarianism? In many respects, our approach was heavily influenced by the conversation in the humanitarian community. Specifically, that community's distinction between religious (or faith-based) and secular agencies, and its current focus on various religious traditions of humanitarian action, imply that religious identity matters. We wanted to turn this assumption into a matter of empirical inquiry. If religious agencies differ from secular agencies, how? And why? How do Oxfam, the International Rescue Committee, and CARE differ from Catholic Relief Services, Islamic Relief, and World Vision International? For several years and through several workshops, we framed our inquiry in these terms and worked through some interesting possibilities.[45]

Perhaps religious organizations are more selective than secular agencies regarding whose suffering matters. Specifically, members of the faithful privilege their own: Christians tend to help Christians, Muslims tend to help Muslims, Jews tend to help Jews, and secular humanists help everyone. Yet each religious community had its own story. Although many Christian aid agencies tended to privilege their own—Catholic Relief Services started by helping Catholics, Lutheran Relief Services with Lutherans—over time even those with rather defined religious orientations broadened the communities they help. Some Christian aid workers and missionaries, for example, cited Christian

Gospel and the obligation to help all of God's children. But even those who preached nondiscrimination tended to use religious criteria to decide whose suffering mattered most. Christian missionaries sometimes decided to focus on those in need who seemed most ripe for conversion or who had not yet heard the gospel; the same Christian workers who insisted that their community was borderless were nevertheless still interested in expanding the community of believers and saw aid as a vehicle of conversion.

Islamic agencies generally tend not to venture outside the *umma*, the Islamic community, and like many of their Christian counterparts they treat charitable activities as a way to strengthen the self, the body and spirit of the sufferer, and the Islamic community.[46] Islamic agencies that acknowledge their preference for helping fellow Muslims will sometimes defend their decision on the grounds that Islamic societies are in great need and it is easier for them to gain access to Muslim populations. They assert as well that, in the current context, working in non-Islamic societies raises suspicion.[47] In short, because religions operate with variegated conceptions of community, religious organizations are likely to use different criteria to decide where to practice and who to help.

If religious agencies are selective, then secular agencies are impartial and are more likely to operate in a morally flat world. Liberal, humanistic beliefs, the argument goes, make it difficult to sustain, at least rhetorically, the claim that some lives are worth more than others; a humanistic tradition is more likely than religious beliefs to lead to principles of impartiality and nondiscrimination and to expand the boundaries of the community and level differences.[48] Richard Rorty argued that (liberal) education, wealth, and security led to broader definitions of the moral community that are related to the centrality of the autonomy and liberty of the individual; the moral community rests on helping even the weakest person, a person valued because of her humanity.[49]

If religious agencies are more likely to help their own, perhaps it is because they have an easier time gaining access to those populations that share their faith. Benthall argues in this volume that cultural proximity plays an important role in how local communities see and understand those who try to help them. Specifically, the more proximate the deliverer of relief is to the recipient, the more likely the recipient will welcome the deliverer and the less work and danger the deliverer can expect to encounter. Walker and his colleagues note in this volume how religious agencies believe they have an advantage over secular agencies precisely because the majority of recipients are religious. Bertrand Taithe suggests similarly in his chapter that religious organizations, because they are religious, will have an easier time than secular agencies communicating with local populations, regardless of their religious orientation, because the discourse of religion is more familiar to most populations than is the language of secular humanism. Yet, as Benthall and Taithe suggest, having a clearly defined religious identity might not always be an advantage. Instead, as many staff from secular agencies observe, being secular, and therefore nonsectarian, brings its own advantages. The softening agent is not their secular humanism, which is far too abstract for most communities in need to interpret, but rather their commitment to universal principles. These repeatedly affirmed principles make their claims to impartiality and neutrality more credible, and therefore local leaders and communities are more likely to accept and trust them.

Religion also might shape willingness to sacrifice and encourage greater stoicism. This is most likely in terms of patterns of giving. In their chapters, both Khan and Bornstein note how Islam and Hinduism, respectively, make charity an article of faith, and there are similar admonitions in other religions, including Christianity and Judaism. The devout are expected to give, and when they give they generally prefer to meet their religious commitments by giving to members of their faith. As Khan argues, Muslims tend to think that only Muslim aid agencies will understand and adhere to the specific rules governing the use of *zakat* funds. Conversely, the general expectation is that religious organizations are best able to draw contributions from their "own," relative to those who are members of another faith or who profess no formal religion whatsoever. Those driven by religious faith also might be more willing to endure hardship and personal sacrifice for a longer period of time. Taithe argues that missionaries are prepared to play the "long game," are more willing to live among the poor, and generally have a more enduring and deeper motivation. In fact, he hints that Catholic missionaries might not mind being martyrs. Walker and his colleagues note how religious commitment and spirituality can motivate and sustain aid workers. Nicholas Kristof, the *New York Times* columnist who has traveled the world bringing attention to silent suffering and neglected injustices, has remarked that the further he travels from the capital city, the greater is the likelihood the aid worker he meets will be from a religious organization.[50] Religious orders are often known for their lifelong commitment to the marginalized and vulnerable, believing that by serving the poor they are serving God. As Taithe puts it in this volume, "missionaries have always played the long game" and missions, whether by choice or circumstance, have been closer to the people than their modern, secular contemporaries.

Religious organizations are more likely to behave consistently with their principles. The devout are known for their uncompromising and unbending devotion to their religious beliefs. The most fiercely devout are "true believers." Can secular humanists also be true believers—in universality and the principles that flow from this belief? Some human rights activists can be as passionate and committed as missionaries, but generally secular humanists are seen as more flexible and far more comfortable with diversity. If religious agencies are indeed less likely to compromise, the reason might have less to do with ideological rigidity and more to do with fewer constraints. Many religious agencies have a built-in constituency that gives with few questions and conditions. For instance, Khan argues that many of Islamic Relief's donors feel it is their "obligation" to give and at various times of the year; therefore Islamic Relief serves as a vehicle for them to fulfill their religious obligations. Secular agencies, such as CARE, depend on governments that set conditions, demand results, and impose metrics. Secular agencies that are relatively free from financial constraints—Doctors Without Borders, for example—can be every bit as single-minded in their commitment to their foundational principles. Differences that are sometimes associated with religion, in other words, might be due to other factors.

Religious identity might shape the social purpose of humanitarian action and the kinds of activities organizations pursue. Missionaries placed considerable attention on education in part because of the belief that individuals needed to read the Bible if they were going to be saved. Muslim agencies might focus on refugee issues because Mohammed was a refugee.[51] Khan notes how Islamic Relief focuses on water because of the numerous references to water and cleanliness in Islamic teachings, but avoids HIV/AIDS because of a perceived association with homosexuality, which, according to some interpretations, is forbidden by Islam. Catholic Relief Services avoids being associated with family planning clinics that offer abortion services. Some religious organizations also see charitable activity as a precursor to conversion.

Perhaps religious belief shapes how religious agencies organize themselves internationally. Religious organizations are more likely to be decentralized than are secular organizations because they rely more on local religious institutions. If so, then, as Barnett argues in this volume, perhaps religious organizations are more accountable to local populations because they are firmly embedded in the local community. In a similar vein, Ferris suggests that religious agencies are more likely to be sensitive to participation in part because they have strong connections to the local populations through religious institutions.[52]

This deep engagement with the local community and responsiveness to its needs may be a result of missionary activity—an individual living for years in one place—or because activities are organized through a local, indigenous church. Religious organizations are less likely to have a traveling class of expatriate professionals who move from one "emergency" to another.

Last, but hardly least, religion, faith, and spirituality might also be important to survival and recovery. Peter Walker and his colleagues argue that there are grounds for exploring the relationship between religious commitment and postconflict recovery. They caution that there is little hard, empirical evidence from the field, but they have been persuaded to explore the possibility for two principal reasons. After years of work in disaster recovery and postconflict reconstruction, they now acknowledge that faith seems to be of profound importance, especially at these soul-crushing moments. Also, there is growing research from the medical community demonstrating, for instance, how various forms of spirituality seem to hasten postoperative recovery. There is a growing literature on the impact of religion on recovery in the related fields of development and postconflict justice.[53]

Beyond the Secular-Religious Divide

The conversations in the workshops were memorable not only because of the identification of plausible connections between religion and aspects of humanitarian action, but also because the "religious" and the "secular" were blending and blurring into each other.[54] We were, in retrospect, buckling under the weight of six limiting preconceptions. First, the religious and the secular are distinct. We did not necessarily subscribe to the version of the secularization thesis that suggested a linear and progressive path away from religion and toward the secular, but we did imagine that they existed in their own containers. Second, we approached the topic as if the secular were the benchmark and the religious were the "deviation" from the mean; our organizing question—What difference does religion make?—started with a secular baseline. Although we did not assign any normative significance, that is, assume that the secular was progressive and religion was regressive, a group of scholars operating at another historical period might have reversed the question and asked, What difference does the secular or the modern make? (In fact, this is how many in religious aid agencies pose the issue.) Third, asking whether religion (or secularism) makes a difference risks turning religion (or secularism) into a variable, thus neglecting religion's (and secularism's) impact in areas such as authority, legitimacy, belief, and justification.

Fourth, our assumption that religious and secular forces could be easily distinguished neglected the worldview of the most important arbiters of meaning: those who receive assistance. It is an article of faith of many aid agencies that recipient communities operate with binaries rather than with fine-grained distinctions in their view of foreign aid agencies; any Western aid agency is also a religious agency. Whether or not agencies explicitly adopt a secular or religious identity often matters little for how they are perceived, explained one MSF staff member as she described her agency's experiences in the field. The omnipresence of religion is apparent in several dimensions. Religion is part of humanitarianism's past and its origins. For many communities, their first encounter with Westerners was with missionaries bearing gifts, and, as Taithe observes in his chapter, aid workers continue to walk that same path and play a similar role. Moreover, secular agencies often work alongside religious agencies, a pattern of fraternal cooperation that can lead local populations to assume they are one and the same. Lastly, humanitarians frequently work in societies in which the religious and the secular are not institutionally or spiritually separated as they are in the West. The distinction has no meaning.

Fifth, we were finding that agencies of the same faith often differed more than faith agencies did from secular organizations. Catholic Relief Services looked a lot more like CARE than it did Samaritan's Purse. Islamic Relief looked more like Oxfam than like the Saudi Arabian-based International Islamic Relief Organization.[55]

And sixth, we relaxed our assumption that the only kind of faith is religious and began to see other kinds. In the humanitarian world, faith-based means religious and nonfaith implies secularism, but religion is not the only kind of faith. The categories of religious and secular obscure the presence of numerous kinds of faith within the humanitarian community. To put the matter bluntly (and following Leo Tolstoy's quip about families), all humanitarian organizations are faith-based—but they are faith-based in different ways. Faith can be generically understood as belief in the divine that does not depend on the existence of God. Liberal cosmopolitanism, particularly those versions that incorporate elements of transcendentalism, can also be understood as part of a faith tradition. Secular humanitarian agencies see themselves as dwelling in a moral universe that transcends the here and now, constituting a faith-based community. As Paras and Stein's chapter argues, the boundaries between secular and religious organizations are fuzzy, since humanitarian values embody the sacred for both.[56]

We consequently became more attentive to processes of boundary creation and boundary drawing, to spaces that were less like demilitarized zones and more like liminal zones. In short, we began to focus on the processes that create and erode the barriers between the secular and the sacred in humanitarianism.

Although secularization is a multidimensional and multifaceted concept, our observation is that humanitarian action is increasingly influenced by the profane, the everyday, and the belief that the world can be reduced to calculations. The growing involvement of nontraditional actors, especially states and commercial organizations, motivated by interests and profit—not care and compassion—introduces an impure element into humanitarianism. The constant need to fundraise and commodify suffering in order to keep the agency afloat financially can sully a humanitarian ethic that is otherwise pure.

Both Barnett and Taithe raise the possibility that secularizing trends can crowd out sacred principles. Organizations are increasingly rationalized, bureaucratized, and professionalized, that is, they are introducing modern secular, operating practices. Efficiency can become a calling, but one that intrudes on spirituality. Although much of the evidence of these developments comes from the world of Christian agencies, Islamic agencies are not immune.[57] The emphasis on means-and-ends calculations and efficiency meant that a more explicit consequentialist ethic displaced a sense of duty.

Religious agencies might be more concerned about these aspects of secularization than secular agencies because they represent a more direct and immediate challenge to their religious commitments. As Barnett suggests and Taithe argues in their chapters, the emphasis on efficiencies in processes and outcomes, the unrelenting need to calculate costs and benefits, the commodification of suffering, the rationalization and professionalization of staff all push the everyday into the humanitarian calling and displace the religious vocation and sense of obligation. There is a constant risk, as agencies compete for funding, that the profane will intrude more and more into the sacred and reduce the space for religious vocation.

But these concerns are not restricted to religious organizations; they are shared by many secular agencies. They too worry that the drive for efficiency, the emphasis on cost-benefit calculations, and the unrelenting focus on outcomes put at risk their sacred vocation and sense of obligation to help any and all who are suffering. They too worry that the professionalization of staff, the rationalization of services, and the constant need to raise funds can shrink the sacred, as the profane and everyday intrudes more and more into their work. For all their differences, secular and religious agencies also worry that the spirit of voluntarism is becoming a quaint and anachronistic value.

Secularization is not only a process but also a strategy. We see this most clearly in the discussion of Islamic Relief, an Islamic agency operating in a Christian world that feels itself a "moral suspect," particularly after September 11. Islamic Relief used secularization quite deliberately as a strategy to reassure

Western governments and donors. It professionalized its staff, opened its financial accounts, and made a major commitment to the transparency of processes and finances in order to ensure legitimacy in a world that was suspicious of Islamic agencies, to satisfy donors who wanted greater transparency, and to distinguish itself from smaller, lesser-known Islamic agencies.[58] There was tension between Islamic Relief's religious vocation and its deliberate embrace of secularization as a legitimating strategy; its leaders were constantly negotiating across these spaces and reshaping the boundaries between the sacred and the profane. Yet, as Khan argues in his chapter, Islamic Relief has developed the ability to speak in different languages to different audiences; it maintains a strong faith identity with accompanying discourse when doing fundraising among Muslim donors but adopts "faith lite" when speaking with Western institutional donors.

Sanctification of humanitarianism refers to those processes that create a sense of the sacred separate from the profane. Humanitarianism was once understood, without question, as part of the sacred. Humanitarianism operates with a number of binaries, but most prominent is the juxtaposition of ethics and politics. The everyday is consumed by politics and power, while the sacred is concerned with saving lives. The everyday is defined by self-interest, acquisition, means-ends calculations, instrumentality, and cost-benefit analysis, but humanitarianism refuses to put a price on life. Humanitarianism lives according to the principles of duty and obligation, not a consequentialist ethic. When people are starving or facing an emergency situation, to stop and ask questions about costs and benefits is not only profane, it is obscene. Unlike the modern world that feeds on structures of exchange, the humanitarian act does not assume norms of reciprocity. It stretches believability to insist that a British public giving help to the famine victims in Biafra imagines these victims might someday return the favor.

Humanitarianism is part of the sacred; so too is humanity. One of the fascinating developments of modern society is the shift of the sacred from God to the individual and the community. To some extent, this outcome was a consequence of anticlerical politics in revolutionary Europe; by shifting the sacred from God to humanity, reformists could reduce the authority and stature of the clerical class. Others championed this shift because it encouraged a more inclusive view of community. But the shift to humanity was not just a result of strategy and politics. It was also a consequence of broader Enlightenment factors that privileged reason over doctrine and human dignity over heavenly ambitions.[59]

Humanitarianism also has its sacred texts, rituals, and spaces. Henry Dunant's *Memory of Solferino* is given great reverence. The humanitarian community has also instantiated a growing number of rituals. There is a Humanitarian Day at the United Nations, commemorating those aid workers who have sacrificed themselves for others, held on August 13 to remember the bombing of the UN compound in Iraq in 2003. The ICRC has sponsored a walk from its headquarters in Geneva to the Italian town of Solferino, enacting the ritual of pilgrimage. And there are the sacred spaces of humanitarianism. In this volume, Paras and Stein write of humanitarian space as part of the sacred—or at least of the efforts of humanitarian actors to sanctify the space.[60] Within the humanitarian community, the ICRC is routinely referred to as the "high priests," a designation that simultaneously mocks a holier-than-thou attitude while also paying respect to venerated status. Humanitarianism is part of the sacred, separate from the everyday.

There is of necessity a constant imperative to sanctify humanitarian action, the attempt to elevate humanitarianism from the everyday. This process is especially evident among (though certainly not exclusive to) secular agencies. Why? Perhaps because within religious discourse, acts of charity and compassion are already defined as sacred. In secular agencies, no such obvious standing exists; it has to be built time and time again. It is the leaders of secular humanitarian organizations who speak repeatedly of the purity of the mission, of the justness of the cause, of the moral community, of the sacredness of the obligation to act, and—in Doctors Without Borders—of the requirement to witness, stand in solidarity, and speak for those who cannot speak, who have been deprived of their voice. This language self-evidently invokes the sacred to separate the moral obligation to humanity from the everyday responsibilities of life. Indeed, the fundamental obligation to relieve the suffering of distant strangers, an obligation shared by all secular humanitarian organizations, is at the core of the sanctity and inviolability of humanitarian space. There are layers of the sacred.

Parenthetically, this suggests that the success of both religion and secular organizations depends on how they are able to navigate the fraught terrain between the sacred and the profane; in this regard, Paras and Stein argue that religious organizations may be at an advantage. Taithe makes a similar point when he argues that the language of missionaries might appear to be more natural to recipients in much of the world than the language of secular humanists. Despite these processes of secularization and sanctification, humanitarianism still operates with the distinction between religious and secular agencies and exists in a world that distinguishes between the religious and the secular. The chapters suggest the importance of history, institutions, and strategy. Most fundamentally, the humanitarian sector is constituted by the modern world. A modern world that operates according to the distinctions between religious and secular organizations will imprint this distinction on the humanitarian world. In other words, the humanitarian sector did not invent these categories; they are an effect of the world in which it exists. Bornstein's chapter captures not only how broader social and cultural distinctions have had an impact on the charitable and relief sectors but also, outside the West, the importance of taking into account the impact of colonialism. In doing so, she points to the enduring role and power of the state.[61] And Taithe's examination of missionary organizations reminds us that there is a long, nearly uninterrupted history in which the secular and the sacred encroach on each other.

Secularization and sanctification are historical processes; they are also strategies used by actors to advance their agendas. There are benefits to promoting secularization just as there are benefits to promoting sanctification. Although the distinction between the secular and the religious is rooted in culture, history, and contingency, this volume is also attentive to how and why both religious and secular agencies work to maintain these boundaries. These agencies do on a smaller scale what secular states and religious institutions have done on a broader canvas for the last several hundred years. One strand of scholarship observes how (1) secular authorities and institutions created rules, discourses, and laws that placed limits on the authority of religious authorities, and (2) religious authorities had a vested interest in maintaining these limits because it helped ensure their autonomy in an otherwise secularizing world in which state authorities were gathering more and more power. For religious institutions, the modus operandi is "Render unto Caesar the things which are Caesar's, and unto God the things that are God's." The identity of many states rests on the guarantee of freedom of worship, religion, and belief. It is in part what they are and who they are. Religious and state authorities both have a vested interest in creating and maintaining separate spheres of authority.

Many of the chapters explain why religious and secular agencies would want to maintain these distinctions. The distinctions that are drawn and defended reflect fundamental interests. For religious institutions, maintaining the distinction between the religious and the secular allows them to operate in a sacred space that might otherwise be denied, while for secular agencies the designation as "secular" allows them to operate in public spaces that are denied to religious organizations. Maintaining this distinction can also be important for fundraising. Hopgood and Vinjamuri identify how religious and secular agencies compete against each other to retain or increase membership, income, and influence in a competitive organizational environment; part of their marketing strategy is to accentuate their religious or secular identity. Khan makes a similar point regarding Islamic Relief, and Taithe also recognizes the importance of competition for creating difference. For some agencies, religious identity is an effective marketing device and gives them access to a built-in constituency, while for secular agencies a nondenominational character can also be part of their appeal to donors. Religious and secular agencies, depending on the circumstances, also accentuate these distinctions in order to gain access to populations in need. For instance, in his chapter Khan notes how Islamic Relief is now considering how faith can be incorporated into program activities, to distinguish itself from (and perhaps gain an advantage over) secular peers and gain legitimacy and acceptance from those in the local community. By positioning themselves as religious or secular, humanitarian agencies help to recreate these distinctions.

Although we have focused on secularization and sanctification as structure, process, and strategy, we also noted that they refer to outcome. One last comment on this point. Secularization and sanctification relate to the competing predictions offered by Durkheim and Max Weber about what will happen to faith in a modernizing environment. Weber believed that a secularizing world would leave no room for a sense of awe, wonder, and the transcendent. It would lead to disenchantment. His argument, closely mirrored by the subtraction thesis, is that secularization includes rationalization; rationalization presumes that there are no forces that cannot, in theory, be understood through calculation and knowledge, and this mastery of the world leads to disenchantment. If humanitarianism is revered because it represents a sanctuary from the everyday world of a liberal, market-oriented world, then the intrusion of everyday practices of measurement, a language of results and outcomes, and a conversation about accountability all risk creating disenchantment within the humanitarian world. Durkheim treated secularization not as the death of enchantment but rather as the source for alternative understandings of enchantment: "Whereas Weber could see in that future [of modern society] only disenchantment and the iron cage of grim bureaucracy, Durkheim saw the possibility of the birth of new gods, that is, innovative, sacred avenues of human flourishing not yet realized."[62] Durkheim's insistence that modern society can create its own form of the sacred offers a sharply contrasting alternative to Weber's emphasis on the relationship between secularization and disenchantment.

Conclusion

Trying to make sense of the relationship between the religious and the secular in the humanitarian world is no easier than doing so in the wider world. Conceiving the multilayered and complex relationship between the two within humanitarianism is challenging because the two concepts define one another, constitute one another, bleed into one another through porous boundaries and shared preoccupation with the sacred and the profane, and push against one another, especially as humanitarian actors reproduce the differences, often for strategic reasons.

As the chapters repeatedly demonstrate, there is no facile way of tracing through the secular and the sacred in humanitarianism—and humanitarianism is very much emblematic of the broader world. Within the humanitarian world, we treat the secular and religious as historically contingent, and as uneven, unsteady, and unstable processes. What counts as the religious and the secular in one historical context might well be very different in another. Even more important, the religious and the secular coexist, mingle, and mutually constitute one another in a constant and evolving dialogue with a sense of the sacred. Indeed, what unites humanitarians, whether they are secular or religious, is their shared sense of the sacred in the work that they do, and the ongoing, difficult, challenging, and demanding dialogue with the profane as they enter into the everyday world to alleviate the pain of those who suffer.

Just as the religious and the secular operate in the plural, so too might the sacred. There are layers of the sacred. A fascinating feature of humanitarianism is that the religious and secular worlds both treat it as part of the sacred, though for different reasons. Here the meaning of the sacred differs for each one, opening up space for contestation of the sacred, for claims of legitimacy and illegitimacy, for charges of appropriation and misappropriation. This kind of fragmentation is common throughout the history of religious organizations and explains the tendency to separate in the name of purity, to divide in pursuit of the holy. Contemporary humanitarianism runs the same risk, and indeed we have seen repeatedly the breaking off of one organization from another. The boundaries between secularism and religion blur and sharpen, sharpen and blur as humanitarianism reconfigures itself again and again in its history. These developments are not recent history; they are part of history. Religious societies and charities, Taithe suggests, were sensitive to the impact of secularizing values such as efficiency and professionalization, worrying that it would chip away at their authority and erode their spiritual commitments. Taithe's attention to historical continuities creates the most explicit linkage between the past and the present and challenges us to put contemporary processes of secularization and sanctification in their historical context. As humanitarians reach out to alleviate the suffering of distant strangers in the early decades of the twenty-first century, the encounter with the religious and the secular takes on new forms and new meanings.

This volume is attentive to the countervailing and constituting trends of secularization and sanctification, and it steers clear of the alternative formulation: whether the secular or the religious has the advantage. Yet many of the chapters nevertheless suggest that if humanitarianism is to have any staying power, not only as a project but also as a saving force for the vulnerable, then succumbing to the excesses of secularization might have a fatal effect. Paras and Stein suggest that humanitarianism must retain a sense of the sacred if it is to operate. Many of the other chapters suggest that fundamental commitments of donors and staff rely on spiritual values. Taithe offers the historically informed prediction that "missionaries win" because they are ready to play the "long game," live among the people, learn the languages, and possibly even recognize the fullest range of needs. At stake, though, is not just which kinds of organizations have an easier time gaining access to those in need, but the very well-being of the recipients. As Walker and his colleagues write in this volume, "If humanitarian aid seeks to support 'life with dignity' and if the vast majority of crisis survivors hold spirituality to be a central component of existence, then we have to ask, Does the negation or assault on a person's spirituality affect their ability to survive in time of crisis? And equally, would supporting spirituality promote survival and recovery?" If there is one moral to this volume, it is: a humanitarianism that loses its sense of the sacred will be a humanitarianism that ceases to exist.

NOTES

1. For summaries of the secularization thesis, see Philip Gorski and Ates Altinordu, "After Secularization?" *Annual Review of Sociology* 14 (2008): 55–85; Warren Goldstein, "Secularization Patterns in the Old Paradigm," *Sociology of Religion* 70(2) (2009): 157–178; Robert Wuthnow, *Boundless Faith: The Global Outreach of American Churches* (Berkeley: University of California Press, 2009), 47–48; Craig Calhoun, Mark Juergensmeyer, and Jonathan Van Antwerpen, eds., *Rethinking Secularism* (New York: Oxford University Press, 2011); and Steve Bruce, *God Is Dead: Secularization in the West* (Boston: Blackwell, 2002).

2. There is a bourgeoning literature on the return of religion in world affairs. For good overviews, see Peter Berger, ed., *The Desecularization of the World: Resurgent Religion and World* Politics (Grand Rapids, MI: Eerdmans, 1999); Monica Duffy Toft, Daniel Philpott, and Timothy Samuel Shah, *God's Century: Resurgent Religion and Global Politics* (New York: Norton, 2011); John Micklethwait and Adrian Wooldridge, *God Is Back: How the Global Revival of Faith Is Changing the World* (New York: Penguin, 2009); Daniel Philpott, "Has the Study of Global Politics Found Religion?" *Annual Review of Political Science* 12 (2009): 183–202; Mark Juergensmeyer, *The New*

Cold War? Religious Nationalism Confronts the Secular State (Berkeley: University of California Press, 1993).

3. Arguably, scholars of international relations were most surprised by these events, in part because they had bought the secularization thesis hook, line, and sinker. For important exceptions, see Daniel Philpott, "The Challenge of September 11th to Secularism in International Relations," *World Politics* 55(1) (2002): 66–95; and "The Religious Roots of Modern International Relations," *World Politics* 52(2) (January 2000): 206–245; Fabio Petito and Pavlos Hatzopoulos, eds., *Religion in International Relations: The Return from Exile* (New York: Palgrave 2003); Scott Thomas, *The Global Resurgence of Religion and the Transformation of International Relations: The Struggle for the Soul of the Twenty-First Century* (New York: Palgrave, 2003); Ron Hassner, *War on Sacred Grounds* (Ithaca: Cornell University Press, 2009), chapter 1; Elizabeth Shenkman Hurd, *The Politics of Secularism in International Relations* (Princeton: Princeton University Press, 2007). For a good overview of the challenge for theorists of international relations (IR) and comparative politics, see Eva Bellin, "Faith in Politics: New Trends in the Study of Religion and Politics," *World Politics* 60(2) (January 2008): 315–347.

4. For statements on IR theory and religion, see John Carlson and Erik C. Owens, "Reconsidering Westphalia's Legacy for Religion and International Politics," in J. Carlson and E. Owens, eds., *The Sacred and the Sovereign: Religion and International Politics* (Washington DC: Georgetown University Press, 2003), 1–37; Scott Thomas, "The Global Resurgence of Religion and the Study of World Politics," *Millennium* 24(2) (1995): 289–299; Scott Thomas, "Religion and International Conflict," in K. Dark (ed.), *Religion and International Relations* (London: Macmillan, 2000), 1–23; Daniel Philpott, "The Religious Roots of Modern International Relations," *World Politics* 52(2) (2000): 206–245; and Jack Snyder, ed., *Religion and International Relations Theory* (New York: Columbia University Press, 2011).

5. Robert Barro and Rachel McLeary, "Private Voluntary Organizations Engaged in International Assistance, 1939–2004," *Nonprofit and Voluntary Quarterly* 37(3) (September 2008): 512–536.

6. Ibid. Also see the data in Rachel McLeary, *Global Compassion* (New York: Oxford University Press, 2009).

7. Barro and McLeary, "Private Voluntary Organizations."

8. Wuthnow, *Boundless Faith*, 6.

9. Ibid., 23.

10. Ibid.

11. Ibid., 1–9.

12. Mamoun Abuarqub and Isabel Phillips, *A Brief History of Humanitarianism in the Muslim World*, (Birmingham, UK: Islamic Relief, July 2009); Amy Singer, *Charity in Islamic Societies* (New York: Cambridge University Press, 2008); and Jon B. Benthall, "Islamic Charities, Faith Based Organizations, and the International System," in Jonathan Alterman and Karin Von Hippel (eds.), *Understanding*

Islamic Charities (Washington, DC: Center for Strategic and International Studies, 2007), 15–31.

13. Carlo Benedetti, "Islamic and Christian Inspired Relief NGOs: Between Tactical Collaboration and Strategic Diffidence?" *Journal of International Development* 18(6) (2006): 849–859; Jonathan Benthall, "The Red Cross and Red Crescent Movement and Islamic Societies, with Special Reference to Jordan," *British Journal of Middle Eastern Studies*, 24(2) (1997), 157–177; Murat Çizakça, *A History of Philanthropic Foundations: The Islamic World from the Seventh Century to the Present Day* (Istanbul: Bogazici University Press, 2000); Jonathan Benthall and Jerome Bellion-Jourdan, *The Charitable Crescent: Politics of Aid in the Muslim World* (London: Tauris, 2003); Bruno De Cordier, "Faith-Based Aid, Globalisation and the Humanitarian Frontline: An Analysis of Western-Based Muslim Aid Organisations," *Disasters*, 33(4) (October 2009), 608–628; Jon Alterman, S. Hunter, and A. L. Phillips, *The Idea and Practice of Philanthropy in the Muslim World*, Muslim World Series, no. PN-ADD-444, Bureau for Policy and Program Coordination, United States Agency for International Development (USAID, 2005); M. A. Mohamed Salih, "Islamic NGOs in Africa: The Promise and Peril of Islamic Voluntarism," in Alex de Waal (ed.), *Islamism and Its Enemies in the Horn of Africa* (London: Hurst, 2004), 146–181; Jon Alterman and Karin von Hippel (eds.), *Understanding Islamic Charities* (Washington, DC: CSIS, 2007).

14. Elliott Dorff, *The Way into Tikkun Olam: Repairing the World* (New York: Jewish Lights, 2007).

15. For a general survey, see Ruben Habito and Keishin Inaba, eds., *The Practice of Altruism: Caring and Religion in Global Perspective* (Newcastle Upon Tyme, UK: Cambridge Scholars, 2006).

16. Jon B. Benthall, "Humanitarianism and Islam After 11 September," in Joanna Macrae and Adele Harmer (eds.), *Humanitarian Action and the "Global War on Terror": A Review of Trends and Issues*, HPG Report 14, 2003 (London: Overseas Development Institute); James Shaw-Hamilton, "Recognizing the Umma in Humanitarianism," in Jonathan Alterman and Karin von Hippel (eds.), *Understanding Islamic Charities* (Washington, DC: Center for Strategic and International Studies, 2007), 15–31.

17. James Cockayne, "Islam and International Humanitarian Law: From a Clash to a Conversation Between Civilizations," *International Review of the Red Cross* 84(847) (2002): 597–626.

18. See, for instance, McLeary, *Global Compassion*.

19. Gorski and Altinordu, "After Secularization."

20. Craig Calhoun, "Rethinking Secularism," *Hedgehog Review* 12(3) (Fall 2010): 35–48; and Calhoun, Juergensmeyer, and Van Antwerpen, *Rethinking Secularism*.

21. For a review of the debate, see Michael Barnett and Tom Weiss, "Humanitarianism: A Short History of the Present," in M. Barnett and T. Weiss (eds.), *Humanitarianism in Question: Politics, Power, and Ethics* (Ithaca: Cornell University Press, 2008).

22. This section draws heavily from Michael Barnett, *Empire of Humanity: A History of Humanitarianism* (Ithaca: Cornell University Press, 2011), chapter 1.

23. Peter Berger, *The Sacred Canopy: A Sociological Theory of Religion* (New York: Anchor Books, 1990), 51. Durkheim's definition is the reference point for most other versions and visions of the "sacred." For a selective but instructive sampling, see W. Richard Comstock, "A Behavioral Approach to the Sacred: Category Formation in Religious Studies," *Journal of the American Academy of Religion* 49(4) (December 1981): 625–643; Roger Callois, *Man and the Sacred* (Urbana: University of Illinois Press, 2001); Mircea Eliade, *The Sacred and the Profane* (New York: Harcourt, Brace, 1959); Matthew Evans, "The Sacred: Differentiating, Clarifying, and Extending Concepts," *Review of Religious Research* 45(1) (2003): 32–47, 562–563; Howard Becker, "Sacred and Secular Societies: Considered with Reference to Folk-State and Similar Classifications," *Social Forces* 28(4) (1950): 361–376; N. J. Demerath, "The Varieties of Sacred Experience: Finding the Sacred in a Secular Grove," *Journal for the Scientific Study of Religion* 39(1) (2000): 1–11; William Gurdon Oxtoby, "Holy (the Sacred)," in Philip Weiner (ed.), *Dictionary of the History of Ideas: Studies of Selected Pivotal Ideas*, vol. II, 511–514 (New York: Scribner, 1973); Vytautas Kavolis, "Contemporary Moral Cultures and `The Return of the Sacred'," *Sociological Analysis* 49(3) (1988): 203–216; Jose Casanova, "The Politics of Religious Revival," *Telos* (Spring 1984): 3–33; Bryan Wilson, "The Return of the Sacred," *Journal for the Scientific Study of Religion* 18(1) (September 1979): 268–280; Daniel Bell, "The Return of the Sacred?" *British Journal of Sociology* 28(4) (1977); Harold Falding, "Secularization and the Sacred and Profane," *Sociological Quarterly*, 8(3) (Summer 1967): 349–364; and Peter Gordon, "The Place of the Sacred in the Absence of God: Charles Taylor's *A Secular Age*," *Journal of the History of Ideas*, 69(4) (October 2008): 647–673.

24. Berger, *The Sacred* Canopy, 26.

25. Émile Durkheim, *The Elementary Forms of Religious Life* (New York: Oxford, 2008).

26. Ibid., 49.

27. Ibid., 40.

28. Berger, *Sacred Canopy*, 25. There are, of course, other definitions of the sacred. See Ron Hassner, *War on Sacred Grounds* (Ithaca: Cornell University Press, 2009), who cites Mircea Eliade, *Patterns in Comparative Religion* (Lincoln, NE: Bison Books, 1996).

29. Berger, *Sacred Canopy*, 25.

30. However, Benthall reminds us that Jews and Christians have more rituals and rules that distinguish the Sabbath from other days of the week.

31. Mark Cladis, "Introduction" to Durkheim's *The Elementary Forms of Religious Life* (New York: Oxford University Press, 2008), xxii.

32. Lynn Cady and Elizabeth Shakman Hurd (eds.), *Comparative Secularisms in a Global Age* (New York: Palgrave, 2010).

33. As with religion, there is a rather large literature dedicated to staking out turf regarding the meaning of secularism. See Gorski and Altinordu, "After Secularization?"; Warren Goldstein: "Secularization Patterns in the Old Paradigm," *Sociology of Religion* 70(2) (2009): 157–178; Robert Wuthnow, *Boundless Faith: The Global Outreach of American Churches* (Berkeley: University of California Press, 2009), 47–48; Slavica Jakelic, "Secularism: A Bibliographic Essay," *Hedgehog Review* 12(3) (Fall 2010): 49–55; Calhoun, Juergensmeyer, and Van Antwerpen, *Rethinking Secularism*.

34. Charles Taylor, *Secular Age*; Karl Marx and Friedrich Engels, "Manifesto of the Communist Party," in Robert C. Tucker (ed.), *The Marx-Engels Reader*, 2nd edition (New York: Norton, 1978), 476.

35. Quite obviously, there are other approaches to the concept of the sacred that have their champions, including those by Talal Asad and Giorgio Agamben. Also see Carolyn Marvin and David Ingle, "Blood Sacrifice and the Nation: Revisiting Civil Religion," *Journal of the American Academy of Religion* 64(4) (Winter 1996): 767–780; Robert Wuthnow, "Beyond the Problems of Meaning," *Meaning and Moral Order* (Berkeley: University of California Press, 1989), chapter 2; and Gordon, "The Place of the Sacred in the Absence of God," 669–677. However, many of these scholars also insist that the sacred need not be limited to God and the divine but rather can be embedded in experiences that suggest transcendence.

36. For a recent and good example of this exercise, see Jonathan Benthall, *Returning to Religion: Why a Secular Age Is Haunted by Faith* (London: Tauris, 2008).

37. For a particularly insightful view, see the distinction between substantivist and functionalist definitions of religion offered by William Cavanaugh, *The Myth of Religious Violence* (New York: Oxford University Press, 2011).

38. *Elementary Forms of Religious Life*, 40.

39. There are a bevy of other concepts used to signify nonreligious faith, including spirituality and hope. For a similar analysis of the concept of hope, see Patrick Deneen, "The Politics of Hope and Optimism: Rorty, Havel, and the Democratic Faith of John Dewey," *Social Research* 66(2) (Summer 1999): 578–598; and Richard Rorty, "Hope and the Future," *Peace Review* 14(2) (2002): 154.

40. John Dewey, *A Common Faith* (New Haven: Yale University Press, 1934), 3, 9.

41. Dewey, *A Common Faith*, 19. The original sentence stated "self is always directed."

42. Charles Taylor, *A Secular Age* (Cambridge, MA: Harvard University Press, 2007).

43. Consistent with these claims, the Pew Foundation reports that a healthy percentage of the people it polled claimed to be atheist and yet believe in some form of the "divine." See http://religions.pewforum.org/reports. See also the very poignant statement by a self-identified atheist on Africa's need for God and evangelism: Matthew Parris, *Times of London*, December 27, 2008. Thanks to Timothy Shah for these points.

44. Cadis, "Introduction," xxviii.

45. For the conference report and the list of participants, see Michael Barnett, Denis Kennedy, Janice Stein, and Laura Thaut, "Religion and Humanitarianism: Floating

Boundaries in a Globalizing World," Centre on Conflict, Development, and Peace-building, Graduate Institute of International and Development Studies, Geneva. For another attempt to ask what is distinctive about religious aid agencies, see Elizabeth Ferris, "Faith and Humanitarianism: It's Complicated," *Journal of Refugee Studies* 24, 3 (2011): 606–625.

46. There seems to be little disagreement that Islamic agencies, empirically speaking, do not generally work in non-Islamic areas, although Islamic Relief, for example, helps everyone who comes to their doors in their clinics in Cairo. They do not ask whether families are Muslim or Coptic. Leaders of Islamic aid organizations explain that Islamic societies are in considerable need, that they have a comparative advantage in Islamic societies, and that non-Islamic societies tend to be hostile and suspicious toward Islamic agencies.

47. However, as Khan points out in his chapter, although this has been and remains largely true, Muslim aid agencies, particularly those with roots in the West, are increasingly working in non-Muslim environments—a development possibly owing to such factors as their perception that they are part of the (Western) international aid community and thus respond where there is need, along with their need to "prove" themselves and demonstrate they are ready to provide aid even when those suffering are not Muslims.

48. See Richard Shapcott, "Anti-cosmopolitanism, pluralism and the cosmopolitan harm principle," *Review of International Studies* 34 (2008): 185–205; and Andrew Linklater, "Towards a Sociology of Global Morals with 'Emancipatory Intent'," *Review of International Society* 33 (April 2007): 135–150.

49. Richard Rorty, "Who Are We? Moral Universalism and Economic Triage," *Diogenes* 173, (Spring 1996): 5–19; Richard Rorty, "Human Rights, Rationality, and Sentimentality," in *Truth and Progress: Philosophical Papers* (New York: Cambridge University Press, 1998), 167–185.

50. Nicolas Kristof and Sheryl WuDunn, *Half the Sky: Turning Oppression into Opportunity for Women Worldwide* (New York: Knopf, 2009), 141–142.

51. Ferris, "Faith and Humanitarianism," 7.

52. Ibid.

53. Toft, Shah, and Philpott, *God's Century*, chapter 7; Harvey Cox et al., "World Religions and Conflict Resolution," in Douglas Johnston and Cynthia Sampson (eds.), *Religion: The Missing Dimension of Statecraft* (Oxford: Oxford University Press, 1995), 266–282; R. Scott Appleby, "Religion and Conflict Transformation," in *The Ambivalence of the Sacred* (New York: Rowman & Littlefield, 2000), 207–244; David R. Smock, "Religion in World Affairs: Its Role in Conflict and Peace," *United States Institute of Peace Special Report* (February 2008); and Gerard Powers, "Religion and Peacebuilding, in D. Philpott and Gerard Powers, eds., *Strategies of Peace: Transforming Conflict in a Violent World* (New York: Oxford University Press, 2010), 317–352.

54. Our goal of attempting to find points of distinction between secular and religious humanitarianism was made deceptively easy, at first, because representatives from

faith and secular agencies project and maintain these distinctions. There is a literature, of course, that works through this process of classification, attempts to distinguish "faith-based organizations" from other kinds, and, like ourselves, discovers
that it is easier in theory than in practice. G. Clarke and M. Jennings, *Development,
Civil Society, and Faith-Based Organizations: Bridging the Sacred and the Secular*
(New York: Palgrave Macmillan, 2008).

55. See Ferris, "Faith and Humanitarianism," for a similar statement. On Islamic Relief
versus International Islamic Relief Organization, see Marie Juul Peterson, "Islamicizing
Aid: Transnational Muslim NGOs after 9.11," *Voluntas* (March 2011).

56. For a comparable conclusion, see Cecelia Lynch, "Religious Humanitarianism and
the Global Politics of Secularism," in C. Calhoun, M. Juergensmeyer, and J. Van
Antwerpen (eds.), *Rethinking Secularism* (Oxford University Press, 2011), 204–224.

57. Andre Wigger, "Encountering Perceptions in Parts of the Muslim World and Their
Impact on the ICRC's Ability to Be Effective," *International Review of the Red Cross*
87(858) (2005): 311–326. Cited from Ferris, "Faith and Humanitarianism."

58. Laura Thaut, Janice Gross Stein, and Michael Barnett, "In Defense of Virtue: Cred-
ibility, Legitimacy Dilemmas, and the Case of Islamic Relief," in Peter Gourevitch,
David Lake, and Janice Gross Stein (eds.), *The Credibility of Transnational NGOs:
When Virtue is not Enough* (Cambridge, UK: Cambridge University Press, 2012).

59. John Micklethwait and Adrian Wooldridge, *God Is Back: How the Global Revival of
Faith Is Changing the World* (New York: Penguin, 2009); Durkheim, *The Elemen-
tary Forms of Religious Life*; Giorgio Agamben, *Homo Sacer: Sovereign Power and
Bare Life* (Stanford: Stanford University Press, 1998); and Daniel Levy and Natan
Sznaider, "Sovereignty Transformed: A Sociology of Human Rights," *British Journal
of Sociology* 57(4) (2006): 657–676.

60. Roger Friedland and Richard Hecht, "The Politics of Sacred Space," in Jamie Scott
and Paul Simpson-Housley (eds.), *Sacred Places and Profane Spaces* (Westport,
CT: Greenwood Press, 1991), 21–61.

61. Rodney Stark, "Secularization RIP," *Sociology of Religion* 60 (1999): 249–273.

62. Cadis, "Introduction," xxxv.

2

Faith in Markets

Stephen Hopgood and Leslie Vinjamuri

WORLD VISION INTERNATIONAL'S annual income is approaching $3 billion, a far cry from the days when not-for-profits were run and staffed mainly by amateur volunteers who did what they could on small and precarious budgets. Along with a handful of other global relief and development organizations—Oxfam, Save the Children, Médicins Sans Frontières (MSF), Catholic Relief Services (CRS), CARE, Plan International, Samaritan's Purse, and the larger Red Cross members of the International Federation of Red Cross and Red Crescent Societies—WVI is at the apex of the $16 billion humanitarian food chain.[1] What is even more notable is that it has achieved this position of dominance within the strongly secular international relief and development world while being an avowedly Evangelical Christian organization. In what is an increasingly competitive market—and we will argue below it *is* a market—WVI has thrived because of, not despite, its religious credentials. Its field operations are in line with secular humanitarian norms, but it raises much of its cash and motivates its work and staff on a religious basis. This mix of secular practice and religious principle has been highly effective. It sells well, which suggests that WVI may be the business model of the future in the humanitarian marketplace.

Competition within this market shapes the strategies pursued by faith-based and secular humanitarian groups; the necessity of securing ever-larger amounts of public and private funds plays an integral role in decisions about humanitarian branding. To survive and thrive, these brands must be carefully calibrated to reflect internal—and especially external—identity claims. External incentives play a (even *the*) major role in the way humanitarians, whether faith-based or secular, present their identity publicly and privately. The two halves of this funding market, public and private, often create conflicting incentives for humanitarians. This is particularly true for many faith-based organizations (FBOs) that must be careful not to undermine their private religious identity when seeking public funds from secular donors. Their reward, for getting the balance right, is a market position superior potentially to that of their secular competitors; a resilient private donor pool, unique brand loyalty, and established religious infrastructure create significant opportunities for FBOs and can facilitate claims to effectiveness.

Our argument has three main elements: that the major Western public funders require humanitarians seeking public money to conduct themselves in a secular fashion operationally; that those who can manage this and also mobilize faith-based support have an edge in a world where religion is increasingly salient and religious giving is more dependable and plentiful than secular giving; and that, in effect, the major secular and religious organizations that dominate humanitarian funding increasingly form an oligopoly in the humanitarian field.[2] To survive in this oligopolistic market, medium and smaller sized INGOs (international nongovernmental organizations) and FBOs have two dominant strategies: alliance formation and specialization (of both products and services). Challenging the oligopoly is possible but massively expensive. The cost of establishing an organizational structure and a brand on a scale that can contend with existing competitors creates a barrier to entry that is virtually insurmountable for most new or smaller humanitarian organizations. Pursuing a balanced strategy in a market structure with these incentives is complex but crucial for smaller humanitarian organizations; a decision to secularize may be the ticket to accessing public funds, for example, but this may deter private donors who prefer to give to more strongly faith-branded humanitarians.

Consider the strategic choices faced by Islamic Relief (IR), a relatively new entrant to the humanitarian world and a non-Christian FBO. To access public funds, it must operate in a secular manner (e.g., not proselytize or discriminate in aid giving or hiring). IR has a motivated though (currently) narrow funding base, but this base is most likely stable since religiously motivated givers tend on average to be more loyal and more generous. If IR seeks to grow, it will need to secure public money or widen its appeal to large numbers of non-Muslims; growth, in other words, depends on maintaining a degree of secularization. But oversecularizing risks alienating more strongly religious supporters who may withdraw funding and instead shift their loyalty and financial support to a rival FBO with a stronger commitment to faith identity; if no such rival existed, we would expect new faith-driven humanitarians to capitalize on this market gap by forming one. IR therefore faces a dilemma: growth is necessary to maintain reliable access to sufficient funds and to gain systematic entry to international funding and crisis situations. Forming an alliance with an oligopoly member or a strategic partnership with another medium-sized organization allows IR to partially overcome this dilemma. Having a specialization (e.g., medical expertise) or a comparative advantage (in IR's case, being able to operate effectively in radicalized Islamic environments) is critical to such alliances. The oligopoly has a "space" for a globally active but effectively secular Islamic FBO. IR has a better chance of moving toward the top of the pyramid than do Christian competitors (the market is too crowded) or Jewish or Hindu ones (the private market may be too small).

We suggest that the best way to understand the behavior of INGOs and FBOs in the humanitarian world is as firms in a market.[3] Rather than maximizing profit, humanitarians raise revenue to fund relief and development operations. They strive to maximize income, minimize costs, increase brand awareness, protect reputation, hire the best staff at close to market rates, market and fundraise, innovate in products and services, and retain existing customers or attract new ones. Their "business" is humanitarian aid: they are delivery machines for this purpose, and over the last forty years they have professionalized and become more commercially astute in order to do this better. The key difference is that most if not all of those who support INGOs and FBOs are purchasing a "product" of which they are not the end user. Humanitarian managers must retain the commitment of these often vocal identity-driven supporters; doing this requires them to be successful both in managing their identity as humanitarians (branding) and in delivering services, since supporters want to identify with the organization as well as be confident in its success. The leading humanitarians market and raise funds on the basis of their unique identity, and they do this to retain a global profile (try to imagine a global crisis without the oligopolists out front).

To be successful in this, humanitarian leaders make certain calculations about their donors. How strongly do an organization's supporters hold to certain values, for example? An organization whose funding base is almost entirely Lutherans or Quakers or Jesuits must always assess how increasing its appeal to a wider audience will affect core membership. How malleable will these faith-driven supporters prove if humanitarians take on work in controversial areas (such as women's rights or population) where the norms of public donors conflict with those of individual members? Are private donors more likely to leave wordlessly and thereby undermine the organization's financial health, or will they stay and protest the change of direction? Some may simply suffer in silence, thereby depriving managers of vital feedback until it's too late.[4]

An FBO such as World Vision that is ecumenical, in terms of both supporters and board membership, and draws from a variety of faith denominations has greater flexibility, to be sure. But its individual members may be less loyal, opting to exit when humanitarian programs appear to contradict deeply held beliefs (especially if their "home" denomination provides an alternative avenue for activism). Maintaining the funding base via strong branding and product awareness becomes a constant concern in such an environment. One long-term danger is that marketing becomes an end in itself to meet organizational identity imperatives rather than a mechanism to fund operations.[5]

Modeling Faith

Our argument challenges previous studies that assume humanitarian practices and strategies are a product of identities endogenous to individuals and organizations.[6] We look primarily to the external environment to explain why humanitarian actors make the branding choices they do, and to account for organizational structure. Arguments that emphasize the role of individual or group identity in shaping organizational practice cannot easily explain the organization of the contemporary humanitarian space or why it has changed over the past two decades.

Much like commercial firms, humanitarian organizations compete to attract donors by adopting, adapting, and projecting identities not simply as a *reflection* of who they are but as a *mechanism* for consolidating and mobilizing members and donations, securing public finance, and gaining access to communities in need. This competition among humanitarians has intensified over time as individual and public donors face proliferating choices about the organizations to which they can donate.[7]

Some scholars have stressed the perverse incentives that competitive pressures engender. Alex Cooley and James Ron argue that these pressures challenge the purity of humanitarianism by causing humanitarians to mute their critique when faced with challenging moral dilemmas.[8] Our work highlights a different aspect of this competition: the tendency of humanitarians to manipulate identity through branding in order to enhance their access to donors and markets. This competition may also have a positive effect: increased (positive) identification between donors and humanitarians may enhance revenue overall as consumers are drawn in by a "product" that closely matches their preference. But it also intensifies competition among humanitarian organizations since survival and growth depend on raising their *own* money. Global organization of the humanitarian space has reproduced a classic dilemma: the tension between the public good and the interests of individual humanitarian organizations means significant energy is diverted into activities designed primarily to maximize market share rather than secure humanitarian gain.

We differentiate between individual and organizational identity. For many, or even most, individual supporters of FBOs and INGOs, identity may be an essential quality that shapes their beliefs and behavior. *Organizational identity*, however, is the product of a more complex set of corporate choices. Organizational leaders must adapt their identity in response to the external incentives they face, as much as to their membership's beliefs. Some U.S. Evangelicals, for example, believe newer members are increasingly liberal and more interested in social service than salvation.[9] This "endogenous" (internal) change alters the scope for FBO leaders to form alliances with other humanitarians, pursue work in controversial areas, diversify fundraising sources, and so on. But what to make of such an internal change is a strategic choice that takes place in the context of external incentives driven by the competition among humanitarians to attract donors. Organizations use their brand (captured in logos, slogans, promotional material campaigns, etc.) to signal, especially to donors and recipients, who they are and why they should be supported. Where managers do not share the identity of the organization's members, the incentive to enhance flexibility will be especially strong if it allows managers to pursue high-growth strategies by accessing new donors and funding sources. Within the organization this can lead to tension with operational staff, however, whose concern is service delivery rather than global branding.

Humanitarian managers may try to restructure their organizations to enhance their flexibility. A franchising model, for example, gives them more control over the global brand. This enables them to adopt a single global message and enhance central capacity while allowing local offices to pursue context-sensitive strategies that maximize their fundraising capacity in local markets. Managers must weigh this against the risk that local franchises may become "rogues" who do damage to the central brand. World Vision has adopted a franchising model; it looks more Evangelical in some places and more secular in others. By contrast, Save the Children and Oxfam are heading in the other direction, toward a more integrated and centralized global brand. The choice of organizational structure—whether to partner locally and co-brand, to franchise under a local brand, or to replicate mini "Save the Children" sections—is a key strategic choice. The "one brand" model may maximize global identity, but it does so at the cost of local initiative and adaptability.

For humanitarians who lack the capacity to adopt a variable branding strategy or to form alliances, vertical investment in a fixed number of geographies and sectors is more attractive. Branding will also be more narrowly defined to fit with the needs and identities that are dominant in local markets. So, for example, small to medium-sized humanitarian FBOs in Islamic states may have little incentive to moderate their faith. Their comparative advantage is proximity and depth. Vertical investment is also essential where barriers to entry and exit are high. The success of Catholic Relief Services, for example, lies in part in its capacity, especially in areas that are hard to access, to link up with small enclaves of priests and nuns whose legitimacy is based on decades of community service. This strategy—which depends on the flexibility of its "Catholic" identity—facilitates both global branding and vertical investment, a tough combination to make effective. INGOs are more constrained because they lack similar local roots; maintaining a local *and* global presence with identical branding is much more difficult. In our model, large secular humanitarian organizations with a high level of organizational capacity, but minimal identity markers, will tend toward global operations, and, to maintain their control over the humanitarian market, the largest INGOs will seek to dominate this market and also control the rules by which it is governed, thereby consolidating the oligopoly into an oligarchy.

The New Humanitarian Space

Since the post-Biafra 1970s, humanitarianism has been both globalized and marketized to produce a humanitarian world characterized by professionalization, bureaucratization, and commercialization.[10] In the past decade, the secular norms that underwrote this world have been challenged by the rise of a competing set of norms, practices, and players inspired and even defined by faith.

Before 2001, getting Western government, UN, and EU funding meant abiding by global secular norms. Discrimination and proselytizing in aid delivery contravene the principle of impartiality, the core ethical principle for the relief and development professionals who dominate access to the field. As a result, religion or "faith" has been absent in most professional development practice and still raises hackles among international activists and civil servants who fear the core rationale for humanitarian relief and development work is being undermined.[11] Some EU aid officials have traditionally seen proselytizing as worse than corruption. But things have changed. As Cassandra Balchin neatly summarizes:

> If you want to get ahead in international development policy today, you've got to use the F-word: *faith-based.*[12]

The increased salience of faith has at least three explanations. First, there is tremendous growth in the number of Christians and Muslims worldwide. A recent Pew Forum poll reports that nine out of ten Africans, for example, consider themselves to be Christians or Muslims, a massive increase in the last hundred years and all at the expense of traditional African religion.[13] In Latin America and Asia, there has been a substantial increase in the number of Evangelicals and Pentecostalists; even in China Evangelical-style Christianity is reported to be rising fast. The Catholic Church remains strong in Africa and is responsible for a remarkably high percentage of social service, health, and education provision south of the Sahara. Indeed, the World Health Organization reports that FBOs are responsible for 40 percent of all health services offered in sub-Saharan Africa.[14] Protestant missionaries are still present in large numbers in many parts of Africa.[15] These developments have various implications. For example they give a potential edge to FBOs that make more of their faith in contexts where a strict secular-religious distinction makes little sense.

Second, policies pursued by U.S. Presidents Bill Clinton and George W. Bush increased the salience, and especially the prevalence, of faith in humanitarianism. Federal government and private funding is the largest source of revenue in the humanitarian market (well over 50 percent), and the United States is home to some of the best-funded and most influential Christian (especially Protestant) churches in the world. In 1996, President Clinton signed legislation on "Charitable Choice," a bill advanced by Senator John Ashcroft, a member of the Assemblies of God Evangelical church (and the attorney general on September 11, 2001). This legislation made it easier for FBOs to bid for U.S. government contracts without suppressing their religious character, obviating the need for them to establish a separate nonreligious nonprofit to offer social services.[16] This was followed by the International Religious Freedom Act of 1998, which made promoting religious freedom a goal of U.S. foreign policy, with the State Department monitoring religious freedom and persecution through an annual report.[17] This opening of religious markets overseas particularly helps large, well-resourced religious organizations, among which Christian congregations are prominent, especially when allied to the growth in Evangelical belief in the global South that guarantees a sympathetic audience.[18]

This shift was accelerated in 2001 by George W. Bush's creation of an Office of Faith-Based and Community Initiatives, explicitly designed to enable more government contracts to be awarded to FBOs (including to churches themselves) that were "pervasively sectarian," provided there was a distinction between where and when service delivery and evangelism took place.[19] In 2002, this office created centers in several government departments, notably USAID, to make sure FBOs were not being disadvantaged. This allowed church groups to use religious structures and have religious symbols on display where U.S. aid was being distributed.[20] It also protected their ability to hire only staff who shared their faith. President Bush also doubled U.S. foreign aid dollars going to FBOs. And DFID, the UK foreign aid department, recently announced it would double the share of its aid funding going through FBOs.

International organizations appear to have followed a similar trend; the World Health Organization has shown an active interest in bringing FBOs into the process of thinking about development.[21] The United Nations Population Fund (UNFPA) has also placed greater emphasis on the need to understand and partner with local faith-based organizations. UNFPA's executive director, Thoraya Ahmed Obaid, talked in August 2009 of the "profound moral authority that religious leaders have, and we are all aware of the fact that religious organizations are the oldest social service providers humankind has known."[22] There has been greater resistance to initiatives designed to integrate faith and faith-based actors, though, within the World Bank, where economists shape development strategies and the commitment to secular norms and principles is especially strong.

Finally, the international politics of the Global War on Terror politicized religious observance and faith identity. In many parts of the world, but particularly in areas where Muslim communities were the targets of U.S. and Western policies designed to "combat radicalism," as in Pakistan, Sudan, and Afghanistan, it became increasingly difficult for secular and in some places Christian humanitarian INGOs to undertake their work. The Taliban sought to drive many international NGOs out of Afghanistan, for example, opening a "local market" for Islamic FBOs. Responses to the tsunami in Indonesia showed similar dynamics.[23]

These three shifts created a humanitarian sphere that, by 2011, was marked by two central facts: an oligopoly of major global providers and increased salience on the part of religion. Together these features have created opportunities for FBOs to access public donor capital and meet local demand for a humanitarianism that is defined by faith.

Public Donors in the Humanitarian Market

By controlling resources, defining access requirements, and monitoring ongoing operations, the United Nations, the European Union, and other multilateral agencies exert a dramatic effect on the organizational structures and branding choices that humanitarians make. The extent to which public donors control humanitarian resources is especially crucial to their ability to shape the humanitarian market. Many humanitarian organizations are dependent on public donors. The size of their global operations would be unsustainable without this funding. World Vision USA, Catholic Relief Services, CARE, and Save the Children USA all rely on substantial sums of USAID money, for example. This diversification (to draw on public, not only private funding) is strategically wise, but it also makes these humanitarian organizations susceptible to fluctuations in public support and dependent on this financing in order to safeguard against a major contraction in their operations. Humanitarian presence at those crises garnering the support of public donors is thus an essential profile-raising activity. By shaping who is present and who is not at these crucial moments, states and multilateral agencies have the power to grant and deny access and legitimacy.

Because resource dependence potentially undermines the independence of humanitarians, most organizations maintain controls on the total percentage of funding they get through public avenues (CRS and CARE take the majority of their income from government sources). Despite this crucial limitation, major Western INGOs have no choice but to take public funds to retain size and access. For those that do refuse, globalization across national contexts creates new pressures to alter this decision. Oxfam America, for example, refuses U.S. government funds on principle, but this also creates a marketing niche that adds political weight to its antipoverty campaigns. The construction of a more integrated and global Oxfam may undermine this choice since other Oxfam sections depend on public money for their operations and it is hard to sustain a global brand without full insider status.

Public donors fail to exert the same pressure on faith-based humanitarians primarily because these FBOs have a more reliable long-term source of private funding. So much so, in fact, that many religious organizations do not apply for government or UN money, choosing instead to guard their autonomy and avoid costly overheads. Access to loyal private membership income makes this possible.[24] Evangelical FBOs especially have maximized their financial autonomy by engaging in relief work where barriers to entry are lower and the need to engage with governments and their complex agendas more limited.

Voluntary cash from members is also more readily available to FBOs for relief work than for longer-term development work since the latter raises trickier issues of conversion and doctrine.[25]

What happens when the conditions imposed for public funding are potentially at odds with the private market? Much secular unhappiness attended the relaxation under President Bush of rules on religious service providers, but faith-based providers are equally committed to safeguarding their identity. President Obama's commitment to ameliorating discriminatory hiring practices provoked a definite reaction. World Vision USA President Richard Stearns argued, "If forced to choose between preserving our faith values or receiving government funds, we would have to walk away from the funding."[26] One way to view this bold statement—putting at risk 28 percent of World Vision USA's 2009 income ($344 million in cash and food)—is as a signal to the Evangelical base of World Vision: our faith is not for sale. World Vision is the ideal-typical example of a secularized FBO. It needs to hold market share against more radical, less secularized FBOs (as well as INGOs). Unlike more radical FBOs, World Vision defends its hiring practices on the basis of the Civil Rights Act of 1964. The organization does not proselytize and serves all, regardless of their faith. And about 17 percent of its employees worldwide are not Christian. But all its U.S. employees are. They sign a statement of faith and abide by a code of conduct that adheres to biblical standards. Extramarital sex and active same-sex relations, for instance, could be grounds for dismissal. Employees gather for weekly chapel to worship and hear Christian speakers and musicians.[27] Nevertheless, its strategy creates room to maneuver against denominational churches such as the Southern Baptist Convention or Rick Warren's Saddleback Church that are raising funds to send missionaries directly into the field.

Religious pressure on "centrist" FBOs is more than theoretical. The website MinistryWatch.com monitors and rates FBOs for the seriousness of their Christian commitment and issues "donor alerts" if they suspect an FBO lacks real commitment (as evidenced by its mission statement and membership in Evangelical organizations). This monitoring of language is an important mechanism by which the depth of faith of FBO brands can be policed; the more definitive the statement, the less room for maneuver, and vice versa.[28] In 2004 MinistryWatch.com issued an alert about the Christian Children's Fund (CCF), alleging it was insufficiently Christian; by 2009 the CCF had dropped the "Christian" and become ChildFund International, simultaneously opening itself up to new, nonfaith-based funding while cutting itself off from the marketing advantages of wider religious branding.[29] MinistryWatch.com reports that, according to the Internal Revenue Service, World Vision is classified as a "church," which would exempt it from the degree of financial transparency it nevertheless insists on demonstrating (even though many churches make use of this reporting leniency). But World Vision's access to *public* funds depends on its greater transparency. MinistryWatch.com also questions whether World Vision has lost its way since the 1980s, when disseminating and preaching the gospel was central to its articles of incorporation. As MinistryWatch.com puts it:

> In part because of its funding from the U.S. Agency for International Development, which forbids the use of government money for proselytizing, World Vision has emphasized its development and humanitarian components over its Evangelical perspective. Although its board of directors is generally Evangelical, many of its contributors are not. World Vision has at times promoted itself as a non-sectarian, humanitarian organization and has downplayed Evangelical components.[30]

The difficulty of the line World Vision walks is clear. Far less reliant on public money than CRS, it always faces the temptation, as Richard Stearns suggests, to rely exclusively on private money. But even if straddling the faith-secular borderline was once an identity-driven decision, it is now a strategy that World Vision is locked into in order to maintain its market share. Would Richard Stearns really walk away from $344 million of U.S. government money because taking it would entail nondiscrimination in hiring practices? Moreover, the vast size and complexity of an organization such as World Vision means that some segments of the professional staff may favor one strategy (e.g., to chase secular humanitarian funds) while another might prefer something different (to move closer to proselytizing). Many local, franchised sections may well proselytize anyway without WVI's central administration being able to effectively prevent them from doing so.

Public funders also shape the humanitarian market by defining access requirements. The terms of legitimacy are set by the UN, the (ambiguously positioned) ICRC, and governments (with some INGO/FBO input). Most important of all is that delivery of relief and development must be nondiscriminatory; *need* is the only legitimate way to choose who is helped and helped first. Proselytizing is explicitly defined as illegitimate. Apart from any direct contractual requirements, various codes of conduct that regulate humanitarian organizations bar proselytizing. The most prominent is the Code of Conduct of the International Red Cross and Red Crescent Movement and NGOs in Disaster Relief, agreed to in the mid-1990s and post-Rwanda. Both INGOs and FBOs drew up this code (including Caritas Internationalis, CRS, Oxfam, Save the Children, and the Lutheran World Federation). Its first three articles are explicit restrictions on discrimination in aid giving and on proselytizing.

The nondiscrimination norm makes the global *public* funding regime essentially secular. Any FBO that seeks to receive UN or government money does so on the basis of the service it provides, not its identity. If public funders judge aid recipients to fall too far to one side of the secular-faith line, they will be excluded. Religious organizations are often reluctant to apply for extensive public funding for this reason. And yet, despite domestic U.S. court cases about proselytizing, the Salvation Army, for example, is providing international relief services. It has received USAID money and was designated a "lead agency" by the UN in the efforts to feed and shelter Haiti's (2010) earthquake survivors.

Most major FBOs are at pains to stress that they are in relief and development work because of their service credentials rather than their faith-identity. FBOs such as World Vision, CRS, and Samaritan's Purse, three of the biggest recipients of USAID money to help with earthquake relief in Haiti, for example, have continually stressed their humanitarian best practices. Any suggestion that FBOs should receive public funds because of their faith status is strongly rejected. According to Ken Isaacs, vice president of Samaritan's Purse:

> It has taken our organization 16 years of building our capacity, honing our skills, and becoming more professional to develop the relationships we have with USAID and other grant-giving entities. We're building latrines and providing clean water. We're not out there with bullhorns trying to win converts.[31]

FBOs are clearly better placed to receive public funds now that the secular-faith line is more blurred. An obvious example of this in action is visible through the importance of religious groups in operations funded by PEPFAR (the U.S. President's Emergency Plan for AIDS Relief). A proportion of PEPFAR money was designated for "HIV/AIDS prevention through abstinence and healthy choices for youth," and these funds have been received by World Vision and Samaritan's Purse, while CRS is the main faith-based recipient of general prevention funds under the program. This emphasis on abstinence or treatment, rather than on distribution of condoms and safe-sex education, reflects the importance, especially at the outset in 2003, of FBOs in PEPFAR, and of the legitimacy accorded FBOs in this instance as specialist service providers. In other words, the public funding market is more subject to norms and practices that emanate from the beliefs of faith-based providers than it once was, and this shift emanates in large part from changes in the United States.

The third mechanism through which public donors shape humanitarian space is monitoring and controlling the distribution of humanitarian aid. Because control can be costly, monitoring and evaluation has been the preferred method of ensuring agents do what the principals want. The Cluster Approach has to some degree shown the counterproductive nature of control by creating the very slowness, bureaucratic inflexibility, and authority problems it was designed to alleviate.[32] Public donors are loath to reabsorb primary responsibility for delivery with all the associated financial and political costs. Increasingly, however, public donors want either more oversight of local implementation or, as in a recent USAID shift, more control over the project specifications themselves. USAID's new administrator, Rajiv Shah, told INGOs and FBOs in June 2010 that stimulating competition between them was going to be a key U.S. government tool for ensuring value for money.[33] Shah told the Interaction Forum in Washington, D.C., about his plans for more competition in procurement reform, more competition being one way for public donors to get better control:

> We simply can't be successful if we work almost exclusively through a small handful of large-contract partners. We need to have a very broad and diverse base of organizations we work with in the NGO community here in the United States and amongst local institutions all around the world. . . . Second, we essentially need to reduce the size of awards and encourage greater competition in our work. I know that we have tools that allow for certain forms of competition, but what we really need is the competition of ideas and the competition of different strategies for doing things like building local capacity in how we execute the work, and building that into our procurement system will be an important focus of mine.[34]

He told them their goal should be to make themselves dispensable by creating lasting local capacity.

> We need to ask your boards to measure success by your ability to create the conditions for your own eventual, long-term exit. This is hard, because nearly every institution I've ever been a part of has often

measured its own metric of success based on its size, based on its budget, based on its staffing. But we need to be the leaders, in this room, that figure out how to put the people we serve and the sustainability of our development enterprise before our own institutional interests.[35]

These major INGOs and FBOs are huge global organizations with billion-dollar incomes, tens of thousands of staff, pension funds, large offices, and infrastructure. Voluntary extinction makes no sense if we see these INGOs and FBOs as firms. Retaining the very best staff when the organization's objective is to "shrink" will be impossible. What Shah does indicate, however, is the one way the "cartel" can be broken. The emergence of Southern INGOs such as the Bangladesh Rehabilitation Assistance Committee (BRAC) gives public funders a local, professional option for direct funding without going through the intermediate process of pushing money through Western INGOs and FBOs. Many of these local organizations are religious, of course, and here FBOs also have an edge: the opportunity to make a case for being better disbursement mechanisms (e.g., through churches and mosques), much as has happened domestically in the United States. Western INGOs can make a case for their superior ability to distribute funds primarily on the grounds of expertise—networks, for example—but if public donors take control of project specifications and have direct access to Southern INGOs with extensive indigenous networks and experience, their dependence on Western INGOs will diminish.

These three very powerful strategies for controlling and shaping the humanitarian market all have a crucial impact on the branding strategies and organizational structures that humanitarian organizations adopt. Through their control of significant humanitarian funds and the ability to define access requirements, public donors exert great control. By then monitoring and controlling the organizations that receive public funds, public donors further define humanitarianism. Large public funders are able to speak with a unified voice and as such can have a much greater say in principle over what INGOs and FBOs can and can't do with public money.

Private Donors in the Humanitarian Market

The market for private donations remains comfortably the largest source of revenue for most INGOs and FBOs, and we expect this market to have a significant impact on the organizational structures and branding choices humanitarians adopt. The private market is composed of individual donors whose choices are in some cases a direct response to humanitarian brands. Humanitarian "brokers" also play a crucial role in the private donor market.[36] These brokers—churches for example—mediate giving by shaping the choices individuals make about the organizations to which they donate. Church-based fundraising functions, for example, sometimes preselect the NGOs who will benefit from the proceeds of an annual meeting. The private market, then, is shaped by a network of institutions that are embedded in local communities; humanitarian organizations often appeal to the preferences of these institutional brokers as well as directly to individual donors. Humanitarian brokers are, if anything, more rather than less likely to be sensitive to changes in an organization's faith identity. They are, in effect, powerful opinion formers that seek to leverage their influence in the humanitarian market by promoting certain actors over others. Consequently their role in structuring donors' choices, particularly but not exclusively in religious NGOs, suggests that humanitarian organizations will be sensitive to what affects their branding in the private donations market.

The success World Vision enjoys in the "Christian" private market may well be explained in part by its independence from specific denominations, giving it a degree of freedom from "brokers." The more ecumenical a religious NGO, in theory the less influence a broker will have; brokers gain more leverage when the target market is narrow but deep because alternative sources of funding supply are scarce for FBOs. This is an impediment to scaling up for all identity-based humanitarian organizations, but especially religious ones within which the hierarchy of authority is more formalized and embedded. Humanitarian organizations that draw on both public and private sources of funding also face difficult tradeoffs, in other words. If Oxfam America starts taking U.S. government money, it may risk losing some of its private donors, though new supporters may come on board. If World Vision is told by the federal government it must end its discriminatory hiring practices, which currently favor the employment of Christians, it may lose a portion of its private income from motivated Christians whose support is contingent on World Vision's commitment to evangelism.

The major INGOs and FBOs have a distinct advantage relative to all others: they hold a cartel-like position in the market. The demands of instant crisis response require organizations to possess a high level of logistical capacity and to finance operations for weeks before government money arrives, enabling this structure to develop. Nevertheless, competition for market share persists among the humanitarians who are members of this oligopoly. Positioning is imperative. If the distribution of private (individual) donors is standard, then it makes most sense to position close to those with centrist views as that will maximize market share; as a result, major secular and faith-based humanitarians have converged close to the "median" private donor and are increasingly indistinguishable.[37] Product and service differentiation among them is small, and the only choice left for consumers to make is over brands: Do they buy their child sponsorship from World Vision or Save the Children USA? There are big cues—religious versus secular being the most obvious—and small ones; CAFOD (Catholic Agency for Overseas Development, the UK's main Catholic relief and development FBO), shapes it AIDS ribbon like a rosary and uses phrases ("acts of mercy") that will chime with those who had a Catholic upbringing. To maximize their private income, organizations that seek a global profile have learned they cannot afford to be too religious (for fear of losing the moderately religious and any secular donors) or too militantly secular (for fear of losing all religious and moderately secular donors). To capture a large share of this private market, humanitarian actors have sought to attract those with whom they share a core identity; INGOs court secular donors, and FBOs court religious ones. But INGOs and FBOs *also seek* to attract moderates who may not share their identity but who will donate to humanitarians whose product and brand is attractive and whose politics or beliefs are not objectionable.

Private donations now outstrip official development assistance. In the case of U.S. NGOs, a fifty-fifty public-private split has become a thirty-seventy split in the last decade.[38] This private money ranges from numerous small-scale donations and membership fees all the way up to huge donations from individual donors and, increasingly important, foundation giving.[39] The development of Internet, Twitter, and Facebook has boosted the small-scale part of this market significantly, especially in emergencies, as can be seen in the speed with which millions of dollars were pledged for Haiti earthquake relief. But they still overwhelmingly go to existing large INGOs and FBOs. In just over two weeks, the American Red Cross received nearly $200 million for Haiti (of which $30 million was donated through $10 texts; CRS received $32 million, of which $13 million was donated online). The *Chronicle of Philanthropy's* figures for giving in the United States in the two weeks after the earthquake in January show income for Doctors Without Borders US of $36.5 million, Oxfam America $11.9 million, Save the Children USA $15.5 million, and World Vision $22 million. U.S. giving totaled $560 million at this stage, compared with the UK equivalent of £50 million ($75 million).

In some instances, efforts to obstruct the potential for private donors to make nonstandard choices of whom to fund have been minimized by the large humanitarian players. In these cases, humanitarian actors have inhibited market dynamics, demonstrating a clear ability to control humanitarian giving. In the UK, rather than emphasize individual appeals, thirteen of the major recipients have formed a Disasters Emergency Committee (DEC) to consolidate giving. Membership of the DEC is carefully controlled and includes commitment to the Red Cross Code of Conduct, which explicitly rules out proselytizing. MSF is the obvious omission from the DEC, declining to be a member. The principle is that the DEC distributes revenue according to the specialist expertise of its members. This mechanism has effectively enabled the DEC to divert funds only to its members and not to other INGOs and FBOs already active on the ground. Indeed, at the time of the March 2011 tsunami in Japan a group of "like minded" Christian FBOs set themselves up in opposition to the DEC. DEC members such as World Vision UK do raise cash for emergencies under their own brands, as well.

How do small INGOs compete with humanitarian oligarchs in such instances? If the dominant humanitarian actors have essentially locked up the market, smaller NGOs face two choices: they can either become a niche provider or form a strategic alliance. Seculars can attempt to create a distinct brand around a product or service that isn't available elsewhere (as in many industries, specialist services are subcontracted). Because identity plays a less prominent role in their support base, these humanitarians need to "find" their funding market. For smaller FBOs, by contrast, this funding market already exists. They can remain as a niche identity that attracts revenue from a distinct religious group (Jews, Lutherans, Jesuits, and so on). Faith-based humanitarians may emphasize their unique capacity to understand and serve local constituents, thereby displacing the threat from seculars or alternative faith actors. In microfinance, Islamic Relief maintains its edge in the Muslim community over other-faith actors by avoiding an interest-rate charge, but also because charitable giving based on *zakat* is an obligation Muslims owe to each other. The loan cost is recovered by imposition of a service charge that enables IR to respect faith practices and norms while both avoiding financial cost and excluding other actors from its protected markets.

Those donors who are *not* indifferent to who provides their "product" will not cross the line—the avowedly secular will not fund CRS, CAFOD, Islamic Relief, or World Vision, and the strongly faithful will look for groups to fund that are closer to their faith positions. This suggests that competition for donors among faith-based actors will be fiercest on questions of faith identity; among secular humanitarians, competition will center more on products and services. "Secular" is not a meta-brand on which INGOs can draw, except in certain narrow circumstances where being pro-abortion, for example, enables a secular brand to distinguish itself strongly from most FBOs (or allows a group to style itself a "representative of the international community," not a claim an FBO could plausibly make).[40] "Faith" *is* a meta-brand, connoting a certain kind of motivation and commitment that all FBOs draw on collectively even before competition begins over *which* faith (one of the competitive advantages nonprofits have over for-profits in attracting social service funding is that their disinterested motivations reassure donors that money will be used for the stated purposes).

Unanchored in a strong, identity-based congregation, and with donors and supporters rather than members, managers of major secular brands, we suggest, will (other things being equal) have more flexibility in strategic direction. Because they are more concerned with outcomes than with the export of identity, the globalization of technology will spur managers of major secular brands toward a global fundraising and media profile; working at the global level can be very lucrative, especially when they can advertise that they are the biggest, that they operate in more countries, that they raise more cash, that they are the world leaders, and so on. Professional INGO managers grow their businesses. This means gaining and protecting market share. Moves toward alliance or division of labor (as with the DEC and clusters) are a way to secure a more permanent and institutionalized position in a particular sector (a mini-monopoly). Secular supporters are less motivated to donate to any particular group even when they are as motivated as religious people to donate in some way (evidence suggests the religious are more motivated givers).[41] Secular brands, then, must work harder to mark themselves out against each other and replenish their support base. Marking out will be in terms of product and service differentiation, especially as their origins recede and they all converge on human rights language as a meta-ethical justification for their work. They face a choice between paying higher costs to try to retain existing members (by providing magazines, for example) or making barriers to exit low and spending heavily on renewing their base with new supporters continuously (lose one, gain one). The dynamics on the secular side are all toward globalization; in other words, big brands, worldwide operations, large-scale marketing, and unique selling points (Save the Children and children, Oxfam and poverty, MSF and medicine, CARE and food). There is also the constant need to position themselves against the Red Cross brand, although that is most acute in emergency and conflict situations. In the UK case, the DEC serves to moderate this competition while in the United States the Red Cross is the dominant emergency brand, having achieved a kind of generic status as *the* emergency NGO.

Things are different for FBOs. They face a squeeze from two sides, but this challenge also presents them with an opportunity denied seculars *and* more strongly faith-based donors. Moderate FBOs have a chance to capture faith-inspired donors *and* secular donors who are indifferent to the identity of the provider but attracted by the specific product on offer. For faith-inspired FBO supporters, a shared identity is central to their donation, and so these donors are less likely to fund secular humanitarians at all.

Faith-based humanitarians may also demonstrate their commitment to nondiscrimination norms and moderation while preserving their core commitment to faith constituents by forming strategic partnerships with other-faith humanitarians. These partnerships ensure certain services are provided to their own faith constituents while respecting the norm of nonpreferential delivery. In Bosnia, World Vision and Islamic Relief traded reconstruction of churches for mosques in a ploy to satisfy secular humanitarian standards while serving their respective faith groups. Christian Aid worked with Islamic Relief to deliver services in Croatia during the war in the former Yugoslavia.[42] In a similar trade, CAFOD delivered crucial faith-services in post-Tsunami Aceh. Muslims in need of prayer kits relied on CAFOD's delivery of 30,000 Qur'ans and prayer mats. Islamic Relief staff admitted they could not have delivered a similar service without risking a backlash from public donors.[43]

World Vision has increased its attractiveness to secular private supporters by branding itself without a religious identifier, unlike, for example, *Catholic Relief Services*. But the World Vision business model also makes it a formidable competitor for church-based organizations. According to the report "The State of Church Giving 2006," the Southern Baptist Convention in 2007 started to raise funds to send twenty-eight hundred missionaries to evangelize to "unreached people" at a cost, the report's authors estimate, of $65,000 per missionary, or $182 million.[44] Raising this sort of money is not only relatively straightforward for World Vision; because its mature and global structure prizes local autonomy, it must also seem to many funders a much more efficient use of resources.

If the world is undergoing a process of rediscovering faith, especially outside the developed North, then an Evangelical FBO such as World Vision is likely to increasingly emphasize its faith identity across the developing world. Indeed, the only reasons not to would be potential loss of public money and access, loss of private secular money, and loss of legitimacy in local markets. The growth in its fundraising outside the United States is testament to the possibility of a nonpublic nonsecular revenue stream, as is the clear recognition that, if the U.S. government seriously tried to restrict World Vision's discriminatory hiring practices, WVI would have no choice but to abandon its USAID funding. And even though World Vision USA's key product—child sponsorship—attracts secular supporters, it's clear from the comments of the organization's president that the target audience for support is Evangelicals interested in working on issues such as poverty.[45]

Medium-sized and smaller FBOs, those in the income range up to approximately $100 million, outnumber their secular counterparts within the top fifty organizations. In this category, donor reliability is greater for the funding of FBOs. This enables the growth of smaller organizations that openly seek to win converts as they deliver various forms of humanitarian assistance. We anticipate that the financial success of those secular INGOs in this midrange will depend on their ability to offer specialist services for successful fundraising, or alternatively, their success in working in partnership with a major INGO. More specifically, identity might sustain a medium-sized FBO (around the $100 million annual income mark), but the narrow service specialization that will sustain a nonglobal INGO is likely to keep them smaller; medium size entails a move away from core competencies toward general advocacy, program work, and fundraising (and so onto the terrain of large INGOs). This leaves us with a religious-secular oligarchy, a majority-religious "middle," and a set of religious and secular small providers in roughly equal numbers.

The plethora of smaller groups is a sign of vitality rather than sclerosis in the humanitarian market. This may be the argument cartel members would ultimately make: they provide complex and expensive generic services that require economies of scale but that also expand the market as a whole. An entire range of niche identity and service providers attract additional private supporters into the marketplace who seek alternatives to the INGOs. The smaller identity and service INGOs and FBOs are organizations that invest vertically, capitalizing on or even creating a narrow but hard-to-replace specialism that gives them privileged entry into particular kinds of local markets.

Conclusion

Humanitarian branding decisions are not only driven by donor strategies; how humanitarians define and project their faith identity is also shaped by faith traditions in the local markets they serve. Where faith is prevalent but politics are secular, the scope for competition along faith lines will be fierce, and we expect humanitarians to engage in strategic manipulation of their faith brands in an attempt to attract private donors. This competition is likely to be even more notable in states with multiple faith traditions and with multiple sects within each of these faiths. Competition between religious providers is especially strong in the United States, where faith is prevalent and politics are secular. Faith-based branding is a much tougher sell in Europe. Not surprisingly, INGOs with European links—MSF, Oxfam and Save the Children—are secular; the major global FBOs—World Vision, CRS, and Samaritan's Purse—are all American.[46]

In states where faith dominates political life, entry to humanitarian organizations outside the fold may be effectively blocked. In Pakistan and Afghanistan, non-Islamic aid agencies have found it difficult and even dangerous to operate among skeptical locals. Faith-based humanitarians who share the local faith have at times resorted to scaremongering to consolidate their advantage. In Afghanistan, Islamic NGOs worked to arouse fears among local constituents by claiming that Christians were conspiring against Islam and seeking recruits to Christianity. Dr. Ahmed Sonoussi, head of the Afghan office of the Lajnat al-Dawa group, labeled Christian NGOs "crusaders" who sought to "poison the minds of Afghans and gradually convert them to Christianity." He later admitted that this claim was part of an effort to raise funds for his organization.[47] The state may also intervene directly to control access. Afghanistan confirmed its status as an "exclusive" faith market in 2001, when it closed the offices of two Christian NGOs, International Assistance Mission and SERVE.[48] So far, CRS has remained active in Afghanistan; having a faith identity, even the wrong one, has been an easier sell than secularism.

Our model suggests that faith-based organizations that do operate in such areas and enjoy privileged access are likely to develop deep roots within single-market structures but may neglect mobility strategies, centered on manipulation of their faith brand, that are necessary for developing and growing a transnational structure. This is especially likely in disaster states, where the potential for an enduring supply of work in a single local market is strong. In markets where the state has intervened more directly to control access, crafty humanitarians may find alternative strategies to secure competitive faith brands. Secular humanitarians have sought to alter their brand by developing strategic partnerships with faith-based humanitarians. These partnerships not only provide them with greater local legitimacy and greater networks, they may also determine whether any access is granted. In Egypt, the government responded to pressure from Islamic NGOs by requiring Western NGOs to work in partnership with local NGOs.[49] In post-Tsunami Indonesia, the government blocked WorldHelp, a Christian organization, from placing children in a Christian orphanage out of fear that this was part of an effort to convert them to Christianity. WorldHelp responded in part by altering the language on its website to deemphasize its focus on Christianity and concern for Islam. It also stopped raising funds that were to be used to rescue children and place them in orphanages.[50]

Understanding INGO and FBO behavior through the lens of brands competing to gain and sustain market share gives a compelling picture of how, despite their normatively rich inner lives, any FBO or INGO aspiring to be a global player must adapt itself to market incentives. This is particularly true now that the market is mature and dominated by an oligarchy. Humanitarians need a lot of cash or a very steady funding supply to buck these trends. They must balance depth and breadth when they are making choices about how to brand and how to organize. Even World Vision, the most successful humanitarian fund-raiser, cannot escape this bind.

This is not necessarily a problem. The humanitarian market has grown in part because every potential donor can now find a product close to what it ideally wishes to fund. Competition has led to market expansion and created an opportunity for more people who need aid to receive it. But competition among humanitarians has also created some more dysfunctional patterns. Fundraising giants such as World Vision crowd others out of the market not because of their superior performance but because they have greater marketing power. Cartels that form among major humanitarian organizations enhance certainty at the cost of innovation. And the difficulties these major providers have in successfully accessing local markets can lead to insufficient accountability, poorly integrated crisis and development response, and exclusionary practices. Understanding how market structures shape faith-based organizations and INGOs (the view from the outside in) tells us as much as, or perhaps more, about what drives the behavior of these organizations as explanations that stress faith-identities or secular principles (the view from the inside out). In this new humanitarian space, the weakening of the secular norm and the new salience of religion may put FBOs in an advantaged position for the humanitarian world that is to come.

Acknowledgment

We would like to thank Michael Barnett and Janice Stein, and also Courtney Bender, Tonya Putnam, Dirk Salomons, and Jack Sndyer for their helpful comments.

NOTES

1. World Vision employs a staggering 40,000 people. See http://www.worldvision. org/content.nsf/about/who-we-are?open&;lpos=top_drp_AboutUs_ WhoWeAre (accessed August 9, 2011).

2. Even a simple list of the top ten humanitarian organizations courts controversy. Data are poor and definition is difficult. Does the ICRC belong here, for example? Food for the Poor and AmeriCares are missing, but each distributed more than $1 billion in aid in 2009 (more than Oxfam). Both are distributors of "gifts in kind" to local providers such as churches and hospitals—medicines for AmeriCares and food for Food for the Poor. AmeriCares is supplied with its medicine and drugs by the U.S. corporate sector, and Food for the Poor works exclusively in Latin America and the Caribbean. Neither is an insider in the USAID-UN-ECHO network that defines who belongs to the oligopoly.

3. This does not mean that their primary values are commercial or that their primary purpose is making a profit; it does mean that INGOs and FBOs are increasingly forced to think and act like firms in a market in order to meet their program objectives, and that those failing to do so risk putting themselves at a competitive disadvantage where members, money, and access are concerned.

4. See Hirschman (1970).

5. Monitoring websites, of which Charity Navigator is perhaps the best known, are constantly vigilant about the percentage of INGO/FBO income spent on the firm rather than its programs (under 10 percent is the desired figure). FBOs may have an edge here if they receive higher amounts of "donated labor" (unpaid voluntary work), thus keeping costs down. Simple products that can be replicated in bulk rather than complex advocacy and operational programs are also attractive, making relief rather than development work more prevalent for many FBOs.

6. See for example Benedetti (2006) and Kniss and Campbell (1997). In a bid to move beyond a sterile faith-secular binary distinction, some scholars have constructed more nuanced and elaborate typologies of the inner lives of FBOs; see Berger (2003), Monsma (1996), Jeavons (1997), Sider and Unruh (2004), Clarke (2008). Laura Thaut (2009), for example, divides Christian humanitarian FBOs into three categories: accommodative, synthetic, and evangelistic. She derives these three types from four variables: mission, ties to religious authorities, staffing policies, and sources of donor support. Accommodative and synthetic FBOs tend to be similar to INGOs in operational terms. The difference comes with the Evangelicals, for whom humanitarian work is more of a means to spread the faith; they are "church-planting organizations."

7. Scholars of the sociology of religion have recognized that *where affiliation is a matter of choice even churches must compete for members*, or risk decline (Finke and

Stark, 1993; Iannaccone, 1998. Cooley and Ron (2002) have used a similar "political economy approach" to show how INGO/FBO competition for money and contracts shapes their (often dysfunctional) organizational behavior, and Eva Bellin (2008: 326) has reviewed research on the politics of religion that treats churches as "economic firms" and stresses how organizational concerns (such as market share) have trumped ideology and belief in explaining church choices; proselytizing religions are particularly concerned about market share, she argues.

8. Cooley and Ron (2002).

9. This is according to the editor of *Sojourners* magazine, liberal Evangelical leader Rev. Jim Wallis, in Janet I. Tu, "World Vision's Richard Stearns Sets out to Put an End to Global Poverty," *Seattle Times* August 23 (2009), http://seattletimes. nwsource.com/html/pacificnw/2009650481_pacificpvision23.html.

10. On the globalization of humanitarianism, see Lindenberg and Bryant (2001): 18–22.

11. Clarke and Jennings (2008).

12. Balchin (2007), 532.

13. Pew Forum on Religion and Public Life (2010).

14. WHO (2007), http://www.chagghana.org/chag/assets/files/FBO%20Meeting%20 report%20_2_.pdf.

15. Hearn (2002).

16. Wineburg et al. (2008), 31.

17. Hertzke (2004).

18. Bush (2009).

19. Ibid.

20. James (2009), 7.

21. WHO (2007).

22. UNFPA (2009).

23. When Sudanese President Omar al-Bashir expelled Western aid groups in 2009 in retaliation for his indictment by the International Criminal Court on charges of crimes against humanity, religious groups (churches and FBOs) were allowed to remain. The allegation was that INGOs were collecting evidence and monitoring human rights abuses under the label of "protection" whereas FBOs were not. This raises a further question about the degree to which INGOs have adopted a broader rights agenda that FBOs have been able to resist.

24. Figures from the Evangelical Council for Financial Accountability (ECFA) in the United States and the *Chronicle of Philanthropy* show that although funding to the country's top four hundred charities fell by 11 percent in 2009 due to the recession, giving to ECFA members only declined 0.1 percent. Interestingly, the ECFA claims that income for child sponsorship—the hallmark World Vision fundraising technique (and one unpopular with many development professionals)—actually rose 25 percent between 2007 and 2009. Simple, highly emotive humanitarian products seem to sell well on a mass basis; see http://www.ecfa.org/Content/2010-ECFA-Annual-State-of-Giving-Report.

25. Kniss and Campbell (1997), 99.
26. Tu (2009). Proselytizing and discrimination are closer than might at first appear to be the case if accessing services requires engagement with faith. The New York Civil Liberties Union won a case in February 2010 against the Salvation Army for proselytizing in the delivery of its social services. Since 2003, the "firewall" between the religious operations of the Army and its social service provision has been weakened, most likely in response to the changes initiated by President Bush (ACLU, 2010).
27. Tu (2009).
28. Kniss and Campbell (1997), 100–101.
29. Cooper (2009).
30. MinistryWatch (2010).
31. Beeson (2010).
32. Humanitarian Policy Group (HPG) Policy Brief 36 (2009), and Dempsey (2010).
33. USAID (2010).
34. Ibid.
35. Ibid.
36. We thank Courtney Bender for impressing on us the significance of brokers in channeling donations among individual faith-based donors.
37. If there is a standard distribution of preferences among private (individual) donors, then the majority are to be found around a centrist position, which means it makes sense for you to position close to those with median views (not too religious, not militantly secular) if your aim is to maximize market share. As with political parties, major secular and faith-based humanitarians have converged ever closer to the median private donor. See for example Downs (1957) and the voluminous work derived from it.
38. Pipa (2008).
39. Kharas (2007).
40. Cooley and Ron (2002), 35.
41. See, for example, Campbell and Putnam (2010).
42. Benedetti (2006); Ghandour (2003).
43. Staff member, Islamic Relief, off-the-record interview.
44. Empty Tomb (2007).
45. Tu (2009).
46. Samaritan's Purse, for example, is run by Billy Graham's son Franklin, who is also president of the Billy Graham Evangelistic Association, which explicitly proselytizes. This link would be a tough sell in Europe.
47. Ghandour (2003).
48. Ibid.
49. Ibid.
50. Cooperman (2005).

BIBLIOGRAPHY

American Civil Liberties Union (ACLU). "NYCLU Settlement Ensures That the Salvation Army May Not Proselytize While Performing Government-Funded Services." ACLU, 2010,

Balchin, Cassandra. "The F Word and the S Word: Too Much of One and Not Enough of the Other." *Development in Practice* 17 (2007): 532–538.

Beeson, Amy. "Who Gets to Give Aid?" *Harvard Political Review* (2010), http://hpronline.org/religion-in-america/who-gets-to-give-aid/.

Bellin, Eva. "Review Article: Faith in Politics—New Trends in the Study of Religion and Politics," *World Politics* 60 (2008): 315–347.

Benedetti, Carlo. "Islamic and Christian Inspired Relief NGOs: Between Tactical Collaboration and Strategic Diffidence." *Journal of International Development* 18 (2006): 849–859.

Berger, Julia. "Religious Nongovernmental Organizations: An Exploratory Analysis." *Voluntas: International Journal of Voluntary and Nonprofit Organization* 41 (2003): 15–39.

Bush, Evelyn. 2011. "Religious Economies and Religious Freedom: A Transnational Approach." In Jeffrey Haynes and Anja Henning (eds.), *Religious Actors in the Public Sphere: Means, Objectives and Effects*. London and New York: Routledge, 2011: 149–166.

Campbell, David E., and Robert D. Putnam. "Charity's Religious Edge." *Wall Street Journal* (December 2010), http://online.wsj.com/article/SB100014240527487037 66704576009361375685394.html.

Clarke, Gerard. "Faith-Based Organizations and International Development: An Overview." In Gerard Clarke and Michael Jennings (eds.), *Development, Civil Society and Faith-Based Organizations: Bridging the Sacred and the Secular*. London: Palgrave Macmillan, 2008.

Clarke, Gerard, and Michael Jennings (eds.), *Development, Civil Society and Faith-Based Organizations: Bridging the Sacred and the Secular*. London: Palgrave Macmillan, 2008.

Cooley, Alexander, and James Ron, "The NGO Scramble: Organizational Insecurity and the Political Economy of Transnational Action," *International Security*, 27 (2002): 5–39.

Cooper, Marty. "Children's Charity Drops 'Christian' Moniker." OneNewsNow (2009), http://www.onenewsnow.com/Culture/Default.aspx?id=525028.

Cooperman, Alan. "Tsunami Orphans Won't Be Sent to Christian Home." *Washington Post* (January 2005) at http://www.washingtonpost.com/ac2/wp-dyn/A7535-2005 Jan13?language=printer.

Dempsey, Benedict. "Hard Lessons for Humanitarian Financing from Pakistan." *Humanitarian Exchange Magazine* 46 (2010) at http://www.odihpn.org/humanitarian-exchange-magazine/issue-46/hard-lessons-for-humanitarian-financing-from-pakistan.

Empty Tomb. "The State of Church Giving Through 2006." Empty Tomb (2007), http://www.emptytomb.org/SCG06.ch8excerpt.pdf.

Downs, Anthony. *An Economic Theory of Democracy*. New York, Harper, 1957.

Finke, Roger, and Rodney Stark. "*The Churching of America 1776–1990: Winners and Losers in Our Religious Economy*." New Brunswick, NJ: Rutgers University Press, 1993.

Ghandour, Abdel-Rahman. "Humanitarianism, Islam and the West: Contest or Cooperation?" *Humanitarian Practice Network* 25 (2003).

Hearn, Julie. "The 'Invisible' NGO: US Evangelical Missions in Kenya." *Journal of Religion in Africa* 32 (2002): 32–60.

Hertzke, Allen D. *Freeing God's Children: The Unlikely Alliance for Global Human Rights*. Lanham, MD: Rowman and Littlefield, 2004.

Hirschman, Albert O. *Exit, Voice, and Loyalty: Responses to Decline in Firms, Organizations, and States*. Cambridge, MA: Harvard University Press, 1970.

HPG Policy Brief 36. "A Clash of Principles? Humanitarian Action and the Search for Stability in Pakistan." Overseas Development Institute (2009), http://www.odi.org.uk/resources/details.asp?id=3765&title=conflict-humanitarian-pakistan-stability-taliban.

Iannaccone, Laurence R. "Introduction to the Economics of Religion," *Journal of Economic Literature*, 36 (1998): 1465–1495.

James, Rick. "What Is Distinctive About FBOs?" *INTRAC Praxis Paper* (2009): 7.

Jeavons, Thomas H. "Identifying Characteristics of 'Religious' Organizations: An Exploratory Proposal." In J. Demerath III et al. (eds.), *Sacred Companies: Organizational Aspects of Religion and Religious Aspects of Organization*. New York: Oxford University Press, 1997.

Kharas, Homi. "The New Reality of Aid." Brookings Institution (2007), http://www.brookings.edu/papers/2007/08aid_kharas.aspx.

Kniss, Fred, and David Todd Campbell. "The Effect of Religious Orientation on International Relief and Development Organizations." *Journal for the Scientific Study of Religion* 36 (1997): 93–103.

Lindenberg, Marc, and Coralie Bryant, *Going Global: Transforming Relief and Development NGOs*. Sterling, VA: Kumarian Press, 2001.

MinistryWatch (2010), http://www.ministrywatch.com/profile/world-vision.aspx.

Monsma, Stephen V. *When Sacred and Secular Mix: Religious Nonprofit Organizations and Public Money*. (Lanham, MD: Rowman and Littlefield, 1996.

Pew Forum on Religion and Public Life. "Tolerance and Tension: Islam and Christianity in Sub-Saharan Africa." Pew Forum on Religion and Public Life, 2010, http://pewforum.org/executive-summary-islam-and-christianity-in-sub-saharan-africa.aspx.

Pipa, Tony. "Private Aid: Boon or Burden." Hauser Center for Nonprofit Organizations, Harvard University (2008), http://hausercenter.org/iha/2008/10/18/private-aid-boon-or-burden/.

Sider, Ronald J., and Heidi Rolland Unruh. "Typology of Religious Characteristics of Social Service and Educational Organizations and Programs." *Nonprofit and Voluntary Sector Quarterly* 33 (2004): 109–134.

Thaut, Laura C. "The Role of Faith in Christian Faith-Based Humanitarian Agencies: Constructing the Taxonomy." *Voluntas: International Journal of Voluntary and Nonprofit Organizations* 20 (2009): 319–350.

Tu, Janet I. "World Vision's Richard Stearns Sets out to Put an End to Global Poverty." *Seattle Times*, August 23 (2009), http://seattletimes.nwsource.com/html/paci ficnw/2009650481_pacificpvision23.html.

United Nations Population Fund (UNFPA). "Cooperation Between Faith-Based Organizations and UNFPA Critical to Maternal Health, Say groups." UNFPA 2009, http://www.unfpa.org/public/News/pid/3310.

U.S. Agency for International Development (USAID). "Remarks by Dr. Rajiv Shah, Administrator USAID." USAID (2010), http://www.usaid.gov/press/ speeches/2010/sp100602.html.

World Health Organization (WHO). "Towards Primary Health Care: Renewing Partnerships with Faith-Based Communities and Services." WHO (2007), http:// www.chagghana.org/chag/assets/files/FBO%20Meeting%20report%20_2_.pdf.

Wineburg, Robert J., et al. "Leveling the Playing Field: Epitomizing Devolution Through Faith-Based Organizations." *Journal of Sociology and Social Welfare* 35 (2008): 32.

3

"Cultural Proximity" and the Conjuncture of Islam with Modern Humanitarianism

Jonathan Benthall

Older Debates

On the need for "cultural sensitivity"—the effort to avoid imposing metropolitan preconceptions when working with local communities—the aid world is broadly agreed, though with room for dissent on specific issues such as gender roles or the economic contribution of children. The debate about "cultural proximity," on the other hand, hinges on whether an assumed commonality between an aid program's implementers and its beneficiaries can be regarded as giving the implementing agency (or its principal representatives) an operational advantage.

The substantive issue is at least as old as 1876. During the Serbo-Turkish war, the Ottoman government complained that the emblem of the newly founded Red Cross gave offense to Muslim soldiers. The Porte was given permission to use the red crescent instead as a national emblem of the movement—thus initiating the "problem of the emblem," which is still not fully resolved today (despite the agreement on a Third Protocol additional to the Geneva Conventions authorizing the use of a third emblem, the diamond-shaped red crystal).

Note: I acknowledge with gratitude a travel grant from the Nuffield Foundation that facilitated my research in Aceh and Mali. Much stimulus has been received from fellow members of the Islamic Charities Project (formerly the Montreux Initiative), administered by the Graduate Institute of International and Development Studies, Geneva, with funding from the Swiss Federal Department of Foreign Affairs. Islamic Relief Worldwide gave permission for me to read and comment on its internal report on orphan sponsorship. CAFOD staff supplied unpublished details about some of their programs. Willem van Eekelen kindly commented on a draft.

The history of what later became officially known as the International Red Cross and Red Crescent Movement may be read by market-oriented analysts as a narrative of sophisticated "branding" *avant la lettre*. But one can invert this argument and interpret visual logos of this kind—like the red poppies of the Earl Haig Fund honoring British and Commonwealth war casualties, or the swaddled Della Robbia *bambino* in the Save the Children Fund's early publicity—as bearing a spiritual or transcendent meaning.

The issue as more recently defined has arisen so far almost exclusively in the context of work in the Muslim world, and "cultural" here becomes a euphemism for "religious." The debate seems to have resulted partly from claims made by Islamic charities themselves for their special aptitude to work with Muslim communities. And partly from the difficulties experienced by non-Muslim NGOs in working effectively and safely in some Muslim majority countries, particularly in the most testing field areas such as Iraq, Afghanistan, and Sudan—difficulties that have increasingly impelled them to consider entering into ad hoc partnerships with Muslim NGOs or to recruit Muslim staff themselves. The incidence of deprivation and distress in many Muslim majority countries is so high that almost every aid agency, of whatever ideological hue, is impelled to intervene to address their humanitarian needs in some way; and it is the extent of these needs that international Islamic charities adduce in defending themselves against the criticism that they concentrate the greater part of their efforts on reaching out to Muslim-majority countries.

The founder of Islamic Relief Worldwide, Dr. Hany El-Banna, claimed in 2001 that his agency was able to bring relief aid to Chechen refugees in Ingushetia, where Western agencies declined to send expatriate staff because of fear of kidnapping and murder. Abdel-Rahman Ghandour quoted this claim in his *Jihad Humanitaire*, published in 2001, characterizing it ironically as an example of "Islamic surplus value." He adduced further evidence from Afghanistan and Somalia that "where other humanitarians have no presence, Islamic NGOs keep watch," and he noted the tension between humanitarian and security concerns that was to become so salient later in the noughties.[1]

An older debate about "comparative advantage," going back to the 1970s, focused on whether it could be shown that NGOs (of all types) performed better than governments in service provision. According to the iconoclastic Norwegian historian Terje Tvedt, the theory of NGOs' comparative advantage was advanced by the American government in the late 1970s and became an "article of faith" for publicists who claimed that NGOs were superior in outreach, effectiveness, flexibility, innovativeness, freedom from bureaucracy, and ability to work with and strengthen local institutions. This became, Tvedt argues, a "list of dogmas," despite having been questioned already in 1982; and the theory could not be substantiated by evidence—both NGOs and governments being heterogeneous in time and space. Moreover, "since the middle of the 1980s the whole issue has been captured by a political-ideological debate about states vis-à-vis civil society, where the NGOs represent the alternative to the rollback of the state."[2]

There are signs that an analogous debate may now be emerging as a contrast between faith-based and secular service provision—for instance, in research projects, largely quantitative in their methods, undertaken by the World Bank's Development Dialogue on Values and Ethics. Particularly thoughtful work has been undertaken by the African Religious Health Assets Programme (ARHAP) at the University of Cape Town, focusing on HIV/AIDS and guided by the assumption that "religion, in its own right, is important to the health of individuals and communities," in contrast to the secularization thesis that used in a crude form to dominate the social sciences.[3] However, as in the former debate about NGOs versus governments, little solid evidence is so far available.

The Christian Precedent

If we look back at the history of humanitarianism, "communitarian aid" has clearly been practiced by Christians and Jews for centuries. St. Paul was, among other things, a formidable fundraiser for support of the poor Christian communities in Judaea: "God loveth a cheerful giver."[4] It is still legal and acceptable in most Western countries to set up a charity for the exclusive benefit of adherents of a particular religion, or for the purposes of proselytism, and it is also legal and acceptable for a charity to have mixed religious and humanitarian objectives. Samaritan's Purse, founded by the Rev. Franklin Graham, and the Saudi-based World Assembly of Muslim Youth are symmetrical examples of these "mixed purpose" charities (though no doubt these organizations themselves envisage their work as a seamless whole). Whereas some Christian NGOs such as Christian Aid and CAFOD (the British arm of Caritas Internationalis) explicitly avoid any form of proselytism, there is some ambiguity in the case of the more Evangelically inspired Christian NGOs such as Tearfund and World Vision. Both these agencies, however, as members of the Disasters Emergency Committee in London, are signed up to the Code of Conduct for the International Red Cross and Red Crescent

Movement and NGOs in Disaster Relief, one of whose principles is nondiscrimination and provision of services on the basis of need alone.

Christian Aid and CAFOD work extensively through partnership arrangements with churches, bishops, and priests in the Christian parts of Africa and in Latin America. This is taken for granted and hardly questioned. I can find little research assessing the advantages to Christian NGOs of "cultural proximity," but these advantages seem to be beyond dispute.[5] The Roman Catholic Church presents a paradox—criticized by its detractors, but maybe part of the recipe for its continued ascendancy despite the scandals of clerical sexual abuse. For at its heart, the Vatican, we find the survival of something like an absolute monarchy, with theatrical pomp and a personality cult of the pope that, with John Paul II, came near to apotheosis. Yet Catholic social teaching includes not only abstract affirmations of human dignity but also more concrete and practical commitments, for instance to the rights of the worker (as early as 1891, in Leo XIII's encyclical *Rerum Novarum*) and the priority of labor over capital (John Paul II's *Laborem Exercens*, 1981). The liberation theology that originated in Latin America in the 1970s and has for many years been disowned by the magisterium in Rome now permeates the Catholic mainstream with the "radical imperative for justice and peace." The Marxist economic analysis, with consequences sometimes verging on revolutionary violence, has been dropped, and Pope Benedict XVI has recently repeated the warning against liberation theology that he enunciated in 1984, as Prefect of the Congregation for the Doctrine of the Faith, in an Instruction entitled *Libertatis Nuntius*. Critics of liberation theology argue that it was mistaken in seeing capitalism as the great enemy, whereas capitalism was exactly what the conquistador oligarchies of Latin America generally lacked, so that stable institutions and a sizeable middle class had not taken root.[6] Benedict, for all his conservatism, accepted in 2007 that "the preferential option for the poor is implicit in the Christological faith in the God who became poor for us, so as to enrich us with his poverty."[7]

In Lusaka, Zambia, the Jesuit Centre for Theological Reflection publishes a monthly "Basic Needs Basket" survey, first launched in 1991, highlighting the devastating impact of Structural Adjustment and now accepted as a major input for policymakers, campaigners, and communities.[8] It exposes the struggle to meet essential needs by comparing the basic cost of living with average take-home wages and general household incomes. According to the Centre, it "transforms from a pure statistical record of history to an active protagonist in the living drama." The Church in Zambia sees its role as helping people to be actors in their own development, rather than passive victims. A program such as the Basic Needs Basket throws into question two sharp distinctions that are often taken for granted: between material as opposed to spiritual needs, and between reflection and action.

Another program, also cofunded from London by CAFOD, is the Pastoral Land Commission in northwestern Brazil. This was nurtured in Rondônia in the 1970s by the Catholic Church, with the aim, through legal advice and education, of enabling farmers to keep their land, which they were often terrorized into losing, and to continue sustainable agriculture as opposed to monoculture. There is an environmental dimension (regenerative management of soil and water) as well as the aim of promoting rural development through family farms. As in the Zambian case, the underlying goal is to help people realize their potential through the conviction that they have a voice and hope. This has been especially important in the troubled history of many Latin American countries, during which the Catholic Church has earned moral prestige through the actions of many charismatic figures. These included Hélder Câmara (1909–1999), archbishop of Olinda and Recife in Brazil, whose campaigns for the poor resulted in his living in constant fear of assassination; Óscar Romero (1917–1980), archbishop of San Salvador, whose condemnation of repression and torture in El Salvador resulted in his being assassinated by a death squad while celebrating mass; and Fr. Ricardo Falla (1932–), the Guatemalan Jesuit anthropologist whose writings have documented the massacres of Amerindian communities such as the Quiche Maya Indians, and defended their human rights.[9]

The two examples given here from Zambia and Brazil of cultural proximity between Roman Catholic donors and beneficiaries may be exceptional in that many Christian NGOs, especially in Europe, have tended to downplay their "faith identity," as explained in the Introduction (Chapter One) to the present book. As Rick James has observed, "An FBO that uses their faith as a decoration for fundraising or only as a founding inspiration is unlikely to be different from a secular NGO. It matters how FBOs choose to operationalize their faith identity in their work. Distinctiveness should not be assumed."[10] This description could be reformulated in the idiom of product branding, favored by Hopgood and Vinjamuri in Chapter Two of this volume and following naturally from the theory of "religious markets."[11] There is no reason religiously inspired institutions should be exempt from analysis in terms of economic competition; but such an analysis is deficient if it does not take account of the gains in spiritual merit that are deemed to accrue to those who perform good works.[12]

Hotelling's Law in economics holds that in many markets it is rational for suppliers to make their products as similar as possible. CAFOD's staff are enjoined to be "bilingual," familiar with the idioms of both development and Christianity. Yet it may be predicted that, as a result of the decline of popular secularization theory and the resurgence of FBOs, many of these organizations will speak with more confidence about the specifically faith-based aspects of their work. For instance, strengthening rural development might come to be represented more explicitly as a way of affirming Catholic family values—though I have not yet seen clear evidence of this.

More generally, it seems that religion is coming to be "mainstreamed" in relief and development. The concept of mainstreaming seems to have originated in education with regard to pupils with "special needs." Gender mainstreaming was formulated in the 1980s, insisting that gender aspects should be made an integral part of policy and practice at all levels of an organization. The pressure for this innovation came more from the donor side than the recipient side; the reverse may be true if religion is now following a similar pattern of mainstreaming as gender—so important is religion in its multiple forms to the lives of most communities that are the "targets" of aid programs.

The present volume is primarily, though not exclusively, concerned with urgent relief aid. (Donor agencies focused on "development" as opposed to emergency relief tend to claim that what they do is quite distinct from "charity." I contend that this is a *déformation professionnelle* of development workers. In the absence of enforceable entitlements for recipients, development programs are, from an analytical viewpoint, forms of charity even though their practitioners disavow the label.) Despite the extensive attention now given to evaluating aid programs from every other point of view, I know of no empirical attempt to assess the extent of "comparative advantage" made use of by FBOs as opposed to secular agencies when responding to crises such as earthquakes, floods, or refugee migrations.

Let us however consider the massive earthquake that afflicted an already immiserated Haiti on January 12, 2010, and the humanitarian response, which was soon criticized for slowness and inefficiency. If one were to estimate how to maximize value for money in the provision of relief aid, it seems probable that Catholic organizations would score highly in a country where some 80 percent of the population is Catholic. Caritas affiliates from the United States, Britain, France,[13] Switzerland, Spain, and the Netherlands already had well-established programs in Haiti with a high proportion of Haitians among their staff, while Caritas Haiti had a presence in every parish in Haiti's ten dioceses. It has been known for many years that, though international search-and-rescue teams have a role after earthquakes, it is limited in scale compared with the work done by locally mobilized teams. It would be instructive to test the hypothesis that—after the unprecedented destruction of governmental buildings and infrastructure, with a death toll of some 220,000, more than this number injured, and almost one-third of the Haitian population affected, in a nation plagued by corruption—the Church networks are likely to have provided some of the most effective and trusted solidarity. This must remain merely a thought, owing to the lack of comparative evidence. If the extensive evaluation literature on the response to the Haiti earthquake mentions the religious dimension at all, it is only fleetingly.[14] However, the effective actions of Church networks in the immediate response to the Haiti earthquake have been underlined by Interaction's director of disaster response, though she also stated that there were serious problems of coordination and communication between the larger international relief effort and *all* local civil society networks.[15] The regional director of a major Catholic aid agency has told me that, from his personal experience, the local churches, both mainstream and Evangelical, were particularly important, during the days and weeks following the Haiti earthquake, in providing space for people to pray, grieve, and somehow survive.

Proximity Within the Islamic Umma

As noted already, it is in the Islamic rather than the Christian world, the presumed *umma* or transnational community of Muslims, that the question of "cultural proximity" has been examined. In 2006–07, Bruno De Cordier asked a number of aid workers in the UK, Pakistan, Tajikistan, and Jordan whether they thought the identity, background, and open or covert Islamic references of Islamic aid organizations brought added value in majority-Muslim contexts. "The vast majority of the aid sector respondents interviewed on this issue think they do, be it with answers ranging from 'absolutely' to 'to some extent'."[16] I shall give some positive examples to support this general case. However, in the small body of research on the topic of cultural proximity, almost all the authors have articulated a number of caveats, for a variety of reasons:

1. Religion is merely one marker of similarity or difference. Others include nationality, language, class, generation, gender, political ideology, and socially defined race.
2. The Muslim *umma* is sharply divided in itself as regards doctrine, religious practice, and relationships with temporal powers—not to mention outright geopolitical hostility in some areas.

3. Though access to operational sites may be facilitated by transnational contacts through religious institutions, once an agency is in the field it is its performance that decides how it is evaluated locally.

4. In some circumstances, an Islamic identity may be a disadvantage for an NGO in that the expectations of Muslim beneficiaries may be unrealistically high.

5. Special political factors may also intervene. In Bangladesh, for instance, Muslim charities are regarded with particular suspicion by the government and the public for historical reasons, because of the secession of former East Pakistan from Pakistan in 1971. Victoria Palmer witnessed an attack by students on an Islamic Relief Worldwide car during her fieldwork in 2008, because they associated anything Islamic with fundamentalism or extremism.[17] In Sudan, Islamic Relief Worldwide has been wrongly suspected of having links with the government or with the militant *janjaweed* and has preferred to employ non-Arab staff in the Darfur region; similar sensitivities have been reported in Ingushetia and Afghanistan.[18]

6. Some of the most professional and effective Islamic charities, such as Islamic Relief Worldwide, have set out to conform to the codes of practice and other norms of the international aid system, and they may be regarded by Muslim beneficiaries in the field, especially in religiously conservative countries, as excessively secularized.[19]

7. There is no evidence for the assumption that Muslim beneficiaries are less able than non-Muslims to respect the neutrality and impartiality of non-Muslim NGOs insofar as these qualities are manifested in practice.[20] In some circumstances, for instance of civil strife, an outsider may be at an advantage in securing trust. International humanitarianism in the field— in common with religious missions and sociocultural anthropology— depends to a great extent for its efficacy on the personal qualities of individuals.

8. The threats to the safety of aid workers—one reason for the appeal of the "cultural proximity" thesis, as mentioned above—are not necessarily alleviated by employment of Muslims rather than non-Muslims, because those militants in Afghanistan or Iraq who attack aid workers tend to have no scruples about killing Muslims.[21]

9. "When organizations are too deeply embedded in local communities in which they operate they risk being co-opted by local elites."[22] (Instrumentalization by elites at all levels is, however, a major endemic problem for aid programs of every description.)

The debate about cultural proximity was probably conducted informally in NGO circles for many years, but in more academic terms it seems to have been launched by a Norwegian researcher, Arne Strand, who drew attention in 1998, on the basis of his relief work in Afghanistan between 1988 and 1997, to the presence in that country of a parallel system of aid—Islamic, mainly Saudi-Arabian—that engaged in no coordination whatever with the Western system. The "livelihood philosophy," Strand noticed correctly, was about to gain favor in Western aid circles—an approach insisting that in relief and development not just the material needs of a population but all aspects of "quality of life" must be catered for.[23] Quality of life must include spiritual needs. "This is evidently," he wrote,

> what the Islamic NGOs have done in Afghanistan since they started their support, focusing on the religious needs of the population. But, the conclusion must be that the religious values and beliefs of the beneficiaries and the relief providers must be the same if it should be accepted for humanitarian agencies to engage themselves in catering for the spiritual needs of the beneficiaries. Otherwise such activities would be a gross violation against the rights of the beneficiaries, as well as against humanitarian norms for relief provision. The other side of this universal approach must be that agencies provide relief to everyone in need, not only to those sharing their own faith or a particular branch of that.[24]

Stimulated by Strand, the argument was taken up by my colleague Jérôme Bellion-Jourdan in our jointly authored *The Charitable Crescent*. The phrase "cultural proximity" must have been doing the rounds already, since he wrote:

> The scenario of confrontation [as opposed to integration or cooperation with the Western aid system] would lead to the promotion of an Islamic alternative to a universal humanitarianism, with a strong claim that secular humanitarianism should be challenged for its lack of cultural sensitivity and replaced by a communitarian approach based on the so-called "cultural proximity."[25]

Shortly afterward, an unsigned editorial in the *International Review of the Red Cross*, introducing a special issue devoted to religion, concluded:

> Notwithstanding the right of NGOs to espouse a particular religious belief, assistance should never be dependent on the recipients' adherence

to those beliefs, and the promise, delivery or distribution of assistance should not be tied to the embracing or acceptance of a particular religious creed. These norms do not exclude the principle of "cultural proximity" or communal aid. Socio-cultural competence has become one of the key qualifications required for all humanitarian action. But that action is centred on human dignity and the welfare of all human beings, which are also the main objectives of all religions.[26]

Carlo Benedetti wrote at about the same time, in an article on the possibilities of collaboration between Christian and Islamic relief NGOs, that

> collaboration is limited to those areas where both a Christian and an Islamic presence are acceptable and accepted by both sides. In other words, the decision to intervene in some areas is relevant for the type of relationship that will exist between Islamic and Christian NGOs. This is reflected in the "cultural proximity" thesis following which Islamic NGOs are better suited, and therefore should be given priority.[27]

My own attempts to explore the question of "cultural proximity" further have partly confirmed the thesis that Islamic NGOs can, on occasion, benefit from a privileged relationship with beneficiaries in Muslim countries. I chose two areas where the population is almost entirely Muslim—Aceh and Mali—so as to eliminate the complicating factor of friction with other religions. Another factor in common was that the majority of the population in both regions had, at least at the time of my research, little interest in religious militancy. In neither case were Islamic charities engaging, or thought to be engaging, on any large scale in programs of proselytism or "reislamization."

Aceh After the Indian Ocean Tsunami

Aceh is the westernmost province of Indonesia. Some 170,000 people in Aceh died as a result of the tsunami on December 26, 2004; 500,000 were made homeless, and 800,000 lost their source of livelihood. Banda Aceh, the provincial capital, lost about one-third of its population and Meulaboh about half, and large areas of both towns were completely destroyed by waves up to twenty meters high that came in as far as five or more kilometers from the shore. The highly publicized tragedy of the tsunami had the indirect effect of encouraging reconciliation between the Indonesian government and the Aceh independence movement—brokered by Finnish mediators and overseen by

European Commission monitors—after a long-running civil conflict. Democratic elections and greater autonomy for the province were introduced. A form of *shari'ah* was implemented that proved highly controversial among the Acehnese, though devotion to Islam has long been an important element in their ethnic identity.

The vast international outpouring of funds for relief and reconstruction was matched in due course by a spate of evaluations, so that when I paid a short visit to Banda Aceh and Meulaboh in April 2007 I felt that my interlocutors were suffering from evaluation overload. A first point to make, however, is that few of the international evaluators acknowledged the key contribution, in the period immediately after the tsunami, of Indonesian Muslim organizations. This was extensive, though relatively spontaneous and fluid. Typically, the international aid agencies ignored or underrated the contribution of local relief workers, both at the time and in their retrospective evaluations. John Ratcliffe's short desk study of the "moderate Islamic role in Acehnese relief operations" is an exception. He records that, according to some estimates, relief workers affiliated to the Prosperous Justice Party (PKS), a mainstream Islamic party, "represented the largest contingent on the ground in the tsunami's immediate aftermath":

> Party workers had established a command center fewer than 24 hours after the tsunami struck, with satellite health clinics over much of the affected region, including in areas unreached by international organizations. Shortly thereafter, the PKS began chartering private jets to fly in additional relief supplies and also provided volunteers to local groups lacking manpower. The rapidity and scale with which the PKS was able to marshal its response indicates excellent contextual knowledge as well as an ease of coordination that largely escaped the international effort.[28]

PKS already had an active humanitarian wing, but the largest direct role was played by volunteers loosely organized under the auspices of religious groups. These umbrella organizations, according to Ratcliffe, covered the Islamic ideological spectrum, including the militant Islamic Defenders Front (FPI), moderate Nahdlatul Ulama, and reformist Muhammadiyah.

> Many of these associations had no particular background in relief provision, and their chief contribution lay in leveraging their convening authority in support of the relief effort. Many of the volunteers, in

turn, were one-time participants responding to an extraordinary event rather than representing an established tradition of organized Islamic charities. This loose organization largely explains the difficulty in taking an accurate census of Islamic actors and is emblematic of the fluidity associated with local Islamic response in extreme situations.[29]

As international agencies became more active, they tended to displace local actors. However, Muhammadiyah in particular, with its extensive networks, was able to form partnerships with international agencies, among them World Vision.

Islamic Relief benefited initially from its existing contacts with Muslim organizations in Indonesia. It had carried out a needs assessment in Indonesia in 1999 and opened an office in Jakarta in 2003. Its contacts enabled it to make a first response within two of three days of the tsunami. But its high reputation, which was evident to me during my visit in 2007—especially as regards reconstruction of houses and schools—was primarily due to good management, as well as to its not having attempted to operate on a scale beyond its capacities, unlike some secular NGOs that are household names in the West. The expatriate staff were remarkably varied in their ethnic back-grounds. Perhaps the most striking advantage of a shared religious identity was the egalitarianism that Islam teaches. One interlocutor told me: "It is good to see Islamic Relief's expats praying and fasting with the people—and the brotherhood spirit during Ramadan. People stand shoulder to shoulder to pray, and the driver may be the prayer leader, with the head of mission behind him."

Muslim Aid, on the other hand, the second largest UK-based Islamic international NGO, owed its equally high reputation in Aceh primarily to the personal abilities of the local head of mission, an Australian convert to Islam with long professional and personal experience in the province. Both agencies seemed to have escaped the onslaught of criticism leveled by local journalists and others against the majority of international aid providers.[30]

Islamic Relief Worldwide in Mali

In one of the world's poorest countries, Mali, especially in the logistically remote northern region where other aid agencies had found it difficult to work, I discovered convincing evidence of an Islamic NGO earning a high degree of trust. Islamic Relief's commitment in the *cercle* of Rharous, Tim-buktu Region, in northern Mali, began in 1997 when it was contracted with the UN High Commissioner for Refugees to help facilitate "reinsertion" of people who had fled as a result of the Tuareg Rebellion, which almost became a civil war between the traditionally nomadic "white" Tuareg and the sedentary "blacks." Islamic Relief enlisted the local imams and village heads as channels of communication with government and NGOs, and the success of this venture gave it the opportunity to develop a range of aid programs, including food security and the drilling of wells. I have written about this as follows:

> There is no doubt that Islamic Relief has achieved an extraordinary degree of entrenchment in the social life of Gourma Rharous [the administrative centre of the *cercle*]. All its staff are from the Timbuktu Region except one who comes from southern Mali. Office hours and appointments with secretaries count for nothing here. Islamic Relief's Tamashek [Tuareg] coordinator, Azarock Ag Inabrochad, compactly built with gimlet eyes, makes himself available to the high and the low of Rharous at any time. His front yard, lit by an electric generator, is a centre where men drop in every evening to discuss problems, make plans, drink tea, and at the appointed times pray together. Islamic Relief never preaches, but slips easily into the daily life of a country where religion and popular culture are closely intertwined.[31]

Having gained a foothold in northern Mali in 1997, Islamic Relief quickly extended its commitment by opening an office in Bamako, the national capital in southern Mali. Some of its programs could just as well have been implemented by secular agencies: the Centre de l'Espoir ("centre of hope"), a clinic for children and mothers in central Bamako; microcredit schemes; a graduate training center for young unemployed graduates; "child-friendly villages" with special emphasis on water, sanitation, and schools. In order to test the theory of "comparative advantage," it would be necessary to compare the performance of an FBO such as Islamic Relief and some of its secular homologues. However, the protean quality of the religious field would call for exceptional clarity in setting up the statistical model.

I shall focus here on a major part of Islamic Relief's portfolio in southern Mali that has a strong religious component: its orphan sponsorship scheme.[32] Orphan programs are a popular, almost universal feature of Islamic charities. The Prophet Muhammad was an orphan. For a Muslim, the gesture of crossing two fingers alludes to a saying of the Prophet that whoever looks after an orphan will be "like this" with him in Paradise. "Orphan" is generally defined as a child who has lost his or her father—that is, the family breadwinner—but

the category may also include children born out of wedlock.[33] Islamic charities provide a wide range of services, from residential homes and day care
centers to individual sponsorship, and paying for school uniforms, textbooks,
or special clothes for festival days.

I visited in 2006 two local orphan care initiatives in Bamako, supported
by Islamic Relief. One was a small residential orphanage, the Association
pour la Protection des Enfants, catering for orphans from the age of one day
old—for instance, when a teenage girl gave birth but was forced to conceal it
from her village—up to the age of five or six, when they were fostered or
adopted by families. This was a typical Malian grassroots association, run by a
dynamic *présidente* and precariously funded from numerous sources.

Another was ALOVE, the Association Locale des Orphelins et des Veuves
("widows"). Whereas widows do not have quite the theological resonance of
orphans in Islam, they have a special place in its early history, especially with
regard to their need for protection. As in other religious traditions, they can
come to be treated as the epitome of helplessness. Widowhood in Mali, as in
most Muslim societies, is still explicitly accepted as a "marked" social condition
rather than, as in modern Western societies, played down.

Hence it was impressive to visit this dynamic organization, founded in the
1990s. Its sixty members were all widows except for a few who were admitted
if, for example, the husband was ill. They met most afternoons to read the
Qur'an together with an imam, and to help each other, but also to help other
widows who were worse off than they were, and to manage a kind of day
kindergarten for orphans that was 50 percent subsidized by Islamic Relief,
which also sponsored many of the individual orphans. The other 50 percent
of the funding came from the Saudi Embassy. The children were accepted
from the age of three. The ladies had a sideline: buying honeycombs from
beekeepers and converting them in a small workshop into three products for
the benefit of the school—honey, soap, and skin cream—so that nothing was
wasted and there were three different markets.

By contrast with these two small-scale initiatives, Islamic Relief's orphan
sponsorship scheme is global, professional, and computerized. At the time of
my visit, some twelve hundred orphans were sponsored in Mali, and a targeted
increase of 2,000 had been agreed with the head office in Birmingham. By
2010, some 27,000 orphans were being cared for worldwide. It has in effect
translated the traditional Islamic concern for orphans into a mechanism that
sets out systematically to bring help to the poorest.

A death certificate and birth certificate are required by Islamic Relief. This
can be a problem because a large proportion of Malian families cannot afford

these documents, so the agency has a special arrangement with the *mairies* to get the necessary documents paid for retrospectively if necessary. The child's family has to accept that he or she is sent to school. An Islamic Relief team verifies the authenticity of the application, seeking out orphans in the poorest villages. Once accepted, Islamic Relief takes responsibility for the child's basic living expenses, health, and schooling, and it also encourages the orphan and his or her family to plan for income generation so as not to be dependent on aid when he or she reaches adulthood. Sponsors pledge about €33 per month[34] and receive reports every year.

Orphan Dilemmas

Child sponsorship has been extremely controversial for many years. The dilemma has been captured with exemplary sensitivity by Erica Bornstein, who was the first social scientist to follow through holistically an instance of North-South charitable funding flows, with ethnographic accounts of individual donors, administrators and beneficiaries. Her case study was the international Christian aid agency World Vision in the 1990s, one of whose activities was organized sponsorship of children in Zimbabwe by Canadian donors. World Vision applied the funds raised to community development projects, while maintaining a one-to-one relationship between sponsors and individual children.[35] This seemed in 2010 to be the norm among aid agencies that still offered child sponsorship schemes, such as Arya Samaj in India, the Hindu reformist movement,[36] or Save the Children USA. Bornstein's 2005 study explores from both sides the awkwardness, with sometimes distressing consequences, of the long-distance relationship between sponsor and sponsored. (We see only one side of this relationship in the schmaltzy drama film *About Schmidt* of 2002, starring Jack Nicholson, in which an American widower finds lachrymose meaning in his life through the drawing sent him by a small boy he has sponsored in Tanzania.)

The objections to child sponsorship programs are well known. They include the risks of friction within the sponsored family (when only one child is sponsored), envy from outside the family, financial abuse by parents or guardians, and overdependency, as well as child protection risks. There is an overall problem of human dignity: sponsors would not, it is argued, demand that their own children compose letters of gratitude to unseen, distant benefactors. These programs are also expensive to administer, requiring regular visits by the agency's social workers, preparation of feedback material for sponsors—such as photographs, health records, and personal letters of appreciation—communication with sponsors, and compliance with child protection laws.

As of 2010, some national offices of Islamic Relief Worldwide were still inviting donors to select children to sponsor from portrait photographs on its website. However, this was now being phased out as a result of a thorough external review of its worldwide orphan program, whose recommendations were recently endorsed in full by Islamic Relief's management. The consultant commissioned to write this report explored all the objections to child sponsorship. Some were general, but the religious character of Islamic Relief introduced specific difficulties. How, for instance, to maintain the principle of nondiscrimination in religiously mixed countries such as India when the easiest way for them to select children is through Muslim institutions? Again, the exclusive concentration on orphans could lead to stigmatization of individuals. He arrived at the conclusion that the objections, though weighty, did not invalidate the program as an overall concept. For instance, to take the "envy" argument, he writes: "communities are complex, . . . many families receive support (from relatives in the village, from remittances, from a government pension) and the NGO support is just one of those drops and is unlikely to tip the balance from 'that's the way the world works' to 'look at them!'"[37]

The consultant's report recommended that the orphan program should be reorganized on two tracks. The first would be improvement of the existing "one to one" program—for instance, eliminating selection by sponsors of children's photographs on a website, which is demeaning to the children; and restricting the scheme to the poorest countries. Second, diversification toward family sponsorship and community programs would open up opportunities for a more participatory form of development.[38] The main theme of the report, on the basis of extensive interviews and observations,[39] was that Islamic Relief's donors extended to it a high degree of trust, and—contrary to worries expressed by some insiders—would not abandon their commitment to orphans if the one-to-one element were to be diluted or even removed. Nevertheless:

> It is the "empathic telescope" effect: our brains are most easily activated when we hear a *single* cry for help, even though the benefit-per-dollar is relatively low. So, while one-to-one sponsorship programmes are unattractive to efficiency-focused institutional donor agencies, they are extremely attractive to individual sponsors.[40]

The clinching argument in favor of developing the orphan program was that it had great religious appeal to Muslim donors as a preferred way for them to discharge their *zakat* obligation. Islamic Relief, already by a long way the market leader in this form of international charity (with a turnover of some £10 million for its 2009 orphan program, an increase of 12 percent over the previous year), saw substantial opportunities for judicious expansion of the department. Hence this is a definite case of "cultural proximity" intensifying the relationship between donor and beneficiary communities, in that Islamic Relief's field activities are located mainly in Muslim-majority countries.

By contrast, however, with the general argument in favor of cultural proximity, which draws attention to local grassroots networks and privileged access through a common religion, the religious aspect of Muslim orphan programs is confined exclusively to the motivation of donors. There is no evidence of any enthusiasm on the recipient side for the religious dimension of orphan sponsorship. But it would be unrealistic to gloss over the fact that marketing to donors, both religious and secular, is an integral part of the humanitarian continuum.

Conclusion

There are arguments for and against the importance of "cultural proximity" in specific cases. A key principle is that of nondiscrimination within a given area, which has been followed by the more progressive Islamic charities such as Islamic Relief and Muslim Aid. (It may be objected that cases of proselytism or discrimination in field operations are occasionally encountered and reported. However, this is also true of Christian agencies formally committed to nondiscrimination. Directives from head office are not always scrupulously obeyed in the field.) Here Hugo Slim's concept of an "interim ethic" in relief aid may be helpful.[41] The "interim ethic" applies to short-term emergency relief, and in these situations of crisis it forbids any form of discrimination within a population of emergency victims. In medium to long-term programs, however—the phases of reconstruction and development—the principle of cultural sensitivity may include sensitivity to particular religious practices. Restricting emergency food aid or shelter, for instance, to co-religionists or potential converts is against the principles endorsed by the leading Islamic agencies (at least those operating from Britain) as much as by the leading Christian agencies, which is to say those that comply with internationally accepted codes of conduct for NGOs. But at the later stage of reconstruction, there would seem to be no ethical reason a religious NGO should not apply funds to rebuilding a mosque or a church. Islamic Relief, however, is so determined to avoid any imputation of proselytism that it has decided never to spend funds on building or repairing mosques, whereas CAFOD does so occasionally on the grounds that mosques are vital cultural resources.

The more conservative Islamic charities—in the main, those based in the petrodollar states—are likely to fall in line gradually with the principle of nondiscrimination, if they have not in some cases done so already. Objective research on Gulf-based charities is still on the whole very difficult to undertake because of their lack of a tradition of transparency and accountability, though these principles have been officially adopted in Kuwait and Qatar.

One reason "cultural proximity" has emerged as a controversial topic is that the growth of Islamic charities has challenged a deep-rooted assumption in the West: that charity is a Judeo-Christian monopoly. As Amy Singer writes in the conclusion to her history of Islamic charity: "Even the current nascent state of charity-philanthropy studies in Islamic studies is sufficient to challenge the long-held perception that western (Judeo-Christian), and most especially the US charitable traditions and practices, constitute the most powerful charity-philanthropy paradigm in history."[42] We may expect more research to be undertaken on charitable traditions outside the Abrahamic traditions. Christianity and Islam, however, as the two principal religions of conversion, are destined to continue to perceive themselves, and be perceived, as having a mutually competitive relationship. This overarching competition does not exclude deep divisions of interpretation and practice within both religions, interacting with ethnic and territorial differences—all of which are reflected in their respective humanitarian activities.

Additionally, the regulatory environment changed after September 11, 2001, though most dramatically in the United States, where an understandable determination to protect the homeland and the interests of close American allies has come to seem, in the eyes of many observers, like a concerted attack on Islamic institutions. Whereas the record of Islamic charities as a whole has not been entirely lily-white, neither was that of the United States charity regulation system in the 1980s when the national policy was to back the *mujahideen* in Afghanistan at all costs in order to help destroy the Soviet system. Many of the mainstream (i.e., non-Muslim) U.S. charities have inferred that attacks on Islamic charities through the U.S. legal system, without realistic rights of defense and appeal, are an attack on the freedom of all relief and development charities to use their judgment to operate effectively in areas of disasters and conflict, taking proper account of security considerations.[43]

Undoubtedly Islamic charities in the West, like other diaspora organizations, have a special potential to mobilize transnational networks in support of local community-based organizations that are often religious in character.

A prime example is the history of the *zakat* committees of the Palestinian West Bank since the mid-1990s. Research suggests that—*pace* the Israeli and U.S. governments—these were developing organically from informal mosque-based committees into more professional charities that had earned an impressive degree of popular trust, in a grim and conflict-torn political context where trust has been scarce. They were "social coalitions" drawing on the symbolic power of *zakat* as one of the pillars of Islam and following locally defined priorities rather than externally imposed aid agendas, while also beginning to raise funds from international sources. Political interference has put their independence in jeopardy since the split between the West Bank and Gaza in 2007.[44] If this analysis is correct, they were before 2007 a good example of what De Cordier, following Olivier Roy, has called "civil society as it is," as opposed to "window-dressing" civil society based on superimposed conceptual templates.[45]

More generally, local *zakat* committees and similar traditional Islamic associations have the advantage of potentially acting as conduits for aid that respond to locally defined priorities while sharing the same symbolic vocabulary as the international Islamic charities (which already make sophisticated use of *zakat* and other key religious concepts to raise funds and awareness). If these circuits of aid are banned, there is a danger of creating a "humanitarian vacuum" that can be penetrated by violent extremist groups. It is believed that Osama bin Laden had personally funded relief and development programs in Sudan and Afghanistan in the 1980s. In Pakistan, after the Kashmir earthquake in 2005 and the floods in 2010, welfare groups closely associated with the extremist group Lashkar-e-Taiba were successful in bringing effective relief aid; and on both occasions, statements attributed to Zawahiri[46] and bin Laden[47] respectively called on Muslims and Arab governments to do more for humanitarian relief and economic development.

Qualified recognition of the value of "cultural proximity" in certain circumstances should not be seen as detracting from the practical potential of non-Muslim aid agencies, both religious and secular, to work effectively in Muslim field areas (provided they exercise cultural sensitivity) and to collaborate effectively with Islamic aid agencies—as do, for instance, Oxfam, CAFOD, the United Methodist Committee on Relief (UMCOR), and the Church of Latter-Day Saints (Mormons) already.[48] I would differ, however, from the *International Review of the Red Cross* editorialist, quoted above, who would assimilate religion to the Dunantian humanitarian ethos—which is historically only a half-truth. Religions have markedly exclusive as well as inclusive properties. It is equally productive to look at all humanitarian and development agencies, even those professing an entirely secular set of values, as variants of faith-based organizations—which is a presiding theme in the present volume. A recent statement by Dr. Hany El-Banna of Islamic Relief that he prefers the concept of "value based organizations" to that of faith-based organizations[49] may be a practical indication that the porosity between the religious and secular, explored in our editors' introductory Chapter One, is now being recognized in a practical as well as an academic context.

Finally, although the academic attention over the last two decades given to NGOs, and more recently to faith-based organizations, has been productive, it needs to be rebalanced toward more understanding of the viewpoints of their recipients or beneficiaries. It seems to be widely assumed that people in need do not care who helps them provided that their needs are met, and this is no doubt true when their very survival is at stake. If, however, we adopt an expanded concept of social security as "the dimension of social organization dealing with the provision of security not considered to be an exclusive matter of individual responsibility"—recently proposed by a group of social anthropologists[50]—we can focus more clearly on aspects of spiritual, emotional, or ontological security, which bring to the fore recipients' relationships with their providers. As an example of how these relationships can be approached, I am currently working with Jacob Høigilt and Emanuel Schaeublin to try to reconstruct analytically the popular view of the Palestinian *zakat* committees before the political split in 2007. These were appreciated not only for their relative financial integrity, but also for the respect paid to recipients (for instance, in small village medical clinics) and for their contribution to maintaining the steadfastness of communities under military occupation. We suggest that, though the quantity of material aid these committees supplied was much less than that coming from international agencies and from the Palestinian Authority, they were iconic of Islamic values of compassion and collective responsibility. One could apply the concept of ontological security to analyze many other cases of humanitarian intervention, but bearing in mind that this aspect of security can actually enhance material vulnerability.

NOTES

1. Ghandour (2001), 332–334, my translation.
2. Tvedt (1998), 128–131.
3. Olivier, Cochrane, and Schmidt (2006), 9.
4. II Corinthians 9:7, also I Corinthians 16:1, II Corinthians 8.
5. Catholic Relief Services (CRS), the U.S. equivalent of CAFOD, decided in the mid-1990s to reemphasize its Catholic identity, integrating "social justice" into its

policies and also extending its connections with local churches worldwide; Barnett (2011), 201–204.

6. Shortt (2006), 78–79; Shortt writes that Benedict's predecessor, John Paul II, "appeared to blow hot and cold about liberation theology" (p. 81).

7. Address to the Bishops of Latin America and the Caribbean, conference hall, Shrine of Aparecida, May 13, 2007. He cited II Corinthians 8:9, which more traditionally has been taken to refer to poverty only in a spiritual sense.

8. For more information, see the JCTR's website at www.jctr.org.zm.

9. Falla (1994).

10. James (2010), 1.

11. The argument can be pushed further. Commercial branding represents "image" rather than conveying a logical message, and it offers consumers "added value" through enabling them to buy into attractive lifestyles at no more than a marginal cost. This can be seen as a form of transcendence or spiritualization of material products, replacing traditional religious symbolism; see Benthall (2008), 63. A clear example is the extremely successful Nestlé subsidiary that markets the proprietary coffee-making process Nespresso. Massive marketing—by means of its "brand ambassador," the film star George Clooney, and the brand slogans "What else?" and "Absolutely divine"—offers membership of the Nespresso Club to consumers of expensive cups of coffee. The value added is access to a daydream of plenitude, hobnobbing with "the sexiest man alive." Clooney's appointment as a United Nations Messenger of Peace supports my suggestion elsewhere that representations of misery in the South are consumables, exported northward and continuously reciprocated by humanitarian aid in a "stable system"; see Benthall (2010), ix–xxvii.

12. It is, however, a common feature of religious traditions to disvalue charity performed in expectation of reward of any kind.

13. Catholic Relief Services, CAFOD, and Secours Catholique.

14. E.g., Rencoret et al. (2010).

15. Linda Poteat, at a public meeting on the Haiti earthquake convened by the Overseas Development Institute, Humanitarian Practice Network, London, on October 26, 2010. See also Duplat and Parry (2010). Interaction is the largest coalition of U.S.-based international NGOs.

16. De Cordier (2009b), 101; see also De Cordier (2008), 42–49; and De Cordier (2009b), 663–684.

17. Palmer (2011), 96–108.

18. Kirman and Khan (2008), 41–50.

19. Palmer (2011).

20. Brikci (2005).

21. Ibid.

22. De Cordier (2009b), 135.

23. "The term 'sustainable livelihood' came to prominence as a development concept in the early 1990s, drawing on advances in understanding of famine and food insecurity

during the 1980s. Much of the literature takes an adaptation of Chambers and Conway's [1991] definition of livelihoods: 'A livelihood comprises the capabilities, assets (including both material and social resources) and activities required for a means of living. A livelihood is sustainable when it can cope with and recover from stresses and shocks.' CARE, UNDP, Oxfam and IISD were some of the early adopters of sustainable livelihoods methodologies. In the late 1990s the sustainable livelihoods approach gained momentum in the UK's Department for International Development (DFID) with investments in research, workshops and the publication of guidance sheets and other papers." www.eldis.org, "Livelihoods Connect."

24. Benthall and Bellion-Jourdan (2003), 84; Arne Strand (1998), 81–82.

25. A later passage in the same book reads: "Western critical thought, much indebted to cultural anthropology, has developed the idea of 'respect for difference' and hence of 'cultural rights'. A number of Islamic NGOs appear to be drawing on this idea in order to develop a doctrine of what might be called 'cultural proximity' or a communitarian approach to aid. It is claimed that women Muslim refugees, for instance, have special cultural needs that can be catered for only by Muslim agencies" (Benthall and Bellion-Jourdan, 2003, 156). This passage appears under our joint authorship, but the thought behind it is Bellion-Jourdan's rather than mine and derives from his earlier doctoral thesis. He was particularly struck by the difficulty experienced in the 1990s by Bosnian Muslims, having lived for decades under Communism, in accepting rules such as the prohibition of alcohol and pork, which was second nature to the staff of Saudi relief agencies.

26. *International Review of the Red Cross*, no. 858, June 2005, Editorial.

27. Benedetti (2006),

28. Ratcliffe (2007), 53.

29. Ibid.

30. For more detail on Aceh, see Benthall (2008a).

31. Benthall (2006), 22.

32. For more detail on southern Mali, see Benthall (2008).

33. Willem van Eekelen points out that the Thokomola Orphan Care Organisation in Durban, South Africa, uses the opposite definition, arguing that young children are more attached to the mother than to the father, and he speculates that this may be especially valid in societies where fathers tend to be mobile. In the United States and Europe, a distinction is often made between "full orphan" and "partial orphan."

34. Up to €48 for children in other countries.

35. Bornstein (2005), 67–95.

36. Bornstein (2010), 134.

37. Willem van Eekelen, personal communication, October 12, 2010.

38. A third recommendation was to adhere more strictly to the concept of "catchment areas," to minimize travel time on the part of IR staff.

39. A total of 115 interviews with sponsors in five donor countries.

40. Islamic Relief internal report.

41. The context of his remarks is the distinction between humanitarian agencies in war-time and multimandate agencies with a vision of the "good society"; see Slim (2004).
42. Singer (2008), 203.
43. Benthall (2010b), 91–121.
44. Schaeublin (2009).
45. De Cordier (2009b), 132.
46. "Al-Zawahiri Urges Pakistan Quake Aid" (2005).
47. Shane (2010). It should be added that mainstream Islamic charities were also active in bringing relief aid to flood victims.
48. There are additional reasons favoring engagement between international agencies and local religion-based institutions. For instance, "Avoiding interaction with religious actors may seem to be a wise move; however, such an approach may create a self-fulfilling prophecy: in refusing to interact with religious actors out of a concern that their influence might be predominantly negative, one risks pushing religious actors towards precisely such unhelpful roles"; in Borchgrevink (2007), 56.
49. Meeting in the House of Commons, London, on Pakistan flood relief, convened by the Muslim Charities Forum, February 1, 2011.
50. Leutloff-Grandits, Peleikis, and Thelen (2009), 2–6.

BIBLIOGRAPHY

"Al Zawahiri Urges Pakistan Quake Aid." Al-Jazeera.net (accessed October 23, 2005), http://english.aljazeera.net/archive/2005/10/200841014315693538.html.

Barnett, Michael. *Empire of Humanity; A History of Humanitarianism*. Ithaca, NY: Cornell University Press, 2011.

Benedetti, Carlo. "Islamic and Christian Inspired Relief NGOs: Between Tactical Collaboration and Strategic Diffidence?" *Journal of International Development*, 18 (2006): 849–859.

Benthall, Jonathan. "Islamic Aid in a North Malian Enclave." *Anthropology Today* (August 2006), 22–24.

———. "Have Islamic Charities a Privileged Relationship in Majority Muslim Societies? The Case of Post-Tsunami Reconstruction in Aceh." Published June 26, 2008a, in the free online *Journal of Humanitarian Assistance* (Tufts University), www.jha.ac.

———. "Islamic Charities in Southern Mali." *Islam et sociétés au sud du Sahara*, 1, new series. Paris: Les Indes savantes, 2008b.

———. *Returning to Religion: Why a Secular Age Is Haunted by Faith*, London: Tauris, 2008c.

———. *Disasters, Relief and the Media*. New edition. Wantage, Oxfordshire: S. Kingston, 2010a.

———. "Islamic Humanitarianism in Adversarial Context." In Erica Bornstein and Peter Redfield, *Forces of Compassion: Humanitarianism Between Ethics and Politics*. Santa Fe, NM: SAR Press, 2010b.

———— and Jérôme Bellion-Jourdan. *The Charitable Crescent: Politics of Aid in the Muslim World*. London: Tauris, 2003 (new paperback edition 2009).

Borchgrevink, Kaja. *Religious Actors and Civil Society in Post-2001 Afghanistan*. Oslo: International Peace Research Institute, 2007.

Bornstein, Erica. *The Spirit of Development*. Stanford: Stanford University Press, 2005.

————. "The Value of Orphans." In Erica Bornstein and Peter Redfield (eds.), *Forces of Compassion: Humanitarianism Between Ethics and Politics*. Santa Fe, NM: SAR Press, 2010.

Brikci, Nouria. "Is Cultural Proximity the Answer to Gaining Access in Muslim Contexts?" *Humanitarian Exchange Magazine*, Overseas Development Institute, issue 29, March 2005, online.

De Cordier, Bruno. ONG islamiques internationales et société civile dans les contextes musulmans: quelle proximité culturelle? *La Revue Humanitaire*, 20 (2008), 42–49.

————. "The 'Humanitarian Frontline,' Development and Relief, and Religion: What Context, Which Threats and Which Opportunities?" *Third World Quarterly*, 30(4) (2009a): 663–684.

————. "The Third Pillar: Islamic development and relief organizations and the humanitarian frontline: a field analysis." PhD dissertation, Ghent University, Faculty of Political and Social Sciences, 2009b.

Duplat, P., and E. Parry. "Haiti: From the Ground Up." Refugees International Field Report, Washington, DC, March 2, 2010, http://refugeesinternational.org/sites/default/files/030210_haiti_groundup.pdf.

Falla, Ricardo. *Massacres in the Jungle: Ixcán, Guatemala, 1975–1982*. Boulder, CO: Westview Press, 1994.

Ghandour, Abdel-Rahman. *Jihad humanitaire: enquête sur les ONG islamiques*. Paris: Flammarion, 2001.

James, Rick. "Faith in Development: Coping with Paradox." *ontrac* (INTRAC newsletter) no. 46, September 2010.

Kirman, Nida, and Ajaz Ahmed Khan. "Does Faith Matter? An Examination of Islamic Relief's Work with Refugees and Internally Displaced Persons." *Refugee Survey Quarterly*, 2008, 27(2), 41–50.

Leutloff-Grandits, Carolin, Anja Peleikis and Tatjana Thelen. *Social Security in Religious Networks: Anthropological Perspectives on New Risks and Ambivalences*. New York and Oxford: Berghahn Books, 2009.

Olivier, J., J. R. Cochrane, and B. Schmidt. *ARHAP Literature Review: Working in a Bounded Field of Unknowing*. Cape Town: African Religious Assets Programme, 2006.

Palmer, Victoria. "Analysing 'Cultural Proximity': Islamic Relief Worldwide and Rohingya Refugees in Bangladesh." *Development in Practice*, 21(1) (February 2011): 96–108.

Ratcliffe, John. "Local Islamic Response to the 2004 Indian Ocean Tsunami and 2005 Kashmir Earthquake." In J. Alterman and K. von Hippel (eds.), *Understanding Islamic Charities*. Washington, DC: CSIS Press, 2007, 52–54.

Rencoret, Nicole, et al. "Haiti Earthquake Response: Context Analysis." London: ALNAP, 2010.

Schaeublin, Emanuel. *Role and Governance of Islamic Charitable Institutions: The West Bank Zakat Committees (1977–2009) in the Local Context.* Occasional Paper. Geneva: Graduate Institute of International and Development Studies, 2009.

Shane, Scott. "Bin Laden Resurfaces in Recordings." *New York Times*, October 3, 2010, A8.

Shortt, Rupert. *Benedict XVI: Commander of the Faith.* London: Hodder and Stoughton, 2006.

Singer, Amy. *Charity in Islamic Societies.* Cambridge: Cambridge University Press, 2008.

Slim, Hugo. *With or Against? Humanitarian Agencies and Coalition Counter-Insurgency.* Geneva: Centre for Humanitarian Dialogue, 2004.

Strand, Arne. *Bridging the Gap Between Islamic and Western NGOs Working in Conflict Areas.* M.A. dissertation in postwar recovery studies, University of York, 1998.

Tvedt, Terje. *Angels of Mercy or Development Diplomats? NGOs and Foreign Aid.* Trenton, NJ: Africa World Press, 1998.

4

Religious Obligation or Altruistic Giving? Muslims and Charitable Donations

Ajaz Ahmed Khan

MUSLIM FAITH-BASED RELIEF and development organizations (FBOs)[1] have traditionally relied predominantly on donations from private individual donors for the majority of their income. Common perceptions regarding such funding have been influential in determining where, how, and with whom Muslim FBOs have implemented relief and development related programs. Although there has been growth in research in recent years examining the role of Muslim FBOs in providing humanitarian aid, as well as the differences among them, the relative emphasis they place on religion, and whether they enjoy cultural proximity among Muslim populations,[2] little analysis exists on the motivations of donors in giving to Muslims charities. This investigation attempts to fill this void by exploring the motivations for charitable giving as well as the expectations and aspirations of individual donors from the United Kingdom to a specific Muslim charity, Islamic Relief. Where appropriate, it refers to Islamic teachings, as these are important in understanding the motivations of many donors, as well as the structure of organizational fundraising and development programs. This investigation both confirms and challenges some common assumptions regarding the motivations of donors. Fulfilling religious obligations was important, but just as significantly donors possessed strong altruistic motivations and a desire to alleviate the poverty and suffering of others. Donors were attracted to Islamic Relief because of its reputation as a reliable, trusted and well-recognized charity and because they believed it promoted a positive image of Muslims and their contributions to British society. By giving to Islamic Relief donors believed they could simultaneously fulfill a range of religious and humanitarian objectives.

Although in recent years Islamic Relief has come to resemble its secular counterparts in terms of its discourse and program operations, this analysis argues that there are limits to any trends toward secularization. In fact, there are important reasons for the organization continuing to strive to distinguish itself from peers and maintaining a strong faith identity.

Islamic Relief Worldwide, usually shortened to just Islamic Relief, is an international relief and development charity founded by Dr. Hany El-Banna in 1984 in Birmingham, United Kingdom, in response to the famines affecting countries in the Horn of Africa. From very modest beginnings, Islamic Relief has expanded considerably; the organization now has programs in more than twenty-five countries in Africa, Asia, Eastern Europe, the Middle East, and most recently the Caribbean. The organization aims to promote sustainable development through work in the sectors of education, health and nutrition, disaster preparedness, water and sanitation, and livelihoods. In addition to its field offices, Islamic Relief has fundraising offices in a further thirteen countries[3] and receives support from tens of thousands of private individual donors who regularly contribute relatively modest amounts of money for both emergency relief and long-term development projects. Private funding from individuals has always formed the bulk of organizational funding, although in recent years an increasing proportion of income has come from institutional donors. Islamic Relief prioritizes income received from private individual donors because it believes that such an approach ensures greater autonomy and flexibility in formulating organizational priorities as well as maintaining a separate identity. It has experienced rapid growth during the last decade in particular, and its annual income reached £58 million in 2009.[4]

The fact that Islamic Relief is a Muslim FBO with its headquarters and almost all fundraising offices in Western Europe and North America no doubt contributes to shaping the organization's identity, and Islamic Relief presents itself simultaneously as both Muslim and Western.[5] It is "inspired by Islamic humanitarian values"[6] and there are frequent references to the Qur'an and *hadith*[7] in its promotional literature and websites. Although the majority of program interventions are similar to those of secular aid agencies, the distribution of food packages during the holy month of Ramadan and of ritually slaughtered meat to coincide with the Muslim festival of Eid-al-Adha[8] are an integral feature of its annual activities. Although they may be of limited long-term development value, such activities are important because they permit donors to fulfill their religious obligations and allow the organization to confirm its "Islamic" credentials among both donors and beneficiaries. The organization has also incorporated Islamic teachings into some operational activities; for example, it developed *shari'ah*-compliant microfinance programs in several countries, and many of its policy positions on issues such as international debt, trade, reproductive health, and the environment are based on Islamic teachings.[9] Interestingly, there is some discussion within Islamic Relief as to whether it is even possible to develop an "Islamic approach to development" to frame the overall work of the organization.[10]

As it grows and attracts greater recognition, it is noticeable that Islamic Relief has tended to employ more secular development language, conform to the codes of practice, and emphasize its commitment to other norms of the international aid system such as impartiality, neutrality, and nondiscrimination.[11] It stresses its policy of working with local communities "regardless of race, color, political affiliation, gender or belief" and aims to "contribute to achieving the Millennium Development Goals."[12] It shares platforms with secular and Christian FBOs in advocacy campaigns on issues such as canceling the debt of the world's poorest countries, raising awareness of the effects of climate change, and promoting fair trade, as well as jointly implementing programs in the field with the same organizations on occasion. Its policy positions respect Islamic teachings but also find convergence in some areas with the policies of secular and Christian counterparts. Highlighting the similarities between Islamic and secular perspectives on development and the search for common ground has been a feature of the organization's activities in recent years. Petersen observed that "as a 'moderate' Muslim organization, Islamic Relief has to promote a secular, almost invisible Islam, and at the same time, underline the strengths and unique qualities of being a Muslim organization—but in a way that does not corrupt the values and principles of mainstream development. In this perspective, Islamic Relief has to be bilingual, mastering the languages of both development and Islam."[13]

There are perhaps two principal reasons for this trend. Firstly, it attracts ever more funding from large Western institutional donors such as the Department for International Development of the UK government (DFID),[14] the Humanitarian Aid Department of the European Union (ECHO), and non-Western institutions such as the Islamic Development Bank. Thus, even though income from institutional donors formed just 8.5 percent of total funding in 2004, it steadily increased to 13 percent in 2005, 21 percent in 2006, 22 percent in 2007, and 24 percent in 2008,[15] and the comparable figure for 2009 was 29 percent.[16] Although welcoming increased institutional funding, particularly from Western donors, because it is seen as conferring acceptance and legitimacy following September 11, 2001, the organization is conscious that the latter should constitute "perhaps no more than one-third" of total income.[17] In order to access such funding it must present its applications and submit reports according to the norms and language employed by such donors.

Secondly, suspicions of Muslim charities following September 11 encouraged Islamic Relief to stress the humanitarian and impartial nature of the organization and promote its image as a "mainstream" development agency sharing many common features with its secular peers. With regard to staff responsible for program implementation, it has emphasized development expertise rather than religious commitment, and it is noticeable that the proportion of non-Muslim staff, particularly in its international headquarters, increased markedly in recent years. At the same time, Islamic Relief has perceptibly increased its representation at discussions and workshops convened by its secular peers and Western institutional donors. These trends are likely to continue as long as Islamic Relief continues to believe that there are operational and fundraising advantages both from being perceived as a "moderate" Islamic, and even "Western," organization and from acting as a possible bridge builder among "Western" agencies, Islamic aid agencies, and even governments in largely Muslim countries.[18]

"Our Donors Are Conservative Muslims"

Within the organization there have always been a number of strong perceptions regarding the motives of individual donors that influence where, how, and with whom Islamic Relief implements emergency relief and development activities.[19] It is assumed that individual donors are Muslims fulfilling their religious obligations and prefer their funding to be used in "traditional" sectors of intervention such as direct provision of water and sanitation, primary health, education, orphans care, and in particular high-visibility emergency projects supporting those affected by natural disasters or conflict. At the same time, there is a belief that support among private individual donors would be less forthcoming for slow-onset emergencies or for interventions in "nontraditional" areas, such as HIV/AIDS and reproductive health, because of their perceived association with sexual permissiveness. Indeed, there is a belief that such activities may actually alienate individual donors, particularly those who hold relatively conservative beliefs, and hence jeopardize the source of a significant proportion of the organization's funding. Fundraising staff particularly believe that individual supporters want most, if not all, of their donations to be spent directly on project implementation rather than in areas such as advocacy and policy change. Furthermore, although donors recognize that administration costs do exist, they prefer them to be kept to the absolute minimum or taken from sources other than their donations. Lastly, there is always the perception that donors prefer their funding to be directed at assisting other Muslims.

However, much of this remains conjecture; in fact, there is relatively little detailed evidence on what actually motivates individual donors and what are their expectations and aspirations.[20] To address these issues, this investigation used data gathered through questionnaires completed by individual donors, as well as through a series of interviews with Islamic Relief staff responsible for fundraising at both the individual and community levels in a number of regions throughout the United Kingdom. The face-to-face interviews with staff were conducted between December 2009 and February 2010; the donor questionnaires were completed between April and July 2010. The question-naires were answered by a random selection of 200 individual donors from the UK who had donated either online or via telephone at least once over the past twelve months. More than one-third of these, 35.5 percent, were regular monthly donors, while another 19.5 percent donated on average at least once every six months. A further 16 percent donated at least once every twelve months, while the remaining 29 percent donated only occasionally and usually in response to an emergency appeal following a natural disaster. Fund-raising staff, some of whom had worked for Islamic Relief for many years, generally had direct contact with donors at fundraising events, collections in mosques or other public places, and through almost daily interaction at Islamic Relief's regional charity shops.[21] Staff also received regular feedback from Islamic Relief's many fundraising volunteers. This analysis, therefore, managed to obtain input from a broad range of donors and fundraising staff. Nevertheless, the information is limited to the extent that it provides an insight into what donors and staff felt at a particular period when the data were gathered and may have been influenced by recent events at the time. These included the earthquake in Haiti and the attempts of a flotilla of aid ships to break the blockade of Gaza. Although limited to Islamic Relief, it is reasonable to assume that the findings may reflect more generally the motiva-tions of individual donors to Muslim FBOs in the UK.

Young, Muslim, and British

Before proceeding to discuss the motivations of Islamic Relief's donors, it might be useful to present some brief information on their general profile as revealed by the survey. Firstly, although it is difficult to be certain about the faith of donors since Islamic Relief does not ask questions regarding religious affiliations, it appears that the overwhelming majority of individual donors are Muslims, confirming an important assumption regarding the constitution of Islamic Relief's supporters. In this survey, 1 percent categorically stated that they were non-Muslims, while another 1 percent of regular donors stated "not applicable" in response to questions relating to *zakat*, indicating most likely that they were non-Muslims as opposed to not meet the minimum level, or *nisab*, for their wealth to be eligible for *zakat*. It appears therefore that only a very small proportion, around 2 percent, of Islamic Relief's donors are non-Muslims. However, even though agreeing with this portrayal of donors, many of the fundraising staff interviewed suggested that when there were public collections or appeals for emergency relief in areas such as Gaza and Iraq the proportion of non-Muslims who donated was much greater.

Secondly, although Islamic Relief attracts support from a diverse range of Muslims, in terms of ethnicity the donor base broadly reflects the general profile of Muslims living in the UK, with the largest number of donors, 74.5 percent, coming from various South Asian communities. Specifically, almost half of all donors, 49.5 percent, described themselves as Pakistani British, 16.5 percent as Indian British, and 8.5 percent as Bangladeshi British.[22] With regard to the ethnic structure of the remaining donors, 8.5 percent described themselves as Arab British, 5.5 percent as White British, and the remaining 11.5 percent as belonging to a variety of other ethnic groups, including Ugandan, Somali, Albanian, Turkish, and Malaysian.[23] Slightly more than half of those surveyed, 53 percent, were women.

Thirdly, Muslims have the youngest age profile of all religious groups in the UK, and this was reflected in the composition of donors. Approximately two-thirds of those surveyed, 68.5 percent, were thirty-five years old or younger and just 12.5 percent were forty-six or older. Generally, older Muslims living in the UK were born abroad and they, as well as those who have settled relatively recently, appear less likely to donate to Islamic Relief. Instead they are probably more likely to make their charitable donations either directly or through family and friends in their country of origin, with whom they tend to maintain strong and direct links. Increasingly, Islamic Relief's donors appear to be second- and third-generation Muslims who were born or raised in the UK, with relatively weaker links with the countries of origin of their parents or grandparents,[24] although many still describe themselves as Pakistani British or Indian British. This is something that clearly Islamic Relief UK has considered as part of its fundraising strategy, since fundraising staff tend to reflect the local communities in which they operate. Thus, those with a Pakistani

Kashmiri heritage are employed in Bradford and those with an Indian Gujarati background are responsible for fundraising in Leicester. In contrast, program staff employed in the international headquarters tend to be from more diverse backgrounds, with many having moved only rather recently to the UK.

Fulfilling Religious Obligations

This investigation found that there were multiple motivations, both religious and secular, behind donations to Islamic Relief. They included desiring to promote positive change in the world, wishing to address fundamental problems such as climate change, feeling good, having compassion for those less fortunate, and even giving simply because someone asked them for a donation. However, there were two principal motivations: first, and in all likelihood something shared with supporters of other humanitarian aid organizations, more than three-quarters of all donors (78 percent) stated they wanted to alleviate the suffering of poor people in developing countries. Second, and perhaps in common with other (particularly Muslim) FBOs, a comparable 76 percent replied that they donated in order to fulfill their religious obligations. Within the latter category, comments typical of many donors were that "charity is an obligation for me," "I need to give my *zakat*," and "Allah will reward me for any charity that I give."

Principles of charitable giving and compassion are enshrined in Islamic teachings through the Qur'an and traditions of the Prophet Muhammad (pbuh[25]). Muslims are obliged to provide for the poor and marginalized through *zakat* (almsgivings), which is payable at a rate of 2.5 percent on a person's wealth above a minimum level or *nisab*. The importance of *zakat* is such that, after the declaration of faith and the compulsory five daily prayers, it is the third pillar of Islam. In addition to this obligatory payment, Muslims are also encouraged to make voluntary contributions, or *sadaqah*, to help the poor and needy and for other social welfare purposes, and also to establish *waqf*. *Waqf* is an endowment (usually a building or plot of land) or trust set up for charitable purposes, typically for education, mosques, or the poor; it involves tying up a property in perpetuity so that it cannot be sold, inherited, or donated to anyone.

Muslims consider undertaking charitable acts as a way of receiving Allah's assistance, atoning for sins, escaping punishment, thanking Allah for his mercies, and bringing a believer closer to Paradise on the Day of Judgment.[26] It is clear that both *zakat* and *sadaqah* play a key role in the religious beliefs of Muslims. Indeed, as Amy Singer observes, "without them faith is incomplete."[27]

Qurbani means "sacrifice" and refers to the ritual slaughter of animals, which can occur at any time of the year but is a requirement among Muslims during the religious festival Eid-al-Adha. Rather than perform the slaughter themselves, many Muslims, particularly those living in the West, simply make payment to a Muslim charity to undertake the *Qurbani* on their behalf and distribute the meat among poor and disadvantaged communities in developing countries. It is clear, therefore, that charitable giving in various forms is an important aspect of the lives of many Muslims.[28]

Although *zakat* and *sadaqah* may be dispensed locally or to poor neighbors, relatively affluent Muslims feel that poorer people living in developing countries, particularly those afflicted by natural disasters and civil conflict, are more deserving recipients. Furthermore, since many Muslims living in the UK are second- and third-generation immigrants, they tend not to have the same strong links with the countries of origin of their parents or grandparents, and they are less likely to send remittances to extended families or neighbors abroad. Instead, they tend to give their *zakat* and *sadaqah* to Muslim FBOs such as Islamic Relief, although they often prefer that this support be directed to those countries with which they have family links.[29] It is also worth noting that many Muslims prefer to give charitable donations anonymously. This follows the advice of a well-known *hadith* stating that one of the seven types of people who are provided with shade on the Day of Judgment are those who give charity so secretly that their left hand does not know what the right hand has given.[30]

In 2009, approximately 6.5 percent of total income received by Islamic Relief was in funds specifically designated as *zakat*,[31] although it is reasonable to assume that many of the donations given as *zakat* were not specified as such.[32] Funding derived from *sadaqah* can be spent across a wide range of activities, but Islamic teachings specify that *zakat* funding can be used only in eight categories specified in the Qur'an: people who do not have anything, so they are in need of asking others for food, clothing, health services, and shelter; the poor who may have money, but it is not sufficient for their basic needs; persons appointed to collect or administer *zakat*; for Allah's cause (which includes every kind of struggle for a righteous cause); debtors; wayfarers or travelers; for freeing captives; and for reconciling hearts.[33] If a person does not fall into any of these categories, then according to Islamic teachings he or she is prohibited from receiving *zakat*, though the person may be eligible to receive other types of charitable donations such as *sadaqah*. Islamic Relief ensures that *zakat* donations are spent only on the permitted categories, and if requested by the donor, funds are allocated to a specific country (most commonly Palestine and Pakistan). Similarly, funding received because of particular campaigns, such as for performing *Qurbani*, is also spent exclusively on a specific project or activity.

There is an assumption that many Muslim donors prefer to disburse their *zakat* to poor Muslims and deem that this is only likely to occur through Muslim charities, which understand the specific religious rules of Islam and, importantly, the obligations and intentions of Muslim donors. An analysis presented by the American Civil Liberties Union notes that some donors expressed a concern that a non-Muslim faith-based charity might even use their donations to promote non-Islamic teachings.[34] There is support for this perspective in the analysis. Donors commented that they preferred to give to Islamic Relief rather than non-Muslim charities because they were concerned not only that their *zakat* must be discharged properly but also because they wanted their funds to be used only for *halal*, or permitted, purposes.

The use of *zakat* funding appears to be one of the most contentious issues facing Islamic Relief. The organization does not restrict *zakat* to just Muslim recipients. Despite this, a number of the organization's fundraising staff and volunteers believed that *zakat* funds should be restricted to Muslims.[35] Almost two-fifths of donors, 37.5 percent, also strongly believed that *zakat* donations should be restricted to Muslims. One regional fundraiser mentioned that "most of the donors I deal with actually believe that our *zakat* donations are restricted to Muslims, in fact if we used *zakat* donations to assist non-Muslims then they would cease giving to the organization altogether."[36] Nevertheless, the majority of donors, 60 percent, felt that *zakat* should be distributed to anyone regardless of faith.

Even though Islamic Relief publicly professes to assist all poor people "regardless of race, color, political affiliation, gender or belief,"[37] there is a widespread assumption both within and outside the organization that it primarily supports other Muslims. One donor's comments were representative of this perspective: "I do not support other charities because I want my donations to go towards helping Muslims." In fact, until early 2010, when it began operations in Haiti in response to the earthquake that devastated the area around the capital Port-au-Prince, all of Islamic Relief's aid programs were implemented in largely Muslim countries and generally among Muslim communities. Even when it worked in majority non-Muslim countries such as China and Sri Lanka, it was invariably in areas with significant Muslim communities. Furthermore, when non-Muslims were the recipients of aid and other development assistance, such as in Sudan and Bosnia and Herzegovina, this was in countries with significant (if not majority) Muslim populations.

However, this investigation revealed that Islamic Relief's UK supporters do wish for their donations to assist non-Muslims, particularly those affected by natural disasters. For example, those affected by the January 2010 earthquake in Haiti were non-Muslims, but Islamic Relief UK over a period of three or four months managed to raise more than £1 million from individual donors for emergency relief operations.[38] Indeed, some donors believed that Islamic Relief should make a concerted effort to assist non-Muslims in order to "show that Muslims are ready to help all those in need," to "show the true nature and generosity and caring of Muslims," to "show Muslims in a positive light," and even to "counteract Islamophobia."

These comments are particularly informative. Since September 11, 2001, and July 7, 2005, Muslims in the West have complained of discrimination, a rising level of suspicion, and even open hostility.[39] More than one-third of donors, 35.5 percent, stressed that one reason for supporting Islamic Relief was they thought it was among the very few Muslim organizations in the UK that were well recognized, were widely respected, and portrayed a positive image of Islam and the work of Muslims. Many donors made reference to supporting Islamic Relief precisely because it presented a "positive image of Muslims in the West"; this was particularly important to them as Muslims living in the UK. Some even wanted Islamic Relief to undertake "inter faith activities wherever possible" and "engage with non-Muslims" in order to "reduce tensions and demonstrate that people of different faiths can work together."[40] It is clear that many donors viewed Islamic Relief as a vehicle to promote a more positive image of Islam and the contributions of Muslims to British society, not just as a relief and development agency.

One suggestion made by a number of donors was that Islamic Relief should allocate some of its funds to development and emergency projects within the UK itself; indeed some donors justified this by remarking that according to Islamic teachings *zakat* funds should be used "close to home." They commented that such activities would also promote a positive image of Muslims, particularly among non-Muslim communities in the UK; it would raise Islamic Relief's profile as well, and encourage people to support the wider work of organization.[41] Referring to flooding that affected parts of southwest England in 2007, one donor commented: "I remember after the flooding in Gloucester when Islamic Relief provided drinking water—this type of help would attract more positive publicity than any amount of leaflets and talking."[42]

At the organizational level, religion is largely relegated to the private sphere, serving as personal motivation and the bedrock of underlying values.

However, Islamic Relief recognizes it is precisely religion that motivates many of its Muslim donors. Asked what he considered the organization's greatest advantage, the chief executive officer remarked, "our name and logo" (a mosque with two minarets),[43] and the organization has clearly formulated its fundraising approach accordingly. It uses frequent references to the Qur'an and *ahadith* in its printed promotional literature, advertisements in Muslim newspapers and Muslim satellite television channels, and on the organization's websites, the latter even offering online *zakat* calculators to assist people in determining their religious dues.[44] Its regular campaigns tend to coincide with Muslim festivals such as Eid-al-Adha and the month of Ramadan, during which Islamic Relief UK generally receives approximately one-third of its annual income.[45] By fundraising at these particular times, through specific media, using religious language, and reminding Muslims of their religious obligations, Islamic Relief manages to reinforce its "Islamic" credentials. Furthermore, fundraising staff, particularly those with direct contact with donors in the community, noticeably conform to religious precepts in appearance, manners, and speech. As highlighted previously, this contrasts markedly with the organization's approach at the operational level, in discussions with secular peer organizations and with Western institutional donors, in which it emphasizes work with communities of all faiths, impartiality, and adherence to common humanitarian standards.

Helping the Umma

Individual donors possessed strong altruistic motivations; one of the primary motivations for donating to Islamic Relief was the desire to alleviate the poverty and suffering of others considered less fortunate, whether Muslims or non-Muslims. However, there appeared to be a strong empathy with the suffering of other Muslims in particular. Approximately 92 percent of respondents confessed they did not hesitate to donate to Islamic Relief or other charities when there was an emergency appeal or when they observed the public suffering and distress of other Muslims elsewhere in high-profile natural disasters, such as the Kashmir earthquake in 2005, or ongoing conflicts in places such as Gaza, Iraq, and Afghanistan. Donors referred to being part of a worldwide Muslim community or *umma*[46] and some even mentioned a well-known *hadith* that states, "The believers in their affection, compassion and love for one another are like one single body. If a part of it suffers from pain, the whole body will suffer in pain."[47] Unsurprisingly, fundraising staff commented that donors were more likely to give in response to sudden-onset natural disasters such as earthquakes and tsunamis featured prominently in the media or to fundraising campaigns during the holy Muslim month of Ramadan, rather than to slow-onset disasters such as drought.

Although many donors felt that Islamic Relief should remain "outside of politics" and "any military affairs," it was also apparent that in instances in which they considered other Muslims to be "victims," particularly because of Western policies perceived to be unjust, donors preferred to channel their support through a charitable organization with a strong, independent Muslim identity. For example, "Islamic Relief should prioritize the Palestinians and the Kashmiris because both are fighting for their lives and homelands"; and "I prefer my donation to be directed to Muslims in war zones such as Palestine, Iraq and Afghanistan." For such donors there was an element of "participating in the struggle against injustice," and "helping the oppressed"; by donating to a Muslim charity they also felt they were to a certain extent helping to counterbalance the influence of "Western aid organizations in Muslim countries some of whom are in places like Afghanistan just to convert the Muslims." Clearly, some donors considered that many Christian faith-based and secular Western aid agencies were not neutral and indeed had an "overly close relationship" with Western donor governments who were considered party to the conflict.

Trust, Reputation, and Recognition

In terms of its annual budget, Islamic Relief is the largest Muslim faith-based humanitarian aid organization in the UK and one of the most internationally recognized Muslim charities in the world. Approximately one-third of respondents, 35 percent to be precise, stated that a main reason for donating to Islamic Relief rather than other charities was that they considered it "a reliable, trusted charity with a good reputation" and "internationally well recognized."

Following September 11 and subsequent suspicions about the activities of some Muslim charities, Islamic Relief made deliberate efforts to present itself as transparent, accountable and adhering to the highest standards of financial reporting—aspects many Muslim donors usually associated with secular organizations. Within the UK, Islamic Relief has established a reputation arguably as the most professional and mainstream Muslim charity; indeed, it is the only Muslim FBO represented on the Disasters Emergency Committee (DEC), a grouping of the largest aid agencies in the UK, and it was the first Muslim member of Bond (the UK membership body for nongovernmental organizations working in international development). Islamic Relief's work has been regularly endorsed by senior officials from the British government,[48] with whom it has a long-term funding agreement through DFID, as well as figures such as the Prince of Wales.[49] It publishes a detailed annual report, and its accounts are regularly audited. Indeed, its financial reports have frequently been awarded the highest ratings by independent charity industry evaluators.[50] Furthermore, through the organization's Development Education Unit it produces educational literature on a variety of development-related issues, which is then disseminated to schools and colleges throughout the United Kingdom. Staff also regularly participate in public events organized to raise awareness of a range of development issues such as international debt and climate change. Fundraising staff commented that the personal contact they and their extensive network of volunteers had with donors at mosques, schools, and the organization's shops probably contributed to developing a "trustworthy" image.

Perhaps unsurprisingly, therefore, donors—particularly those who were younger—stated they supported Islamic Relief rather than other Muslim charities in part because it had a good reputation and they felt they could trust the organization to spend their donations transparently and accountably. Indeed, more than two-thirds of donors, 70.5 percent, stated that one main reason for supporting Islamic Relief was that they considered it a trustworthy charity. Donors derived satisfaction from knowing their money was used for the purposes given and were confident their donation would reach the intended beneficiary; indeed, they regularly received an up-to-date progress report on orphan sponsorship or other more general information detailing how funds were used. This legitimacy was often contrasted with other smaller Muslim charities and the frequent mosque and door-to-door charitable collections that are a common sight in Muslim communities throughout the UK, which appeared to be less accountable and transparent. A donor commented, "Once I give money to the charity collectors that come knocking on my door, I have no knowledge where it goes and how it is actually used." In a similar vein, donors mentioned negative stories about misgovernment and corruption in developing countries and their concerns about the effectiveness of their individual contributions, and indeed whether their donation would actually reach beneficiaries. Another donor commented that he preferred to donate to Islamic Relief because he did not want "money falling into the westernized puppet governments who keep money for themselves." In this respect, individual donors are mirroring their institutional counterparts and are increasingly concerned with issues relating to performance, transparency, and accountability.

Clearly, Islamic Relief enjoys a relatively privileged position in attracting donations because it has been the foremost Muslim international development charity in the UK, with frequent appearances in the national media and growing funding from institutional sources. However, this situation is rapidly changing as the growth of other Muslim FBOs in the UK means donors have a choice of organizations.[51] Furthermore, the fact that Islamic Relief is attracting institutional funding and becoming highly visible results in some donors considering that it has enough money and no longer needs their relatively small donations anymore: "You have so much money now that I feel my donation is better used in a smaller charity."

It is apparent from the preceding discussion that Islamic Relief's constituency differs from its Western, more specifically secular or non-Muslim FBO peers. Indeed, one regional fundraiser commented, "Our donors are Muslims and if they do not donate to us they are likely to give to one of the other Muslim charities rather than Oxfam or Save the Children."[52] Rather, it shares donor constituency with other Muslim charities and is facing strong competition for individual donor funds from the growth and burgeoning professionalism of other Muslim FBOs in the UK. Unsurprisingly, though the organization has readily collaborated with secular and Christian FBOs in national campaigns as well as project implementation overseas, it rarely does so with other British Muslim FBOs.

In order to keep the support of individual donors, particularly those who donate to fulfill religious obligations, Islamic Relief has recognized that it must maintain a strong Islamic identity. Perhaps as a response to the "drift toward secularization" expressed by some donors and staff, and to safeguard its Islamic ethos, the organization felt obliged to establish an Islamic Values Committee in June 2010. The committee comprises senior staff and trustees and is entrusted with safeguarding the Islamic nature of the organization.

Perennial Concern over Administration Costs

The issue of administrative costs in Muslim charities is something that has consistently generated much debate among both donors and the charities themselves. Partly this is because, as with any charitable donation, donors are concerned that as much of their funds as possible reach the intended recipients. However, it is also in part because there are differing theological interpretations as to whether those who administer charitable activities are allowed to cover their administrative expenses from *zakat* funds. Although there is consensus that a proportion of funds can be used to cover the costs of collecting and distributing *zakat*, the influential Muslim scholar Mufti Taqi Usmani has argued that this is applicable only in the context of an Islamic state in which those entrusted with collecting *zakat* are under constant observation and monitoring.[53] In contrast, he argues, since there is no recognized authority to scrutinize the performance of NGOs and other private development organizations, they are not therefore entitled to use *zakat* monies to cover administration expenses. He concedes that although they may collect and distribute *zakat*, they can do so only on a charitable basis, without deducting any amount to cover the costs of administration. Usmani's opinion seems to be the dominant perspective in the Hanafi School of *fiqh*, or Islamic jurisprudence, generally followed by Muslims originating in South Asia, hence the vast majority of Islamic Relief's donors in the UK. Despite this, Islamic Relief has a policy of deducting administration costs from *zakat* funds, although it ensures that the proportion is no more than 17 percent.[54] In contrast, other large Muslim charities in the UK, such as Muslim Hands and Ummah Welfare Trust (UWT), pointedly claim not to deduct any administration costs from public donations.[55] Rather, they claim to cover all staff salaries, administration, and fundraising costs through the Gift Aid Scheme,[56] and in the case of UWT also through income from recycled clothes as well as profits from its charity shops.

This investigation found that a significant proportion of Islamic Relief's donors, 37 percent, were unhappy with administration costs being deducted from their donation, although this did not deter them from actually donating. Indeed, some donors confessed they were actually unaware that Islamic Relief deducted a proportion of their donation to cover administrative costs. Approximately one-third, 31 percent, were unconcerned, commenting that "administration costs must be taken for the charity to survive," while a further 32 percent were happy with the level of administration costs. Some felt that Islamic Relief should be more transparent as to what percentage of administration costs was deducted and for what purposes it was used. Others expressed the view that administrative costs should be kept to a competitive minimum, or that Islamic Relief should follow the example of other charities and "use Gift Aid contributions to cover administration costs."

Changing Donor Aspirations

The traditional focus of Muslim FBOs, among them Islamic Relief, is largely on satisfying the basic needs of the poor and providing care for orphans.[57] Confirming initial assumptions, this analysis found that this emphasis was also reflected in the desires of donors. When asked in which three sectors they would prefer their donations to be used, 86.5 percent prioritized provision of basic needs and 76 percent welfare of orphans.[58] This is usually understood as donors wishing to see provision of food for those who are hungry; emergency relief during disasters; access to clean water through digging wells and drilling boreholes; and sponsoring orphans. Such projects are attractive to many donors because they can be clearly identified, furnish obvious and generally immediate evidence of donors' generosity and produce tangible outcomes.

However, it is important to note that there are also theological reasons for this emphasis, as each of these activities is clearly encouraged in the Qur'an and *ahadith*. For example, during the festival of Eid-al-Adha, when each Muslim family that is able sacrifices an animal (most commonly sheep), Prophetic tradition recommends that the family eat one-third themselves, offer another one-third to friends and neighbors, and donate one-third to the poor. As Singer has observed, not only does charity accompany many Islamic festivals but it is also "a canonically acceptable substitute to replace a variety of ritual obligations."[59] Thus, if a Muslim is unable to fast during Ramadan, for example due to illness, he or she must feed a needy person every day; so under certain circumstances, the obligation of fasting can therefore be replaced by an act of charity. Indeed, those who refuse to share their food are considered outside of Islam. The Prophet Muhammad said, "He who sleeps on a full stomach whilst his neighbor goes hungry is not one of us."[60] There are a number of verses in the Qur'an that demand kindness toward orphans, promising rewards for those who care for them and warning of punishment for those who mistreat them. Indeed, the Qur'an even compares the person who mistreats an orphan with a nonbeliever: "See the one who denies the religion, then such is the man who repulses the orphan with harshness and does not help feed the poor."[61] This message is reinforced by various *ahadith*. Raising and crossing his middle finger and forefinger, the Prophet Muhammad said, "I and the guardians of orphans are like this"[62] to illustrate their closeness. Also, "The best house among the believers is the one in which an orphan is treated well and the worst house among the believers is the one in which an orphan is mistreated."[63] Similarly, there are numerous references to water and cleanliness in Islamic teachings. Water is also a necessary element of regular Muslim purification rituals, most commonly those performed before prayer. The digging of a well is regarded as an act of particular merit. When the Prophet Muhammad came to the city of Medina, he found only one well, from which Muslims bought drinking water. So his companions purchased the well and made it *waqf*. Indeed when asked, "What sort of *sadaqah* [charity] is best?" he replied "Water."[64] It is unsurprising, therefore, that programs that focus on feeding the poor, providing relief to those affected by natural disasters, furnishing access to clean water, and caring for orphans all have a particular resonance for Muslim donors and figure prominently in the activities of Islamic Relief and indeed other Muslim charities.

Support for such activities remains popular with donors, but it is also noticeable that donors were attracted to longer-term development projects that promoted economic independence and self-reliance among poor people. Donors considered that beneficiaries in such projects were proactive in addressing their poverty, and therefore deserving of "a hand up," and not seen as passive victims. More than half of the donors, 52 percent, wanted Islamic Relief to prioritize enabling poor people to become self-sufficient in the future through, for example, provision of microfinance, skills training, and marketing assistance. This sentiment is perhaps indicative of wider changes in donor behavior and Islamic Relief's donors; second- and third-generation Muslims with a higher level of disposable income are more and more resembling donors to secular aid organizations in terms of the issues they wish the organization to address. In fact, it has been argued that individual donors are becoming concerned with more abstract and intellectually challenging "big picture" causes such as human rights and climate change.[65] Islamic Relief's campaign of "Dignity not Charity," for example, which focused on promoting provision of small loans for poor people to establish and expand businesses, was met with great interest from donors in 2008.[66]

Interestingly, 12 percent of donors felt that Islamic Relief should prioritize addressing topics traditionally considered "taboo" for Muslim charities, such as reproductive health and HIV/AIDS. There was further support for this perspective during interviews with Islamic Relief fundraisers who considered that donors were in favor of the organization addressing "sensitive" issues, particularly when the impact of such issues on poverty was clearly explained and, importantly, they were made aware that Islamic Relief had sought the opinion and support of Islamic scholars before developing and implementing programs. Some donors even felt it was more appropriate for Islamic Relief as a Muslim FBO to address such sensitive issues rather than leave this to secular Western organizations—believing that the organization was likely to develop and implement programs in sensitive areas according to or at least respecting Islamic teachings. This is an interesting and important development; it indicates that, provided the organization seeks and obtains the necessary religious support, it has the backing of individual donors to address issues traditionally considered taboo for Muslim charities—perhaps strengthening any privileged access it may possess among Muslim communities.[67]

Maintaining a Faith Identity amid Secularization

This analysis both confirms and challenges some common assumptions regarding the motivations of Muslim donors, with specific reference to one Muslim FBO, Islamic Relief. The vast majority of Islamic Relief's individual donors in the UK are Muslims. They were strongly motivated to donate in order to fulfill their religious obligations, but equally importantly they also possessed strong altruistic motivations and a desire to alleviate poverty and suffering. Many preferred to donate to Islamic Relief rather than a non-Muslim faith-based or secular organization because they believed a Muslim organization better understood their religious obligations. It is important to note, however, that donors were not exclusive in their support of Islamic Relief; an overwhelming majority, 83.5 percent, of respondents professed that they also supported other charitable initiatives. Although these occasionally included prominent secular British charities such as Cancer Research and Save the Children, most tended to be other Muslim FBOs such as Muslim Aid, Ummah Welfare Trust, and Muslim Hands. Only a relatively small proportion, 16.5 percent, were exclusive in donating only to Islamic Relief.

In general, donors are supportive of assisting non-Muslims, although not necessarily with *zakat* funds. Nevertheless, donors assume that Islamic Relief will use donations largely to support Muslims, or at least prioritize them. It is apparent that Muslim donors were particularly motivated to give when they observed the public and high-profile suffering of other Muslims in places such as Kashmir, Palestine, Afghanistan, and Iraq. This analysis reveals that donors are supportive of the traditional focus of Islamic Relief on provision of emergency relief, water and sanitation, and orphan care. However, it is also apparent that donors are, in fact, willing to support a range of interventions, among them long-term empowerment of the poor through building self-reliance and even programs in such sensitive areas as reproductive health and HIV/AIDS, which have usually been the preserve of secular aid agencies.

Donors considered Islamic Relief to be one of the leading Muslim aid organizations; consequently it enjoyed a greater level of trust and recognition than other Muslim charities. This credibility has enabled it to attract many donors who feel they can trust the organization to spend their donations transparently and accountably. Despite having a strong Muslim identity and entrusting the organization to discharge their religious duties, donors were clear that Islamic Relief was not a "religious" organization that undertook *da'wah*.[68] However, they did recognize and indeed supported Islamic Relief because they considered it one of the few organizations that promote a positive image of Islam and the contributions of Muslims to British society. Indeed, they took pride in Islamic Relief having become a widely recognized and respected organization even among non-Muslims, with its achievements regularly being lauded and endorsed by governmental and other establishment figures. Some donors are even keen that it increase visibility further by extending its work to include interfaith activities and programs with poor and disadvantaged communities within the UK.

It was noticeable in recent years that Islamic Relief has tended to use the language and conform to the codes of practice and norms of its secular peers not only in order to attract institutional funding but also to maintain its legitimacy after September 11. It has downplayed its religious identity. However, even though this trend may continue, particularly in respect to program implementation, the organization still receives the majority of its income from the private donations of tens of thousands of individuals, many of whom are attracted by Islamic Relief's strong identity as a Muslim FBO. Furthermore, it also realizes that it is a partner much sought after by Western institutional donors, secular agencies, and non-Muslim FBOs, precisely because of its religious identity. The former may wish to appease Muslim constituencies and work with "moderate" Muslim organizations; the latter may wish to benefit from Islamic Relief's perceived privileged access among Muslim communities. It appears, therefore, that there will be limits to any trends toward "secularization," as Islamic Relief realizes that there are many advantages originating from its emphasis on faith-based identity. It continues, therefore, to use frequent references to religious teachings in fundraising campaigns, which also tend to coincide with Muslim festivals. The simultaneous Western and Muslim identity is both a result of circumstances and a deliberate choice, a reflection of the wishes of its donors and indeed staff who themselves are Muslims living in the West. It is probably also the case that Islamic Relief adapts itself and accentuates Muslim or Western characteristics according to the audience, stressing Islamic inspiration to Muslims and emphasizing conformity with common humanitarian standards and practices to secular and Western audiences.

NOTES

1. Although this is a contested term, for the sake of simplicity this analysis uses FBO. Clarke defines an FBO as "any organisation that derives inspiration and guidance for its activities from the teachings and principles of the faith or from a particular interpretation or school of thought within that faith"; Clarke and Jennings (2008), 6.
2. For example, see Alterman and von Hippel (2007); Benthall and Bellion-Jourdan (2009); and de Cordier (2009), 608–628.

3. These are the United Kingdom, France, Netherlands, Belgium, Germany, Sweden, Switzerland, Italy, United States, Canada, South Africa, Malaysia, and Mauritius.

4. Islamic Relief (2010), 43. This figure includes only income raised in the UK and sent by fundraising offices from abroad; it does not include income received directly and spent locally by field and fundraising offices.

5. Islamic Relief is one of a growing number of Muslim FBOs located in the UK; the other larger organizations are Muslim Aid, Muslim Hands, Human Appeal International, and Ummah Welfare Trust.

6. Islamic Relief (2010a), 2. Recently, however, it has been proposed that the organization, rather than simply being "inspired by faith values," change to "one that is inspired and guided by them in terms of the approaches we adopt and guidance we provide staff." Islamic Relief (2010b), 3.

7. Sayings attributed to the Prophet Muhammad; the singular is *hadith*.

8. This festival falls toward the end of the annual pilgrimage to Mecca, or Hajj, and commemorates the willingness of the Prophet Abraham to sacrifice his son Ismail as an act of obedience to Allah.

9. For further details, see http://www.islamic-relief.com/Indepth/Default.aspx?depID=6.

10. See, for example, Khan, Tahmazov, and Abuarqub (2009).

11. Islamic Relief is committed to various initiatives regarding delivery of humanitarian aid, including the Code of Conduct for the International Red Cross and Red Crescent Movement and NGOs in Disaster Relief, the Sphere Project, and People in Aid.

12. Islamic Relief (2010a).

13. Petersen (2010), 22.

14. In 2006, Islamic Relief agreed to a five-year Partnership Programme Arrangement (PPA) with DFID, the first time that the latter had signed such an agreement with a Muslim FBO. All PPAs were renegotiated for 2008–2011 and Islamic Relief's funding for this period was £2.39 million. Interestingly, in the agreement DFID specifically requested Islamic Relief to "present an Islamic perspective on a range of issues including debt and finance, reproductive health, HIV/AIDS and gender," recognizing that as a faith-based rather than secular organization it has a particular contribution to make.

15. Islamic Relief (2009), 84.

16. Islamic Relief (2010a), 43.

17. Personal communication with chief executive officer of Islamic Relief, June 10, 2008.

18. For example, the former president of Islamic Relief, Dr. Hany El-Banna, was invited by the Humanitarian Affairs Commission, the body entrusted with overseeing the activities of all international NGOs in Sudan, to speak to its many staff on "Western" concepts of development and the motivations of "Western" aid staff in 2007.

19. Personal communication with chief executive officer of Islamic Relief, June 10, 2008; and with Islamic Relief regional fundraisers on December 9–10, 2009; January 4, 2010; and January 27, 2010.

20. In a personal conversation with the director of Islamic Relief UK on June 15, 2010, he confessed that the organization has relatively little detailed evidence on what actually motivates its donors or "supporters," as they are more commonly referred to. Organizational research is limited to two unpublished internal memos: Islamic Relief (2008) and Rabiya (2009). Perceptions of what motivates donors are largely the result of informal feedback from regional fundraisers and call center staff.

21. Islamic Relief has seven charity shops in the UK, located in the major cities of Birmingham, Bradford, Cardiff, Glasgow, Leicester, London, and Manchester.

22. The UK has a Muslim population of approximately 2.8 million, accounting for 4.6 percent of the total population. Data retrieved December 20, 2011, http://pewforum.org/future-of-the-global-muslim-population-regional-europe.aspx.

23. According to the last UK census of 2001, 43 percent of Muslims living in the UK have Pakistani heritage, 17 percent Bangladeshi, and 9 percent Indian, while 4 percent described themselves as White British. Data retrieved on August 3, 2010, from http://www.statistics.gov.uk.

24. Personal communication with Islamic Relief regional fundraisers.

25. Abbreviated form of "peace be upon him," which is a customary utterance among Muslims after mentioning the Prophet's name.

26. For a longer discussion, see Krafess (2005), 327–342.

27. Singer (2008), 218.

28. An investigation titled *Philanthropy for Social Justice in the British Muslim Societies* carried out by the Centre for the Study of Islam at the University of Glasgow in 2006 estimated that British Muslims donated the equivalent of £90 per month, whereas the general UK population in comparison donated £12.55, although it is likely that this relatively high figure included remittances abroad. Quoted in Islamic Charity and Development Aid, presentation made by Islamic Relief at the Foreign and Commonwealth Office, London, February 27, 2007.

29. Personal communication with Islamic Relief regional fundraisers.

30. This is reported in Sahih Bukhari, vol. 8, book 82, *hadith* no. 798, available at http://www.cmje.org/religious-texts/hadith/bukhari/082-sbt.php. There is actually similar advice in Christian teachings: "When you give to the needy, do not let your left hand know what your right hand is doing, so that your giving may be in secret. Then your Father, who sees what is done in secret, will reward you" (Matt. 5:33–36.4).

31. Islamic Relief (2010a), 58.

32. Personal communication with Islamic Relief finance manager on February 17, 2010.

33. Chapter 9, verse 60 of the *Qur'an* as translated by Asad (2008).

34. American Civil Liberties Union (2009), 106.

35. Personal communication with Islamic Relief regional fundraisers.

36. Ibid.

37. Islamic Relief (2010a), 2.

38. Islamic Relief USA also managed to raise approximately US$2.5 million for relief operations in Haiti, and the organization as a whole received a donation of US$5

million from the Islamic Development Bank (personal email communication with Islamic Relief staff member responsible for coordinating emergency relief operations in Haiti, August 2, 2010).

39. See for example, Murshed and Pavan (2009).

40. Interestingly, the head of Islamic Relief UK was asked to form part of an interfaith delegation that met with Pope Benedict XVI on his visit to the UK on September 17, 2010.

41. Also interestingly, Islamic Relief USA has adopted this approach through, for example, providing emergency relief to those affected by Hurricane Katrina in 2005 and an annual campaign to provide food, clothing, blankets, and first aid to homeless people in cities across the United States.

42. Islamic Relief distributed 5,000 liters of bottled drinking water among (non-Muslim) vulnerable people.

43. Personal communication, June 10, 2008.

44. Islamic Relief's main website is http://www.islamic-relief.com; the UK office has a separate fundraising website as well (http://www.islamic-relief.org.uk). Fundraising offices in other countries tend to have their own websites; for example, Islamic Relief USA maintains http://www.islamicreliefusa.org.

45. Email correspondence with the personal assistant to the head of Islamic Relief UK, October 12, 2010. When there is a major emergency during Ramadan, as happened in 2010 with the floods in Pakistan, this proportion may increase to almost one-half.

46. This is commonly used to refer to all Muslims wherever they may be. However, in the constitution of Medina that was negotiated by the Prophet Muhammad in 622 AD with the leading clans of the city of Medina, even Jewish and pagan citizens were included as members of the *umma*.

47. This is reported in Sahih Muslim, book 32, *hadith* no. 6258, available at http://www.cmje.org/religious-texts/hadith/muslim/032-smt.php.

48. For example, at an *iftar* (the meal to break the fast) Ramadan dinner organized by Islamic Relief in London on August 16, 2010, and also attended by the secretary of state for international development, Andrew Mitchell, Deputy British Prime Minister Nick Clegg commented: "I come here full of admiration for what Islamic Relief does. What you are doing is an example to us all. You are responding with moral and organizational leadership which I think, frankly, has been lacking from the international community as a whole." Available at http://www.islamic-relief.com/NewsRoom/4-308-nick-clegg-celebrates-Ramadan-with-islamic-relief.aspx.

49. At its twenty-fifth anniversary dinner on December 17, 2009, HRH the Prince of Wales commented, "Islamic Relief's fine achievements bear witness to the energy, dynamism and selflessness of our British Muslim community." Available at http://www.islamic-relief.com/NewsRoom/6-2-275-hrh-the-prince-of-wales-praises-islamic-relief-s-work-over-the-past-25-years.aspx.

50. For example, Islamic Relief USA received the highest rating of four stars for its financial transparency and organizational competence from Charity Navigator, the

largest American charity evaluator, for the seventh consecutive year in 2010. Similarly, the Institute of Chartered Accountants in England and Wales (ICAEW) awarded Islamic Relief second place in the ICAEW Charities Online Financial Report and Accounts Awards in July 2010, from a list of the leading one hundred fundraising charities in the UK.

51. There are now eleven Muslim FBOs in the UK that focus on international aid and development having an annual income of more than £1 million; for further details see Khan et al. (2009), 3.

52. Personal communication with Islamic Relief regional fundraiser on January 27, 2010.

53. For further details of Mufti Taqi Usmani's opinion or *fatwa*, see http://qa.sunnipath.com/issue_view.asp.

54. Personal conversation with Islamic Relief's internal auditor, October 25, 2010.

55. For example, UWT states: "100 percent of your donation will reach those in need. Not a single penny will be taken from your donation," Ummah Welfare Trust (2010), 20.

56. The Gift Aid scheme is for gifts of money by individuals who pay UK tax. Gift Aid donations are regarded as having basic rate tax deducted by the donor. Charities take the donation—which is money on which tax has already been paid—and reclaim the basic rate tax from the UK government. The basic tax rate is 20 percent, so this means that if a donor gives £10, it can be worth £12.50 to the charity, provided the donor is a UK taxpayer.

57. Opinions of various staff from the international projects division of Islamic Relief, gathered through meetings on February 24, 2010.

58. By way of clarification, in Islam an orphan is generally defined as a child who has lost his or her father, who is the family breadwinner.

59. Singer (2008), 73.

60. Book VI, 61, no. 122 in Azami (2005).

61. Chapter 107, verses 1–3, Asad (2008).

62. Sahih Bukhari, Book 8, Vol. 73, *hadith* 35. Available at http://www.cmje.org/religious-texts/hadith/bukhari/073-sbt.php.

63. Ibn Majah (2007), *Kitab Al-Adab, hadith* 3679.

64. Sunan Abu Dawud, Book 9, *hadith* 1677. Available at http://www.cmje.org/religious-texts/hadith/abudawud/009-sat.php.

65. Alan Clayton, (2009).

66. Personal communication with head of Islamic Relief UK, January 24, 2010.

67. Of course, this is not a straightforward process; there is a range of religious perspectives. Reflecting its status as "Western," "Islamic," and mainstream, Islamic Relief has felt it appropriate to seek the assistance of the European Council of Fatwa and Research and build relationships with orthodox, widely recognized, and internationally respected Islamic institutions such as Al Azhar University in Cairo. A delegation from the university most recently visited Islamic Relief's international headquarters in the UK on October 11, 2010.

68. *Da'wah* is literally translated from Arabic as "making an invitation," although often it is understood as "preaching Islam," particularly through construction of mosques and distribution of written religious material. Essentially, *da'wah* has two dimensions, external and internal. External *da'wah* is to invite non-Muslims to Islam and teach them about Islamic beliefs and practices. Internal *da'wah* is to teach Muslims about aspects of Islam.

BIBLIOGRAPHY

Al Qazwini, Imam Muhammad Bin Yazeed Iban Majah. *English Translation of Sunan Iban Majah with Commentary*. Riyadh, Saudi Arabia: Darussalam, 2007.

Alterman, Jon B., and Karin von Hippel, eds. *Understanding Islamic Charities*. Washington DC: CSIS Press, 2007.

American Civil Liberties Union. *Blocking Faith, Freezing Charity: Chilling Muslim Charitable Giving in the "War on Terrorism Financing."* New York: ACLU, 2009.

Asad, Muhammad, trans. *The Message of the Qur'an*. Dorset, UK: Book Foundation and Orca Book Services, 2008.

Azami, Iqbal Ahmed. *Imam Bukhari's Al-Adab al-Mufrad: A Code for Everyday Living—The Examples of the Early Muslims*. Leicester: UK Islamic Academy, 2005.

Benthall, Jonathan, and Jerome Bellion-Jourdan. *The Charitable Crescent: Politics of Aid in the Muslim World*. London: Tauris, 2009.

Clarke, Gerard, and Michael Jennings, eds. *Development, Civil Society and Faith-Based Organizations: Bridging the Sacred and the Secular*. Basingstoke, UK: Palgrave Macmillan, 2008.

Clayton, Alan. "Good People: A Work in Progress." *International Journal of Nonprofit and Voluntary Sector Marketing*, 14 (2009): 387–393.

De Cordier, Bruno. "Faith-Based Aid, Globalisation and the Humanitarian Frontline: An Analysis of Western-Based Muslim Aid Organisations." *Disasters: The Journal of Disaster Studies, Policy and Management*, 33(4) (2009): 608–628.

Islamic Relief. *UKCC Top Donors Campaign*, London: Islamic Relief, 2008.

———. *Annual Report and Financial Statements 2008*. Birmingham, UK: Islamic Relief, 2009.

———. *Annual Report 2009*. Birmingham, UK: Islamic Relief, 2010a.

———. Islamic Relief Global Strategy 2011–2015 Final Draft. Birmingham, UK: Islamic Relief, 2010b.

Khan, Ajaz A., Ismayil Tahmazov, and Mamoun Abuarqub. *Translating Faith into Development*. Birmingham: Islamic Relief, 2009.

Krafess, Jamal. "The Influence of the Muslim Religion in Humanitarian Aid." *International Review of the Red Cross*, 87(858) (2005): 327–342.

Murshed, Syed Mansoob, and Sara Pavan. *Identity and Islamic Radicalization in Western Europe*. MICROCON Research Working Paper 16. Brighton, UK: MICROCON, 2009.

Petersen, Marie J. *Islamizing Aid: Muslim NGOs After 9/11*. PSA Conference Proceedings, 2010, http://www.psa.ac.uk/Proceedings.aspx?JournalID=5 accessed December 7, 2010).

Rabiya, Isma'il. *Top Donor Campaign*. London: Islamic Relief, 2009.

Singer, Amy. *Charity in Islamic Societies*. Cambridge: Cambridge University Press, 2008.

Ummah Welfare Trust. *10 Years of Serving Humanity*. Bradford, UK: UWT, 2010.

5

The Role of Spirituality in Humanitarian Crisis Survival and Recovery

Peter Walker, Dyan Mazurana, Amy Warren, George Scarlett, and Henry Louis

DOES A PERSON'S degree of spirituality make a difference to their ability to survive and recover in times of crisis, and if it does, can and should humanitarian aid agencies seek to support spirituality? This chapter explores what we know about the relationship between spirituality and well being, particularly in traumatic environments and humanitarian crises. We examine the evidence on how humanitarian aid agencies interact with the spiritual lives of their beneficiaries and how spirituality within some agencies may determine how and where they provide aid. We end by describing what we believe is much-needed field-based research to shed empirical light on the survival value of spirituality and the possibilities for affecting it through aid interventions. Along the way, we dwell for some time on the problem of understanding and measuring the phenomenon of spirituality and its effects on people's physical and mental health, particularly following trauma or crisis. This is important since religion and spirituality are so rarely viewed through the empirical lens but rather, and all too frequently, as unquestionable beliefs not amenable to analysis.

We start with the humanitarian enterprise. At heart, it is a deeply moral and ethically driven endeavor. It works to provide lifesaving aid and protection for people caught up in extreme crisis, regardless of their race, religion, wealth, or nationality. It is a direct expression of the belief that humanity is one family.

The ethic of impartial lifesaving aid has been captured and codified in international law, most obviously in the Geneva Conventions, which seek to limit the extremes of warfare and its effect on those not directly engaged in fighting.[1] It is also captured in the Universal Declaration of Human Rights, where not only the physiology of survival (the right to food and shelter) is enshrined but also humanity itself (the right to life with dignity).

In recent years, as the humanitarian enterprise grows, it has sought to further codify behavior and competence in a series of global standards and codes. The NGO Code of Conduct, the Sphere Standards, and the operational handbooks of UNHCR and the World Food program serve as examples.[2] These standards tend to deal with the physiology of survival in crisis. They seek to define what is needed in terms of food, water, health care, and shelter. They allude to the need to protect crisis survivors from violence and sexual assault, and in the case of refugees unjust repatriation. Also recently, there has been increased attention paid to the psychological needs of survivors, many of whom suffer deeply traumatic experiences. Standards and codes of psychological support are being drafted,[3] and aid agencies, with varying degrees of success, are starting to implement psychosocial support programs. The notion of seeking to support "life with dignity" is expanding, from a limited notion of feeding the physical body to a more expansive notion of providing psychological support for families and for administering to the traumatized and tortured mind.

All of these developments are seen as shared ground between the increasingly secular industrialized and urbanized North that funds and largely staffs the senior echelons of aid agencies, and the populations they seek to assist. Yet for the vast majority of humanity, and certainly in those countries where most humanitarian crises take place, there is another, fundamental dimension to people's lives. For most of humanity, religion and spirituality are central,[4] and for many spirituality is the bedrock on which individual and social behavior is based. Spirituality for most is not confined to a Sunday (or Saturday or Friday) morning but is pervasive. It offers an explanation for one's selfhood and one's relationship to the world, past, present and future. It acts as an anchor for hope.

If humanitarian aid seeks to support "life with dignity" and if the vast majority of crisis survivors hold spirituality to be a central component of existence, then we have to ask, Does the negation or assault on a person's spirituality affect his or her ability to survive in times of crisis? And equally, would supporting spirituality promote survival and recovery?

Is there a causal correlation between the strength of a person's or a community's spirituality or religiosity and the ability to survive and recover from crisis or trauma? Is this sufficiently important, so that aid agencies should take spirituality into account in their programming and even program to support spirituality as they now program to support a sense of home, not just shelter, and mental well-being, not just physiology?

We set out to explore these questions with some hesitation because we are entering the realm of deeply held personal beliefs. For many, discussion of spirituality and religion cannot remain objective and dispassionate, and for many they are simply not amenable to scientific and empirical investigation. We hold otherwise. Spirituality can be studied with the same objectiveness and rigor as any other naturally occurring phenomena. Its study does not require belief, just an openness to inquire and question.

What Is Spirituality?

We are seeking to understand the role of spirituality, not religion. We have a problem, though, with terminology. For many, the terms *religion* and *spirituality* are interchangeable. Today, the former is apt to refer to something akin to "institutions and systems consisting of organizational structures, codes of behavior, and symbol systems defining assumptions and beliefs designed to create within people powerful, comprehensive, and enduring world views and attitudes."[5] In contrast, *religiousness* is the term used in much of the literature to refer to the subjective, to what individuals experience and do with their religion.

The distinction between religious and spiritual is a fairly recent one that has developed in response to widespread disaffection with institutional religion and religious practice in Europe and America, a disaffection that began sometime in the 1960s and led to marked decreases in church attendance and institutional affiliation.[6] The fundamental assumption behind making this distinction is that people can be spiritual without being religious, by subordinating themselves to something experienced as sacred but without the trappings, ideology, or history associated with a religious institution. For example, one can be spiritual by taking up some noble cause (feeding the poor, overcoming racism) or by living a healthy lifestyle—by making sacred a moral principle, or the body itself. However, even though the distinction between religious and spiritual is important to some, the results of empirical research suggest it is not so important to the vast majority.[7]

The language used and spirit behind the effort to distinguish religion from spirituality derives from research carried out in Western cultures, where religion so often means the Abrahamic traditions (Christianity, Judaism, and Islam). In cultures where spirits and ancestors are more salient than belief in a supreme God, and where religion is treated as something other than a matter of institutional affiliation and loyalty, the distinction between religious and spiritual is even less clear—and less important.

All this points to the need for more qualitative, grounded research on the meaning of spirituality for those actually being studied, or in the case of humanitarian relief, for those helping as well as being helped. Without at least some understanding of the spirituality of individuals, it is impossible to say with any precision just how spirituality figures into recovery from disasters.

In seeking a way out of this dilemma, many researchers now focus on the notion of faith. This is a term referring to the overlap between religious and spiritual; it frees researchers of spirituality from being limited to measuring beliefs and institutional practices. More important, it is the term that best describes the hard-to-measure but central phenomenon that explains so much about why and how humans often prove resilient in the wake of hardships and disasters.

Faith defined broadly is much more than belief. Wilfred Cantwell Smith,[8] arguably the last century's dean of comparative religious studies, defined faith as

a quality of the person . . . an orientation of the personality, to oneself, to one's neighbor, to the universe; a total response; a way of seeing whatever one sees and of handling whatever one handles; a capacity to live at a more than mundane level; to see, to feel, to act in terms of, a transcendent dimension.[9]

Faith defined in this way allows a researcher to look for individual meanings embedded not simply in institutionally sanctioned beliefs and practices but also in actions expressing whatever an individual takes to be sacred and in whatever an individual has put his or her trust. A dance, a sharing of food, a simple gesture of compassion can each be an act of faith, depending on the person and circumstances. Faith, so defined, need not refer to religious faith. For example, classical Greece and Rome furnished a secular faith, which is, says Smith, "a living tradition with its own metaphysical underpinning, its own great champions and even martyrs, its own institutions, its own apprehension of transcendence, and . . . its own type of faith."[10]

Faith, as defined here, bears directly on the work of humanitarian crises and provision of aid—because it refers to that which can sustain individuals in times of disaster and extreme hardship.

From here on in this chapter, we use the term *faith* rather than religiosity or spirituality.

Measuring Faith

In the social sciences, the accepted practice when attempting to measure a complex phenomenon such as faith is to first differentiate component parts. For the purpose of studying faith in the context of humanitarian crises and relief, some components of faith may be assumed to be more relevant than others. For example, understanding spiritual coping may help explain how people cope with extreme suffering in humanitarian crisis; therefore understanding how to measure and research coping, especially "religious coping," is crucial.[11]

As for qualitative methods, there are a number of examples of excellent ethnographic research that have direct relevance to studying faith, humanitarian crises, and recovery from crisis. Examples include qualitative studies of how religion and faith have been used to cope with hardships incurred by ethnic-racial identity,[12] sexual orientation,[13] and gender.[14]

There is, then, a body of research providing a plethora of scales available for use in testing hypotheses and carrying out quantitative research on faith, humanitarian crises, and humanitarian aid. In addition, there is a body of research supplying excellent examples of qualitative methods for shedding light on the connections between the faith of individuals and their capacity to cope with extreme hardships, both physical and psychological.

The Relationship Between Faith and Health Outcomes

"In times of crisis," wrote psychologist Paul Johnson, "religion usually comes to the foreground."[15] Anecdotal accounts[16] and large-scale empirical studies[17] support this assertion. For example, religion came to the fore in a nationwide survey of stress reactions in the United States following the September 11, 2001, World Trade Center attacks.[18] Expressions of religious faith (e.g., personal prayer) were the second most common method of coping (90 percent), after talking with others (98 percent). Such expressions were also prominent in a sample of people paralyzed in serious accidents.[19] When asked to explain their severe misfortune, the most common response to the question "Why me?" was that God had a reason. Examples such as these abound in the social science and medical literatures.[20]

Why, then, is recovery most readily sought through faith pathways? According to Janoff-Bulman,[21] trauma shatters our assumptive world, and so the process of recovery from trauma involves building a new assumptive world, one that somehow incorporates the powerful new trauma-related information about oneself and one's context; faith may be uniquely capable of aiding this process.[22] For many, faith serves as an integrating and stabilizing force for interpreting traumatic events.[23] By giving meaning and coherence to traumatic experiences, faith may support their psychological integration.[24]

In addition to being a pervasive dimension of life, faith appears to be a uniquely powerful one. Numerous studies have shown that faith coping predicts recovery from trauma and crisis above and beyond the effects of secular coping measures.[25] For example, one study of churchgoers coping with negative life events found that both faith coping methods and secular coping methods explained unique proportions of variance in several adjustment indices.[26]

What, then, makes faith-based methods of coping so special? When confronted with extreme adversity, especially uncontrollable situations that test the limits of personal power and control, "The language of the sacred—forbearance, mystery, suffering, hope, finitude, surrender, divine purpose, and redemption—and the mechanisms of religion become more relevant" than secular (Western) methods of coping through efficacy, agency, and control.[27] In this way, faith may uniquely equip individuals to confront their finitude. Indeed, faith-based coping methods appear to be more helpful during highly stressful situations than during periods of low stress.[28]

At this point, we need to flag a caveat. Virtually all the literature on the connection between faith and health outcomes is based on research conducted in the North, predominantly America and Europe, and most of this literature focuses on populations of Christian or Jewish faith. The literature hypothesizes that what it is reporting on is a deep-seated relationship stemming from universal notions of faith. This may well be true, and indeed in this chapter we take it as a working hypothesis, but the caveat stands that the sampling on which this hypothesis is based is highly skewed to the North and to predominantly Protestant Christian populations.

Four Major Religious/Spiritual Functions and Their Promotion of Resilience

What, then, does faith actually do for you? Pargament and Cummings highlight four major functions as particularly relevant to the process of resilience in the face of adversity: (1) the search for meaning; (2) the quest for emotional comfort or anxiety reduction; (3) promotion of a sense of social interconnectedness; and (4) communion with the sacred.[29] These faith functions are not mutually exclusive; people may pursue any one or all of these ends.

Moreover, these ends may be pursued through a variety of religious and spiritual means that reflect diverse beliefs, emotions, practices, and relationships.

The Search for Meaning

Adjustment to major trauma and loss may require more "meaning making" than active "problem solving" per se, as only cognitive adaptation can transform the meaning of such events.[30] Park and Folkman sought to model how faith aids meaning.[31] Their model differentiates between two levels of meaning: systems of global meaning and situational meaning. The former involves general beliefs, assumptions, and expectations, which structure general goals, while the latter is based on appraisals of a specific event, initial causal attributions about why it happened, judgments regarding any discrepancy between the event and one's global meaning system, and determination of actions to be taken to cope with the event. Discrepancy between global meaning and situational meaning (i.e., the degree to which appraised meaning contradicts global beliefs and goals) represents a crisis of meaning and determines the amount of stress caused by the event. Accordingly, to assuage their distress, individuals must reduce this discrepancy by altering either their perception of the event or their beliefs, assumptions, and expectations about the world or themselves. This meaning-making process is known as *reappraisal*.

Faith may play an important role throughout this meaning-making coping process, affecting both global and situational meaning making.[32] For example, Banerjee and Pyles examined the meaning and role of faith in the lives of eight African American women participating in a welfare-to-work program.[33] In-depth interviews revealed that possession of a religious or spiritual global meaning system was associated with inner peace, self-esteem, and perseverance. As one woman put it:

> Spirituality causes you to be calm when you want to go off, when you're just fed up with things, when you just don't think that you can keep going. My spirituality makes me know that God is in control no matter what the situation looks like, and . . . keep pushing on and asking for his strength so that I don't quit.[34]

Another study of accident victims with temporary and permanent disability provides evidence of the link between faith attributions and recovery.[35] Forty-one patients (sixteen to forty-two years of age) were interviewed one and three weeks after their accident. Among the permanently disabled,

attributions to karma or God's will were positively correlated with psychological recovery, as measured by positive attitude, the expectation of recovery, the belief that they must be proactive in the recovery process, and plans
for resuming life following recovery. This correlation was seen at both times
of measurement.

The Quest for Emotional Comfort or Anxiety Reduction

Another important function of faith that may promote resilience is the
quest for emotional comfort or anxiety reduction.[36] A variety of studies
have identified a link between faith and positive emotional outcomes.[37]
Koenig examined the effects of religious involvement on time to remission
of depression in a sample of depressed inpatients with congestive heart failure or chronic pulmonary disease or both.[38] Group-related and private
religious activities—i.e., frequent religious attendance, prayer, Bible study,
and high intrinsic religiosity—predicted a 53 percent increase in speed of
remission.

Positive religious and spiritual coping strategies have also been linked to
reduced depression. Bosworth et al. examined the relationship between faith
coping and depression, both cross-sectionally and longitudinally, in a sample
of 114 geriatric patients.[39] After controlling for clinical, social support, and
demographic measures, the researchers found positive faith coping inversely
related to depression scores.

Promotion of a Sense of Social Interconnectedness

When facing major trauma and loss, many people turn to their faith-based,
spiritual communities for social support. During these difficult times, faith
communities may function to promote a sense of social interconnectedness
or "relational resilience."[40] Gillum, Sullivan, and Bybee investigated the
role of faith in recovery from domestic violence.[41] They interviewed 151
women and found that the majority (97 percent) relied on spirituality or
God as a means to cope with and heal from the violence. Among nonwhite
women, greater religious involvement (as defined by frequent religious service attendance and the belief that one's place of worship is a source of
strength and comfort) was positively related to perceived social support.
Similar findings were reported in another study of African American survivors of domestic violence.[42] More recent research has provided comparable
findings.[43]

Communion with the Sacred

As we have seen, faith may foster meaning-related resilience, emotional resilience, and relational resilience. In addition to these more secular functions, faith may also function to conserve itself in the face of adversity, by fostering communion with the sacred or "religious/spiritual resilience."[44] Indeed, in response to trauma and crisis, many people employ faith to seek religious and spiritual ends in and of themselves.

There is a great deal of evidence that faith is resilient to acute, multiple, and prolonged stress.[45] Falsetti et al. examined changes in religious and spiritual beliefs following traumatic events, such as sexual assault, serious physical injury, homicide of family members or close friends, disasters, and military combat.[46] For those participants who endured multiple traumas (68 percent of the sample), 73 percent reported no changes in faith beliefs following a second trauma.

Although there is abundant evidence that faith effectively functions to conserve itself in the face of adversity, a handful of studies contradict this trend. Fontana and Rosenheck examined the effects of traumatic exposure on strength of religious faith among veterans treated for posttraumatic stress disorder.[47] Veterans' experiences of killing others and failing to prevent the death of fellow soldiers were found to weaken their religious faith. Nevertheless, the majority of studies point to the resilient nature of religiousness and spirituality.

We have, then, a coherent picture building up of the nature of faith as a pervasive trait of humanity and as playing a positive role in the health outcomes of people caught up in crisis and subject to trauma. We have caveats, the most critical being that the body of research we can draw on is predominantly focused on North America and Europe and on Christianity (and in particular, Protestant Christianity). There is, however, a big enough body of evidence to allow us to move forward and examine the role of faith within humanitarian aid as it is presently practiced and to speculate as to how we might research more specifically the role of faith in health outcomes in the types of crisis that are typically the focus of humanitarian agencies.

In summation, we have a body of research, albeit mostly on Northern and Christian communities, which lends evidence of a strong correlation between the strength of someone's faith and the speed and completeness of their recovery from trauma. In addition, we have a theory explaining this correlation in terms of a causal relationship, noting four ways in which faith affects health outcomes. In short, it is reasonable to suppose that something real, measurable, and effective is going on here, a phenomenon that might be enhanced and used in crisis response to aid recovery.

Spirituality in the Humanitarian Crisis Setting

Having described and defined the phenomena of faith, we now move on to examine what we know about how it affects humanitarian aid, through the aid institutions, through the aid workers, and through aid programming.

Humanitarian agencies implicitly acknowledge that there is more to survival than preserving physiology through supplying water, food, shelter, and medical care. Most agencies already recognize the need to additionally help protect people from violence and provide for their psychological support needs. The question that arises therefore is whether humanitarian assistance should and could include interventions that capitalize on individuals' and communities' use of faith to recover from crisis and catastrophe.

Most of the present case-load of the international humanitarian community is in countries where spiritual and religious concepts and practices form an integral part of people's lives and worldviews. A Gallup poll conducted in sixty countries to mark the beginning of the new millennium found "Eighty-seven percent of respondents say they consider themselves to be part of some religion, and only 13 percent declare that they belong to none." In Africa, the Middle East, and Asia, the figure can rise to as high as 99 percent of respondents declaring religious affiliation.[48]

There is a long history linking religious faith and humanitarian values. Walker and Maxwell show that many humanitarian agencies have their roots in religious motivation and how notions of altruism, which underpin humanitarian action, are deeply entwined in the social and personal behavior expressions of most world religions.[49] Dulles shows clear linkages between Christian and humanitarian values, as does Wechsler for Judaic values.[50] Krafess reflects on the role of Islam in shaping Islamic-based humanitarian agencies, and Gres (2010) shows how secular- and religious-based humanitarianisms are becoming increasingly intertwined in today's operating environment.[51]

What then does the literature tell us about the way faith manifests itself within the humanitarian aid agencies and how it is explicitly used in their programming and internal support services?

Use of Religion and Spirituality by Aid Agencies

Religious nongovernmental organizations (RNGOs) practice a form of humanitarian aid that is ideologically guided by faith traditions. RNGOs believe this gives them privileged access to faith-based communities, and professed advantages over secular agencies under certain circumstances. RNGOs' practices are varied and share faith-based values' embedded ideas of empathy and compassion. In this section we present a typology of RNGOs focusing on their (1) religiously guided missions, (2) significance in terms of wealth, and (3) humanitarian practices. In doing so, we examine the empirical evidence supporting the claim that RNGOs have a special place in the community of humanitarian aid agencies.

The mission statements of RNGOs lend ideological direction to religious humanitarian aid practices by using faith-based traditions to provide guiding principles. For example, the mission statement of World Vision International, one of the largest Christian nongovernmental organizations (NGOs) operating today, states that it is a Christian humanitarian aid organization "inspired by [their] Christian values" to "serve all people regardless of religion, race, ethnicity or gender."[52] Muslim Aid, another large humanitarian aid group, states in its mission statement that their "vision is the alleviation of poverty, education for all and the provision of basic amenities for those in need; in order to create a world where charity and compassion produce justice, self reliance and human development," and that they are "guided by the teachings of Islam."[53] Some RNGOs possess more specific spiritual messages. For example, the mission statement of Haddassah states that it "is a volunteer women's organization whose members are motivated and inspired to strengthen their partnership with Israel, ensure Jewish continuity, and realize their potential as a dynamic force in American society."[54] RNGOs are not always inspired by one specific faith tradition. For example, the Sunray Meditation Society describes itself as "an international spiritual society dedicated to planetary peace."[55]

In financial terms, RNGOs boast financial statistics comparable to those of the world's largest secular NGOs. In 2001, the Mennonite Central Committee's (MCC) annual budget was $63 million; Mercy Corps, $87 million; Aga Khan Foundation, $99 million; World Vision International, $525 million; and Catholic Relief Services (CRS), $373 million.[56] These compare favorably in size and wealth to well-known secular NGOs such as Oxfam GB (whose 2009–10 income was £318 million),[57] and CARE USA (whose program expenses totaled $589 million in 2006).[58] Furthermore, some RNGOs such as World Vision International ($1.22 billion as of 2009)[59] and CRS ($768 million in 2009)[60] have experienced significant increases in funds over the past several years.

As for the services provided by RNGOs, many fall within religious communities that match their own faith traditions. This gives RNGOs a familiar clientele base and facilitates access and assistance. Jonathan Benthall writes that, in the post-tsunami area of Indonesian Aceh, Turkish Muslim aid groups were able to help Indonesian Muslim communities with specialized access and ease. In his words, "It seems likely that a common religious, or religio-political, heritage did make access easier for the TRCS [Turkish Red Crescent Society]."[61] Despite their geographic and cultural differences, groups from Aceh and Turkey found common ground in their shared faith tradition, making it easier for them to work together. Parenthetically, non-Muslim groups such as Catholic Relief Services were excluded from directly funding construction of a mosque in Aceh on the grounds that it was forbidden by Islamic religious rules.[62]

RNGOs also provide services that meet specific tenets of their associated religions. For example, Jamal Krafess writes that "Islamic humanitarian agencies came into being and assumed the task of distribution using *zakat* and other forms of charity donations mainly in developing countries. . . ."[63] Benedetti touches on how many Islamic RNGOs work in countries "with a very strong Islamic presence, both in the *dar al-Islam* and in territories on the border of it as a sub-Saharan African, Muslim Kosovo etc." In addition, there are a number of groups, such as Islamic Relief, that provide services for a more religiously diverse clientele.[64]

Kirmani and Khan also argue that the religious identities of RNGOs sometimes give their organizations privileged access and trust not extended to secular organizations. One example is the work that Islamic Relief has done in Somalia over the past few years. Islamic Relief has been able to

> make important inroads into various parts of the country, especially in south and central districts . . . those familiar with Islamic Relief's work in Somalia point to the importance of being identified as a "Muslim organization," in terms of gaining access into Muslim communities, as compared to secular International Non Governmental Organizations (INGOs) or non-Muslim Faith Based organizations (FBOs) working in the region.[65]

There is also significant cooperation among religious aid groups. Our research uncovered many examples of RNGOs of different faiths cooperating with each other in relief efforts. For example, in Ingushetia Islamic Relief worked closely with the UK-based Catholic Agency for Overseas Development (CAFOD) to provide basic services for Chechen refugees.[66] Nawyn, in her study on the use of faith in providing for refugees, found through fifty-eight interviews with U.S.-based refugee resettlement and assistance organizations that interreligious cooperation was often an advantage for humanitarian aid groups. Furthermore, on many occasions RNGOs have provided aid for groups from different faith traditions, even those known for their opposition to the faith tradition of the RNGO. For example, the Hebrew Immigrant Aid (HIA) society was able to provide food baskets for Muslim refugees. A worker at the HIA society reported she felt it was her religious duty as a Jewish person to help those in need.[67]

Unlike secular groups, RNGOs often provide specific material services that help to meet the *religious* needs of communities affected by traumatic stress or disaster. For example, at the Bosnian and Herzegovinian American Community Center in Chicago, Ramadan calendars were passed out as a tool for cultural and ethnic reconstruction. Islamic Relief has supplied Ramadan meals for displaced Muslim communities and has coordinated proper slaughtering of animals, *Qurbani*, during the festival Eid-al-Adha.[68]

Many RNGOs facilitate reconciliatory dialogue in conflict and postconflict communities. In Bosnia and Herzegovina, three ethnoreligious groups (Orthodox Christians, Catholic Christians, and Bosnian Muslims), all claiming local ethnic heritage, have used religion as a reconciliatory tool. The organization Abraham, run by laypeople invested in the study of religion, "aims to instill tolerance and respect toward other people, worldviews, and religions" within the ethnic conflict of the region by hosting events that "include gatherings and debates, peace building training sessions and seminars for members as well as public lectures, conferences and rallies, and collaboration on joint declarations and publications."[69] The International Multi-religious Intercultural Center (IMIC) is another group "with the aim of preventing divisions among people based on religion."[70] The IMIC works with academics and intellectuals, including the Academy of Arts and Sciences and the University of Sarajevo, to promote religious understanding.

Abraham and the IMIC are examples of RNGOs working directly on reconciliation. Others have acted as a third party to facilitate peace talks. In 2004, the International Scholars Annual Trialogue (ISAT) involved RNGOs in peace talks in Macedonia, attempting to quell ethnoreligious conflicts between Albanian Muslims and Macedonian Christians.[71] The humanitarian aid group Christians Associated for Relationships with Eastern Europe (CAREE) was one such sponsor of that dialogue.

RNGOs often support refugees. In our research there are many examples of host communities and humanitarian groups assisting displaced refugees. Gozdziak writes that "in the United States, eight of ten major resettlement agencies are faith-based"[72] while Mayer states "'The majority of organizations that resettle refugees in the United States are faith based, either Christian or Jewish, although they may have supporters from other religions."[73]

Some RNGOs actively spread their religious message by *proselytizing*. These missionary activities are more concerned with spreading one particular faith tradition regardless of the religious identity of those who are in need. Many of these proselytizing groups are Christian RNGOs. Clarke writes "In 2001, an estimated 350,000 Americans travelled abroad with Protestant missionary agencies, and donations to such agencies totaled $3.75 billion, a 44 percent increase in 5 years "[74] Although most proselytizing has come from Christian RNGOs, a growing number of Muslim and non-Christian groups are striving to spread their own faith traditions through proselytizing in the humanitarian setting. Clarke continues that groups such as the World Muslim League and the African Muslim Agency "fund local *madrasas*, which reach large sections of the population, promoting conservative Islamic movements such as Wahabism and Salafism which, traditionally, had little purchase in African societies."[75] Despite significant financial support and successful permeation of faith-traditions into communities needing humanitarian aid, proselytizing remains an area of concern for many in the field of humanitarian aid who fear that it undermines the reputation of aid agencies as impartial, neutral, and independent providers of assistance in times of crisis.

The literature described above posits a positive role for the religious nature of NGOs, but almost all of the evidence given is anecdotal, in the form of case studies or the opinions of aid workers. Furthermore, most of the published studies are self-analytical; the senior officer of an Islamic agency writing about his experiences in that agency, the senior evaluator for a Christian agency writing about her experiences and findings in that agency's programs. Very little external, objective research has been carried out to date in this area.

Spirituality as a Personal Prop for Aid Workers

Religious conviction and spirituality can motivate aid workers. Specifically, individuals' own convictions may lead them to volunteer or seek employment with a RNGO from the same faith tradition as their own. More generally and regardless of which type of NGO volunteers and workers join, simply providing help for those in great need can take on spiritual meaning and resonate with personal beliefs.

In RNGOs, religion seems to provide a common bond among workers. Nawyn writes, "For faith-based NGOs, common religious values between an

NGO and a faith community facilitate recruitment of volunteer labor and in kind donations."[76]

Many RNGOs have memberships composed of workers who follow the same religion. Indeed, a recent court ruling in the United States allows one of the largest faith-based agencies there, World Vision USA, to dismiss employees who are not professed Christians, the ruling opining that, although World Vision USA provides humanitarian assistance, it is in essence a religious body.[77] Flanigan writes that a good many workers think the common religious bonds between a like-minded staff result in less conflict and greater trust among workers. She quotes one worker as saying, "Because of our religion, there is trust among our group and our members, and this gives us more power. We also have aligned goals, and we are very organized, which provides us power."[78]

Not only in RNGOs but in humanitarian aid agencies in general, religious conviction and spirituality often lend meaning to the work being done. In our research we find words such as "love," "caring," and "equality" used to describe the motivation behind humanitarian action. Flanigan notes the importance of such words in her study of RNGOs operating in Lebanon. Many workers within the Lebanese humanitarian aid community felt that religion brought benefits to their work, including credibility, compassion, commitment, safety, and trust among workers. One aid worker with a Christian RNGO commented, "We are just trying to reflect Christ's love to those needy people. We are just trying to tell them that God cares, that our Lord cares about them, and we are just trying to fulfill the ministry that is assigned to us."[79]

Indeed, for some aid workers providing humanitarian aid is a form of religious charity. A member of a Shiite Muslim RNGO pointed out that the *hadith*, a Muslim religious body of text, says that "the principal role of the human being is to serve other people."[80]

Krafess writes that helping those in need is a basic tenet of the Muslim religion, and that such help is comparable to humanitarian action. Islamic tenets of charity, such as *zakat*, require Muslims to give alms to the poor. However, our research turned up only a limited number of examples where RNGOs and their workers directly addressed the idea of fulfilling *zakat*.

Spirituality can also act as a coping device for aid workers. Laidig and Speakman make note that many humanitarian aid workers are victims of secondary traumatic stress disorders and that spirituality can be a method for their coping with stress.[81] Weinrich et al. also report that religion was highly valued in a sample of disaster relief workers in the wake of a class 4 hurricane.[82] After three weeks of disaster relief work, three-quarters of the sample reported that religion was a primary positive coping strategy.

Nevertheless, evidence linking spirituality and aid workers is thin and largely in the form of anecdotes. For now, at least, these assumed relationships remain largely untested.

Do No Harm? Spirituality in Aid Programming

Almost all studies on the relationship among religion, spirituality, and health have been carried out in the North. There are a few exceptions, which explore this relationship in situations closer to the humanitarian crises we are interested in. In a qualitative study of how victims cope with the stress of being affected by mustard gas in the Iran-Iraq war of the 1980s, Ebadi et al. find that "effective spiritual coping strategies help individuals to find meaning and purpose in their illness. Identifying the coping strategies used by this patient group and reinforcing them can lead to an enhanced ability to deal with the illness."[83]

Brune et al. studied 161 refugees in Scandinavia, all suffering from post-traumatic stress disorder (PTSD), coming from a variety of countries in Africa, Asia, and Latin America.[84] They found that possession of a firm belief system was an important predictor for a better therapy outcome. Ai et al. and Orosa et al., working with different refugee groups, have demonstrated similar correlations.[85]

Ojalehto and Wang have reviewed the current literature on children's spiritual development, particularly for those caught up in forced displacement.[86] They take a human rights rather than a health perspective but tentatively assert that faith does have a positive effect on child development in these dark environments: "Although preliminary findings strongly suggest the positive role of spirituality in war-affected children's development, the field of spiritual development is still emerging, and there is virtually no empirical attention to refugee children's spiritual development."

In 2006, the aid agency World Vision commissioned a study of its post-tsunami relief programs in Indonesia and Thailand. In addition to seeking to report the standard indicators of changes in food security, health, access to water, and the like, they also sought to explore, through focus groups and semistructured interviews, what they termed the "emergence of hope":

Eight topics were explored with the emergence of hope focus group participants to measure if hope for a brighter future is emerging and growing among tsunami-affected communities, and if there have been changes in hopefulness since the baseline. The themes discussed

included good memories, dealing with past traumas and current difficulties, planning for the future, self esteem and the role spirituality
plays in feeling hopeful.[87]

The methodology was refined and in 2008, in the eastern Democratic
Republic of Congo, World Vision surveyed fifty-three focus groups across
twenty-three local and refugee communities who had received humanitarian
aid from the agency. They reported, "Faith plays a significant role in the lives
of community members; the majority of the groups report a gain in strength
and hope through belief in their higher power.[88]

So even though the literature looking specifically at the role of spirituality
in the context of humanitarian crises is extraordinarily thin, what does exist
seems to support the Northern-based research reported earlier in this chapter.

Two of this chapter's authors (Walker and Mazuranna) have extensive experience working in humanitarian assistance operations for aid agencies and carrying out livelihood- and human rights-based research in conflict zones. Our
anecdotal observation is that aid efforts can both bolster and undermine faith.
We have seen faith reinforced where aid agencies recognized its local importance. One large agency operation in Afghanistan today realized that most of
its local Afghan employees had only a very rudimentary knowledge of their
religion, coming as they did from remote rural settings. The aid agency helped
find an Imam who would come into their office and offer classes on the Koran
and spiritual guidance for those who wished to attend. Attendance was high,
and the agency reports that workers commitment to the mission of the agency
seemed to grow. We should note that this was an avowedly Christian agency.

On the negative side, the authors have witnessed incidents where both
Christian and Islamic agencies made receiving relief aid conditional on beneficiaries converting to the agency's preferred religion. In other instances the
pressure is less direct, and aid is not conditional on conversion, but proselytizing is a strong part of agency activities. In Northern Uganda, we observed
how the undermining and denigrating of local spiritual values, belief systems,
and practices has significantly decreased survivors' sense of hope and confidence in the future.

Future Research?

We have reviewed in this chapter the nature of spirituality and faith; sought
to show how it might influence health outcomes, particularly following stress
and trauma; and shown that, at least in the North, there is strong evidence

that such a relationship exists and can be explained through the phenomenon of faith. We have shown that faith-based agencies believe their faith makes a positive difference in their ability to program effective aid, though we temper this with the observation that these studies are almost all subjective and anecdotal. In a similar vein, there is some evidence that faith can play a role in helping individual aid workers both directly in their work and as a coping mechanism for the more stressful side of their work. And finally, we cite the lamentably few studies that have looked at the role of faith in helping people recover from the types of trauma we most often encounter in humanitarian crises.

Thus from the Northern-based literature, the few Southern-based crisis studies cited earlier, and our own anecdotal evidence, we believe there is a strong case to be made for the critical role supporting faith can have in improving survival and recovery from the trauma of a major humanitarian crisis.

However, this case is still largely hypothetical. It needs to be backed up by solid, field-based research on communities affected by crisis—to test both the hypothesis that the faith-recovery relationship, observed in the North among populations of monotheists, also holds true in the South and across a much larger range of faith traditions; and the notion that this relationship can be harnessed as a positive asset in aid programming. Specifically, we believe the research needs to address four questions.

First, in the environments of conflict, gross violations of human rights, and humanitarian crisis, what is the relationship between the strength of spiritual or religious belief and practice on the one hand, and both personal and community recovery from crisis on the other?

Second, what is the evidence for aid agency interventions affecting people's faith, and through this their ability to withstand and recover from crisis?

Third, if such a set of relationships exists, how might aid agencies use this in their programming to best support, and at a minimum not undermine, spirituality and religion as an aid to recovery?

Finally, if such programming is possible, can it be shown empirically to aid recovery?

If these questions can be answered and if it is shown that faith has a measurable effect on recovery, then the path is open for aid agencies to program for faith support in the same way they now do for environmental sustainability, gender sensitivity, and psychosocial support.

If, however, the research fails to demonstrate such a relationship, then it will raise serious questions about the role faith presently has in humanitarian aid. As we write, there is a strong push for aid workers to become more professional, and for development of an agreed set of core competencies and a core value statement, which could be universally adopted, learned, and examined such that aid workers could acquire the equivalent of internationally recognized professional qualifications. What place, then, do faith and religion have in a system that is essentially based on the notion of impartial nondiscriminatory aid, and a community of practice that is essentially a meritocracy? We live in interesting times.

NOTES

1. Fred L. Borch and Gary Solis, *The Geneva Conventions* (London: Kaplan, 2010).
2. Peter Walker and Daniel Maxwell, *Shaping the Humanitarian Word* (New York: Routledge, 2008), chapter 6.
3. UN Inter Agency Standing Committee, *IASC Guidelines on Mental Health and Psychosocial Support in Emergency Settings* (Geneva: IASC, 2007).
4. World Religion Database, http://www.worldreligiondatabase.org.
5. Fritz K. Oser, W. George Scarlett, and Anton Bucher, "Religious and Spiritual Development Throughout the Life Span," in W. Damon and R. M. Lerner (eds.), *Handbook of Child Psychology: Theoretical Models of Human Development*, vol. 1, 6th ed. (Hoboken, NJ: Wiley, 2006).
6. Brian Zinnbauer, Kenneth I. Pargament, Brenda Cole, Mark S. Rye, Eric M. Butter, Timothy G. Belavich, Kathleen M. Hipp, Allie B. Scott, and Jill L. Kadar, "Religion and Spirituality: Unfuzzying the Fuzzy," *Journal for the Scientific Study of Religion* 36, 4 (1997): 549–564.
7. Peter C. Hill and Ralph W. Hood (eds.), *Measures of Religiosity* (Birmingham, AL: Religious Education Press, 1999).
8. Wilfred Cantwell Smith, *Faith and Belief: The Difference Between Them* (Oxford, UK: Oneworld, 1998); Smith, *Patterns of Faith Around the World* (Boston: Oneworld, 1998).
9. Smith, *Faith and Belief*, 12.
10. Ibid., 134.
11. Kenneth I. Pargament, David S. Ensing, and Kathryn Falgout, "God Help Me: Religious Coping Effects as Predictors of the Outcomes of Significant Negative Life Events," *American Journal of Community and Psychology* 18, 76 (1990): 793–824; K. I. Pargament, *The Psychology of Religious Coping: Theory, Research, Practice* (New York: Guilford Press, 1997).
12. Susan Kwilecki, *Becoming Religious* (Cranbury, NJ: Associated University Press, 1999); Linda Juang and Moin Syed, "Ethnic Identity and Spirituality," in Richard M. Lerner, Robert W. Roeser, and Erin Phelps (eds.), *Positive Youth Development and Spirituality: From Theory to Research* (West Conshohocken, PA: Templeton Foundation Press, 2008), 262–284.
13. Patrick Love, Marianne Bock, Annie Jannarone, and Paul Richardson, "Identity Interaction: Exploring the Spiritual Experiences of Lesbian and Gay College Students," *Journal of College Student Development* 46, 2 (2005): 193–209.

14. Anna Mansson McGinty, "Formation of Alternative Femininities Through Islam: Feminist Approaches Among Muslim Converts in Sweden," *Women's Studies International Forum* 30, 6 (November–December 2007): 474.

15. Paul Emmanuel Johnson, *Psychology of Religion* (Oxford, UK: Abington Press, 1959), 82.

16. Ani Kalayjian, Nicole Moore, Judy Kuriansky, and Chris Aberson, "A Disaster Outreach Program for Tsunami Survivors in Sri Lanka: The Biopsychosocial, Educational, and Spiritual Approach," in Ani Kalayjian and Dominique Eugene (eds.), *Mass Trauma and Emotional Healing Around the World: Rituals and Practices for Resilience and Meaning-Making*, vol. 1: *Natural Disasters* (Santa Barbara, CA: Praeger/ABC-CLIO, 2010), 125–150; Ani Kalayjian, Beverly Musgrave, and Chris Aberson, "Psychosocial and Spiritual Impact of 9/11 Terrorism on Mental Health Professionals in America," in A. Kalayjian and D. Eugene (eds.), *Mass Trauma and Emotional Healing Around the World*, vol. 2: *Human-Made Disasters*, 327–342.

17. Andrew J. Weaver, Laura T. Flannelly, James Garbarino, Charles R. Figley, and Kevin J. Flannelly, "A Systematic Review of Research on Religion and Spirituality in the Journal of Traumatic Stress: 1990–1999," *Mental Health, Religion & Culture* 6, 3 (2003): 215–228.

18. Mark A. Schuster, Bradley D. Stein, Lisa H. Jaycox, Rebecca L. Collins, Grant N. Marshall, Marc N. Elliott, Annie J. Zhou, David E. Kanouse, Janina L. Morrison, and Sandra H. Berry, "A National Survey of Stress Reactions After the September 11, 2001, Terrorist Attacks," *New England Journal of Medicine* 345, 20 (2001): 1507–1512.

19. Ronnie J. Bulman and Camille B. Wortman, "Attributions of Blame and Coping in the 'Real World': Severe Accident Victims React to Their Lot," *Journal of Personality and Social Psychology* 35, 5 (1977): 351–363.

20. Ivanka Choumanova, Stan Wanat, Ronald Barrett, and Cheryl Koopman, "Religion and Spirituality in Coping with Breast Cancer: Perspectives of Chilean Women," *Breast Journal* 12, 4 (2006): 349–352; Betty Ervin-Cox, Louis Hoffman, and Christopher S. M. Grimes, "Selected Literature on Spirituality and Health/Mental Health," in Richard H. Cox, Betty Ervin-Cox, and Louis Hoffman (eds.), *Spirituality and Psychological Health* (Colorado Springs: Colorado School of Psychology Press, 2005), 284–315; Charles H. Hackney and Glenn S. Sanders, "Religiosity and Mental Health: A Meta-Analysis of Recent Studies," *Journal for the Scientific Study of Religion* 42, 1 (2003): 43–55.

21. Ronnie Janoff-Bulman *Shattered Assumptions: Towards a New Psychology of Trauma* (New York: Free Press, 1992).

22. Laura T. Matthews and Samuel J. Marwit, "Meaning Reconstruction in the Context of Religious Coping: Rebuilding the Shattered Assumptive World," *Omega: Journal of Death and Dying: Special Issue* 53, 1–2 (2006): 87–104.

23. Robert A. Emmons, Patricia M. Colby and Heather A. Kaiser, "When Losses Lead to Gains: Personal Goals and the Recovery of Meaning," in Paul T. P. Wong and

Prem S. Fry (eds.), *The Human Quest for Meaning: A Handbook of Psychological Research and Clinical Applications* (Mahwah, NJ: Erlbaum, 1998), 163–178.

24. Harold George Koenig, *In the Wake of Disaster: Religious Responses to Terrorism & Catastrophe* (West Conshohocken, PA: Templeton Foundation Press, 2006); Julio F. P. Peres, Alexander Moreira-Almeida, Antonia Gladys Nasello and Harold George Koenig, "Spirituality and Resilience in Trauma Victims," *Journal of Religion & Health* 46, 3 (2007): 343–350.

25. Hayden B. Bosworth, Kwang-Soo Park, Douglas R. McQuoid, Judith C. Hays and David C. Steffens, "The Impact of Religious Practice and Religious Coping on Geriatric Depression," *International Journal of Geriatric Psychiatry* 18, 10 (2003): 905–914; Eileen J. Burker, Donna M. Evon, Jan A. Sedway and Thomas Egan, "Religious Coping, Psychological Distress and Disability Among Patients with End-Stage Pulmonary Disease," *Journal of Clinical Psychology in Medical Settings* 11, 3 (2004): 179–193.

26. Pargament et al., "God Help Me."

27. Kenneth I. Pargament, "Religious Methods of Coping: Resources for the Conservation and Transformation of Significance," in Edward P. Shafranske (ed.), *Religion and the Clinical Practice of Psychology* (Washington, DC: American Psychological Association, 1996), 232.

28. Peter Fischer, Tobias Greitemeyer, Andreas Kastenmüller, Eva Jonas, and Dieter Frey, "Coping with Terrorism: The Impact of Increased Salience of Terrorism on Mood and Self-Efficacy of Intrinsically Religious and Nonreligious People," *Personality and Social Psychology Bulletin* 32, 3 (2006): 365–377; Kenneth I. Maton, "The Stress-Buffering Role of Spiritual Support: Cross-Sectional and Prospective Investigations," *Journal for the Scientific Study of Religion* 28, 3 (1989): 310–323.

29. Kenneth I. Pargament and Jeremy Cummings, "Anchored by Faith: Religion as a Resilience Factor," in John W. Reich, Alex Zautra, and John Stuart Hall (eds.), *Handbook of Adult Resilience* (New York: Guilford Press, 2010), 193–211.

30. Crystal L. Park, "Religion as a Meaning-Making Framework in Coping with Life Stress," *Journal of Social Issues* 61, 4 (2005): 707–729.

31. Crystal L. Park and Susan Folkman, "Meaning in the Context of Stress and Coping," *General Review of Psychology* 1 (1997): 115–144.

32. Neal Krause, "Religious Meaning and Subjective Well-Being in Late Life," *Journals of Gerontology: Series B: Psychological Sciences and Social Sciences* 58, 3 (2003): S160–170; Shirley A. Murphy, L. Clark Johnson, and Janet Lohan, "Finding Meaning in a Child's Violent Death: A Five-Year Prospective Analysis of Parents' Personal Narratives and Empirical Data," *Death Studies* 27, 5 (2003): 381–404.

33. M. M. Banerjee and L. Pyles, "Spirituality: A Source of Resilience for African American Women in the Era of Welfare Reform," *Journal of Ethnic & Cultural Diversity in Social Work: Innovation in Theory, Research & Practice* 13, 2 (2004): 45–70.

34. Ibid., 60.

35. Ajit K. Dalal and Namita Pande, "Psychological Recovery of Accident Victims with Temporary and Permanent Disability," *International Journal of Psychology* 23, 1 (1988): 25–40.

36. Pargament and Cummings, "Anchored by Faith."

37. Marvin W. Acklin, Earl C. Brown, and Paul A. Mauger, "The Role of Religious Values in Coping with Cancer," *Journal of Religion and Health* 22, 4 (1983): 322–333; Randy S. Hebert, Qianyu Dang, and Richard Schulz, "Religious Beliefs and Practices Are Associated with Better Mental Health in Family Caregivers of Patients with Dementia: Findings from the Reach Study," *American Journal of Geriatric Psychiatry* 15, 4 (2007): 292–300; Kenneth S. Kendler, Xiao-Qing Liu, Charles O. Gardner, Michael E. McCullough, David Larson, and Carol A. Prescott, "Dimensions of Religiosity and Their Relationship to Lifetime Psychiatric and Substance Use Disorders," *American Journal of Psychiatry* 160, 3 (2003): 496–503.

38. Harold George Koenig, "Religion and Remission of Depression in Medical Inpatients with Heart Failure/Pulmonary Disease," *Journal of Nervous and Mental Disease* 195, 5 (2007): 389–395.

39. Bosworth et al., "Impact of Religious Practice."

40. Pargament and Cummings, "Anchored by Faith."

41. Tameka L. Gillum, Cris M., Sullivan, and Deborah I. Bybee, "The Importance of Spirituality in the Lives of Domestic Violence Survivors," *Violence Against Women* 12, 3 (2006): 240–250.

42. Christina G. Watlington and Christopher M. Murphy, "The Roles of Religion and Spirituality Among African American Survivors of Domestic Violence," *Journal of Clinical Psychology* 62, 7 (2006): 837–857.

43. William J. Strawbridge, Sarah J. Shema, Richard D. Cohen, and George A. Kaplan, "Religious Attendance Increases Survival by Improving and Maintaining Good Health Behaviors, Mental Health, and Social Relationships," *Annals of Behavioral Medicine* 23, 1 (2001): 68–74.

44. Pargament and Cummings, "Anchored by Faith."

45. Sain Cotton, Christina M. Puchalski, Susan N. Sherman, Joseph M. Mrus, Amy H. Peterman, Judith Feinberg, Kenneth I. Pargament, Amy C. Justice, Anthony C. Leonard, and Joel Tsevat, "Spirituality and Religion in Patients with HIV/AIDS," *Journal of General Internal Medicine* 21 (2006): S5–13; Hebert et al., "Religious Beliefs and Practices"; Sherry A. Falsetti, Patricia A. Resick, and Joanne L. Davis, "Changes in Religious Beliefs Following Trauma," *Journal of Traumatic Stress* 16, 4 (2003): 391–398; Jose Parappully, Robert Rosenbaum, Leland van den Daele, and Esther Nzewi, "Thriving After Trauma: The Experience of Parents of Murdered Children," *Journal of Humanistic Psychology* 42, 1 (2002): 33–70; Karolynn Siegel and Eric W. Schrimshaw, "Perceiving Benefits in Adversity: Stress-Related Growth in Women Living with HIV/AIDS," *Social Science & Medicine* 51, 10 (2000): 1543–1554.

46. Falsetti et al. "Changes in Religious Beliefs Following Trauma."

47. Alan Fontana and Robert Rosenheck, "Trauma, Change in Strength of Religious Faith, and Mental Health Service Use Among Veterans Treated for PTSD," *Journal of Nervous and Mental Disease* 192, 9 (2004): 579–584.

48. Gallup Poll, "Religion in the World at the End of the Millennium." Results available at http://www.gallup-international.com/ContentFiles/millennium15.asp (accessed September 12, 2011).

49. Peter Walker and Daniel G. Maxwell, "Origins of the International Humanitarian System," in *Shaping the Humanitarian World* (New York: Routledge, 2009), 1–12.

50. Avery Cardinal Dulles, "Christianity and Humanitarian Action," in Kevin M. Cahill (ed.), *Traditions, Values and Humanitarian Action* (Bronx, NY: Fordham University Press, 2003); Harlan J. Wechsler. "For the Sake of My Kin and Friends: Traditions, Values and Humanitarian Action in Judaism," in Cahill (ed.), *Traditions, Values and Humanitarian Action.*

51. Jamal Krafess, "The Influence of the Muslim Religion in Humanitarian Aid," *International Review of the Red Cross* 87 (2005): 327–341; Dijana Gres, "The Ambivalence of Religion Within the Framework of Secular Humanism: The Case of Faith-Based Humanitarian Organisations" (master's thesis, University of British Columbia, 2010).

52. World Vision International mission statement, http://wvi.org/wvi/wviweb.nsf/maindocs/7A0A54FD44BC11C38825737500737C8A?opendocument.

53. Muslim Aid mission statement, http://www.muslimaid.org/index.php/about-us.

54. Hadassah mission statement, http://www.hadassah.org/site/c.keJNIWOvElH/b.5572905/k.A1D7/Our_Mission.htm.

55. Sunray mission statement, http://sunray.org/dotnetnuke/AboutUs/SunrayMeditationSociety/tabid/57/Default.aspx.

56. Julia Berger, "Religious Nongovernmental Organizations: An Exploratory Analysis," *Voluntas* 14, 1 (March 2003): 15.

57. Oxfam GB annual reports and accounts, 2009–10, http://oxfam.org.uk.

58. CARE USA; see http://www.care.org/about/faqs.asp?s_src=REDPSRCH10.

59. World Vision International 2009 Annual Report, http://www.worldvision.org/resources.nsf/Main/annual-review-2009-resources/$FILE/AR_2009FinancialHighlights.pdf.

60. Catholic Relief Services 2009 annual report, http://crs.org/about/finance/pdf/ar_2009.pdf.

61. Jonathan Benthall, "Have Islamic Aid Agencies a Privileged Relationship in Majority Muslim Areas? The Case of Post-Tsunami Reconstruction in Aceh," *Journal of Humanitarian Assistance* (2008), http://sites.tufts.edu/jha/archives/category/jonathan-benthall.

62. Ibid.

63. Krafess, "Influence of the Muslim Religion in Humanitarian Aid."

64. Carlo Benedetti, "Islamic and Christian Inspired Relief NGOs: Between Tactical Collaboration and Strategic Diffidence?" *Journal of International Development* 18, 6 (2006): 849.

65. Nida Kirmani and Ajaz Ahmed Khan, "Does Faith Matter: An Examination of Islamic Relief's Work with Refugees and Internally Displaced Persons," *Refugee Survey Quarterly* 27, 2 (January 2008): 41–50.

66. Ibid.

67. Stephanie J. Nawyn, "Faithfully Providing Refuge: The Role of Religious Organizations in Refugee Assistance Advocacy," *Center for Comparative Immigration Studies.* Working paper 115. University of California San Diego (2005).

68. Kirmani and Khan, "Does Faith Matter."

69. Branka Peuraca, "Can Faith-Based NGOs Advance Interfaith Reconciliation?" United States Institute of Peace Special Report (2003), http://www.usip.org.

70. Ibid.

71. David Smock, "Divine Intervention: Regional Reconciliation Through Faith," *Harvard International Review* 25, 4 (Winter 2004): 46–50.

72. Elzbieta M. Gozdziak, "Spiritual Emergency Room: The Role of Spirituality and Religion in the Resettlement of Kosovar Albanians," *Journal of Refugee Studies* 15, 2 (June 2002): 136–152.

73. Jean-Francois Mayer, "'In God Have I Put My Trust': Refugees and Religion," *Refugee Survey Quarterly* 26, 2 (January 2007): 6–10.

74. Gerard Clarke, "Faith Matters: Faith-Based Organisations, Civil Society and International Development," *Journal of International Development* 18, 6 (August 2006): 835–848.

75. Ibid.

76. Nawyn, "Faithfully Providing Refuge."

77. Ninth Circuit Court Ruling on *Spencer v. World Vision Inc.*, filed August 23, 2010, http://www.ca9.uscourts.gov/datastore/opinions/2010/08/23/08-35532.pdf.

78. Shawn Teresa Flanigan, *For the Love of God: NGOS and Religious Identity in a Violent World* (Sterling, VA: Kumarian Press, 2010).

79. Ibid.

80. Krafess, "Influence of the Muslim Religion in Humanitarian Aid."

81. Joan Laidig and Danielle Speakman, "The Role of Spirituality in Understanding and Coping with Traumatic Stress in Humanitarian Aid Workers," Headington Institute. *Continuing Education Series* (October 2009): 33–35.

82. Sally Weinrich, Sally B. Hardin, and Maggie Johnson, "Nurses Respond to Hurricane Hugo Victims' Disaster Stress," *Archives of Psychiatric Nursing* 4, 3 (1990): 195–205.

83. Abbas Ebadi, Fazollah Ahmadi, Mostafa Ghanei, and Anoshirvan Kazemnejad, "Spirituality: A Key Factor in Coping Among Iranians Chronically Affected by Mustard Gas in the Disaster of War," *Nursing and Health Science* 11, 4 (2009): 344–350.

84. Michael Brune, Christina Haasen, Michael Krausz, Oktay Yagirna, Enrique Bustos, and David Eisenman, "Belief Systems as Coping Factors for Traumatized Refugees: A Pilot Study," *European Psychiatry* 17, 8 (2002): 451–458.

85. Amy L. Ai, Christopher Peterson, and Bu Huang, "The Effect of Religious-Spiritual Coping on Positive Attitudes of Adult Muslim Refugees from Kosovo and Bosnia." *International Journal for the Psychology of Religion* 13, 1 (2003): 29–47; Francisco José Eiroá Orosa, Michael Brune, Katrin Huter, Julia Fischer-Ortman, and Christina Haasen, "Belief Systems as Coping Factors in Traumatized Refugees: A Prospective Study," *Traumatology* 17, 1 (2011): 1–7.

86. Bethany Ojalehto and Qi Wang, "Children's Spiritual Development in Forced Displacement: A Human Rights Perspective," *International Journal of Children's Spirituality* 13, 2 (2008): 129–143.

87. TANGO International, *End of Project Study of the Tsunami-Impacted Communities of Southern Thailand: A Multi-Component Review* (London: World Vision International, 2006).

88. K. Duryee and M. Kawaharada, *WV Eastern DR Congo Assessment Report May/June 2008* (London: World Vision International, 2008).

6

Religious Giving Outside the Law in New Delhi

Erica Bornstein

Introduction

The extent of religious giving in India is tremendous. Some estimate that the equivalent of $92 million is donated to Hindu shrines every year.[1] Religious giving encompasses daily donations to local temples, pilgrimage offerings, gifts to beggars on the street, and donations to religious charitable trusts and nongovernmental organizations (NGOs). It includes cash donations, gifts-in-kind, service via volunteer labor (*seva*), and gifts remitted electronically via the Internet. Religious giving is not regulated by the state and does not confer tax benefits on donors, and as such it is of concern to the government and to organizations that aim to make charitable work "accountable."[2] In fact, most giving to charity in India falls under this rubric. One study documented that giving to "individuals in distress, known to oneself, and to beggars" takes up about 77 percent of the donations to individuals, while only 21 percent goes toward organized secular humanitarian efforts. NGO activists lament that this ad hoc charity takes precedence over philanthropy for long-term change and development.[3] Another study found that Indians donate large amounts in cash or in kind at temple shrines.[4] For example, one of the most famous temples in India (Shri Thirupathi Devasthanam Trust) receives approximately $41 million annually in cash donations. Pilgrims also donate gold, jewelry and other valuables. Additionally, the sale value of hair donated by pilgrims comes to roughly $4.36 million annually. Mata Vaishno Devi Shrine in Jammu has an annual income of about $16 million, mainly from offerings by devotees. Thousands of other temples, gurudwaras (Sikh shrines), dargahs (Muslim shrines), churches, and other institutions across India likewise receive significant donations.[5]

Religious donations support more than places of worship. They also support charitable social service programs sponsored by religious organizations. In everyday practice, the humanitarian endeavors of religious charity—such as feeding the poor, caring for the infirm, and providing education and medical care for those without resources—may not look different from those of its secular counterpart. However, religious charity and secular humanitarianism have been legally segregated into two distinct fields in India, and in this chapter I examine how and why charity developed this divide.[6]

The chapter is structured around three legislative contexts, during which the divide was recodified: in the introduction of British Trust law in colonial India, in the formation of the secular constitution of early postindependence India and Personal Law, and in the regulation of contemporary NGOs through Tax Law. After outlining the scope and practice of Hindu religious giving—or *dān* (donation)—I examine how, during the period of colonial "noninterference" in Indian religion and custom, distinctions between religious and secular giving were legally codified. This era was marked by the emergence of British Trust law, founded in dialogue with its Indian colony. At independence, reform movements involved in the nationalist struggle continued to influence the regulation of religious donation (as "custom") through what is now called "Personal Law." Today, as India's secular state considers once again whether or not to tax and regulate religious giving and Hindu dān, I bring the history of state regulation of charitable activity to bear on current NGOs. My analysis draws on a concept pioneered by legal anthropologist Sally Falk Moore,[7] *the semiautonomous social field*, to explore how the realms of custom and formal law, although segregated by code, may coexist and inform each other.

Politically, debates over secularism and religion in India are heated—calling into question the status of minority rights, religious politics, and the governmental power of the state. India's population is majority Hindu and contains a diverse religious minority for whom the tensions of secularism are great, evidenced by repeated outbreaks of violence that have occurred between Muslims and Hindus since Partition in 1947.[8] Historically, and in the present, the secularity of charitable donation has also occupied an arena of contest. That dān and religious charity stand outside the field of territorial secular law, in the field of personal law, is an issue for NGO activists who aim to make charitable activity a realm of social change that empowers the poor and needy. For religious charitable organizations and donors, however, the fact that religious donations are neither calculated nor taxed may constitute a strategic political stance defying intervention from the state. Partha Chaterjee, following Foucault, has pointed out how membership in cultural and religious group-based identities may facilitate a strategic autonomous stance in Indian secular law, against further governmental intrusion by the state.[9] Although he does not discuss religious donation, I draw on his argument to articulate the strategic politics of donation outside secular law. My focus is primarily on Hindu giving, but similar arguments could be made for the Islamic injunction to give through *zakat* and the legislation of *waqf* committees in India.

It is worth noting at the outset that religious giving is not a mere artifact of tradition. Instead, we must consider it a vibrant contemporary practice that works alongside, and is framed by, the humanitarian efforts of secular NGOs and the Indian state. It is also important to clarify in this introduction that the contemporary constitution of India offers a unique case of secularism that integrates religious law in civil personal law.[10] Personal law, which governs donations to religious endowments, also regulates (for Hindus, Muslims, Parsis, Christians, and Jews) marriage, dowry, divorce, parentage, legitimacy, guardianship, wills, inheritance, and succession.[11] Most NGOs are registered with the state as either Trusts or Societies, and donations to Religious Endowments, Religious Charitable Trusts, and Religious Societies are dealt with differently than those given to trusts and societies that are not identified as religious, with different acts pertaining to the two legal spheres. In other words, donations in India take one of two roads, depending on their religious or secular framing. How these roads came to be formed and the efforts to maintain them are the subject of this chapter.

Who Gives

Although it is difficult to quantify the scope of religious giving, partly because it is untaxed, uncalculated, and unaccounted for by institutions, one NGO in New Delhi attempted to map its scope.[12] Through the marketing firm AC Nielson in 2001, it surveyed sixty-four hundred upper- and middle-income households in fourteen cities with a population of more than one million people (representing roughly 28 percent of the urban Indian population). The survey found that 96 percent of households gave something to charity, and the total amount was a sizable US$8.25 million.[13] In case one is inclined to think these donations are for strictly religious purposes and are not linked to secular forms of social welfare, the Nielson study also asked questions regarding the intended purpose of the donations: 28 percent gave to support the priest, 10 percent gave for educational activities, 8 percent for health activities, 43 percent for developing physical infrastructure, and 20 percent for social service activities (the realm of NGOs).[14] Thus individuals give to religious organizations for religious purposes, for infrastructure, and for more general purposes of social welfare. Many of the temples that receive religious donations have a social service wing that feeds the poor and offers ayurvedic and allopathic medical care, for which doctors donate their time.

Another study, conducted on places of worship and donation practices in New Delhi, focused on fifteen religious organizations randomly selected on the basis of importance and visibility.[15] In the group were six Hindu temples; one Jain temple; the Delhi Gurudwara Prabandhak Committee which covered ten Gurudwaras; the Waqf Board (which dealt with entire offerings and donations made by the Muslim community for charitable and religious purposes); one Sufi Dargah; one Ashram; and two New Age Ashrams. Again, although it is difficult to calculate the extent of religious donation as the amounts may be small and anonymously given in temple donation boxes, there were specific devotee patterns that emerged: out of seventy devotees interviewed, 40 percent said they wanted their donations (offerings) to be used for welfare purposes, 30 percent wanted them to be used for religious purposes, and 30 percent wanted them to be used for both.[16]

In contrast to donations to organizations that were categorized as religious, secular NGOs did not have such a good reputation. In the same study:

> When asked what they thought about NGOs, 50 percent of devotees called NGOs corrupt, 30 percent said they didn't know too much about them, and 20 percent said the NGOs should tie-up with the temple to use the money in the best possible way. As for the religious leaders, hardly any of them were interested in forming partnerships with NGOs. Out of the 15 heads of institutions interviewed, only six held a positive opinion about NGOs. Seven had mixed feelings, and two were highly critical of them. Four of them wanted to associate with NGOs, while another four said they didn't have the resources to associate with them.[17]

These same patterns emerged in my own ethnographic work on charitable giving in New Delhi, which indicates that the pattern is widespread and persists.[18]

Sacred Ideas

Sacred ideas structure Hindu donation. Dān, in Hinduism, is a particular form of donation that does not require a "return," at least in this lifetime.[19] Many expect *punya*, or merit, from giving dān. It differs from Marcel Mauss's classic conception of giving as requiring a reciprocal relation of obligation.[20]

In contrast to reciprocal giving, those who give dān in Hinduism strive to release themselves from any future contact with the recipient of their gift. Dān is a "pure" or "free" gift; yet it is not free of danger. In Hindu scripture and in some ritual practices, it is through dān that evil, sin, and affliction are ritually transferred from donors to recipients.[21] In the *Bhagavad Gita*, dān is a gift that is offered through desireless action.[22] With Hindu religious donation, one "gives in order to forget." There are proper recipients for dān, as well as proper times and places to give it—religious institutions and holidays being among the best.[23]

Yet I found this was being challenged in the course of my research on the contemporary practice of dān in urban New Delhi. The notion, like all cultural forms, is lived and changing. If one takes a ride on any New Delhi street, one is likely to encounter beggars demanding dān. Outside temples, the poor gather to receive dān from devotees and temple priests. Increasingly, urban Indians prefer to give dān to organizations such as orphanages, where they can "see the results over time" and "make spontaneous visits," instead of giving it to a pandit (pundit) or priest at a temple. People give dān in the form of water, rupees, or rice out of their doorways in urban Delhi to beggars, mendicants, and *sadhus* (world renouncers). People also consider donations to schools for the education of impoverished girls, and philanthropy to humanitarian NGOs more broadly, to be forms of dān.[24] Dān, one can say, has become a catchall term for many types of religious charity, whether motivated by duty, habit, or spontaneous desire. Dān has also become a trope through which many Indians understand humanitarian activity more broadly. In 2004–05, I conducted an ethnographic study in New Delhi on religious and secular humanitarian activity that was informal, relatively unorganized (at least in terms of institutions), and under the radar of the state. In this research, most urban Indians referred to their work—whether caring for orphans, giving donations at temples, or helping educate poor children in slums—as dān. Orphanages accepted the sponsorship of girls' education and marriage through dān.[25] One of the most holy forms of dān is *gupt dān* (anonymous dān), which like all religious dān poses a problem of regulation for the state.[26]

Religious Giving in "Hindu Law"

Hinduism, like Islam, integrates what can be considered ancient law that may be textually referenced by the Smriti literature (Laws of Manu), the concept of *dharma* (duty or righteous action), and Dharmashastras.[27] This scriptural authority, with multiple referents, was codified during British colonial rule, before which the textual referents were fluid and less authoritative. Some have argued that the category of "ancient Hindu Law" as a legal category may have arisen from the influence of colonial attempts to govern Hindus.[28] Before the British arrived in South Asia, there was law but in both Hindu and Islamic religious law there was no concept of "equality before the law." Within particular regions, religious laws governed different people, such that Muslims and Hindus coexisted under separate customary legal rubrics. Even during Muslim rule, if Hindus paid their taxes they could be ruled by their own customs and religious laws, including those that governed donation.[29] Like *zakat*, which is one of the five pillars of Islam (see Benthall 1999, also Benthall chapter in this volume), in Hinduism dān is considered a duty and is connected to *dharma*. It is important to reassert that there was not one scriptural authority that codified Hindu law; codification occurred through interaction with British colonial legislative rule.[30]

"Hindu law" is also referenced today; it is not a static, ancient practice. As a contemporary legal category, it is constantly mediated by the legislative present.[31] Thus, when we analyze different eras of regulatory practice toward giving—especially where religious giving is made to stand for "tradition or "culture"—we must explore how the categories of the past are interpreted today, and how categories of the present (such as secular humanitarianism) are in dialogue with those of the past.[32] This co-constitution is a critical aspect of my argument. When we think of the category of *religious giving* as one that is recognizable and legislatable, we must think about how this category came to be, whose interests the category serves, and what is at stake in preserving the category as an identifiable realm, exempt from regulatory practice such as tax. To understand why religious giving is part of "culture" and left to its own devices, we must examine the historical relationship between religious giving and regulatory bodies.

Scholars of colonial India have documented how "tradition" was codified in dialogue with colonial attempts to understand and govern it.[33] Law and traditional practices in precolonial India were not determined exclusively by interpretations of religious texts but had other bases for their authority, such as customary practice, that varied widely across Hindu communities, interpreted and enforced by community councils, not priests. It was the British who gave power to pundits and religious texts to define what constituted "tradition." For example, in an analysis of *sati* (widow immolation), Uma Narayan and Lata Mani have shown how colonial administrators and Indian reformers relied on scriptural privilege and textual authority to authenticate "tradition," and how the logic of official discourse on Hindu custom was provided by pandits at courts.[34] The colonial debates surrounding sati questioned whether or not it could be legislatively prohibited. If a practice were to have a basis in scripture, it was feared, there would be indigenous outrage at its prohibition. Hence the British studied tradition through pandits in order to understand and regulate what they considered custom, which included religion; colonial intervention in customary practice was not about progress for Indian culture, but about governance. If officials favoring the abolition of sati considered their agenda part of maintaining and protecting religious tradition, then before tradition could be protected it had to be identified, and colonial intervention involved protecting religious tradition from pandits who were seen to hold a monopoly over its knowledge. Although the scriptural texts that were seen to be authoritative were written in various periods (Srutis, Dharamashastras, Smritis), the older texts were assumed by the British to have greater stature. Later, for Indian reformers such as Rammohan Roy in 1818, the very same scriptures were used to argue *against* sati practice. Both abolitionists (Indian reformers) and colonial officials used Brahmanic scriptures as justification for their position. Thus "Hindu Law" as a scriptural referent is partly a colonial byproduct, codifying the equation of scripture with tradition that arose in the colonial era. It deserves mention in this historical overview that contemporary Hindu fundamentalists also use scripture to justify their nationalist claims. From this brief survey, we can see how the category of religious giving may have emerged from earlier attempts to define, legislate, and codify its practice.

Religious Communities and Abstract Publics in British Trust Law

When the British colonized the region, they refrained from legislating what they considered "custom" (including religion). Following a strategy of indirect rule that was also employed in southern Africa, custom was governed through Personal Law.[35] Parallel institutions, such as *panchayats* (local village courts led by elders) emerged as alternative forums to colonial civil courts for dispute settlement. These traditional forms of rule were not simply premodern legal forms. Their existence was enhanced and legislated by colonial law, in what Sally Falk Moore has termed a "semiautonomous" social field. Thus the domain of tradition is not in opposition to modernity; it is constituted by it as such. In 1772, the East India Company instituted a body of "civil administrators," and Warren Hastings introduced uniform criminal law to provide "equality before the law."[36] In the early phase of this civil administration,

Brahmin pandits and Muslim jurists were appointed and consulted to develop what became Anglo-Hindu and Anglo-Muslim Personal Law. In 1864, the Hindu pandits and Muslim jurists were eliminated from the British system of government, and British judges interpreted personal law without native assistance.

Britain's secularity and some of its legal institutions were constituted through encounter with the colonies. Peter van der Veer articulates this argument through the example of the British concept of a "Christian self," which was connected to notions of progress and modernity largely created in dialogue on encountering colonial others.[37] Christian missionaries in colonial India, carrying out the white man's burden, articulated a particular relationship among religion, secularism, and progress. Missionaries demanded the secularity of the state and operated in a public sphere distinct from it. For both India and Britain, categories of modernity, religion, and secularism were co-constituted in relation to each other.

During this era, new legal forms governing charitable trusts and mortmain emerged simultaneously in Britain and in its Indian colony.[38] The legal form of the Trust in Britain was a precursor to the corporation and was based on F. W. Maitland's "tripartite contract" among (1) donors, (2) beneficiaries of the donor's gift, and (3) trustees that administer the gift.[39] In Victorian England, the trust concept encompassed both "private trusts," designed for the benefit of dependents such as widows and children, and "public charitable trusts." The distinction between private and public charitable trusts was imported to India in the 1880s, the same period in which the distinction was being codified in England.

In British case law, there was a shift in the concept of charity from benefiting the community to one benefiting an abstract notion of the public, an additional distinction to that between customary and secular law. The Charitable Trusts Act of 1887 (amended in 1891) clarified procedures for public charitable trusts. In England, a charitable gift was one given with the clear intention of *public benefit* to an *abstract public*: "If the intention of the donor was to benefit specific individuals, the gift was not considered charitable."[40] If the donor aimed to accomplish the abstract purpose of relieving poverty, or advancing education or religion without giving any particular individuals the right to claim the funds, the gift was charitable. Charitable gifts were thus defined as benefiting only abstract others, such as causes, not specific individuals. This distinction was critical to the emergence of the trust as a legal concept. By the turn of the century, the trustee had become the model figure of an ethical subject. Charitable purposes included relief for the poor, education, medical need, and "advancement for any other object of general public utility, but does not include a purpose which relates exclusively to religious teaching or worship."[41] Here we see how, and when, religion was segregated from charitable purpose.[42]

In practice, religious giving in India did not fit the British distinction between public and private social welfare. Dān, gifts given through *dharma*, relied upon an ethic of duty, at times given to specific persons such as a priest or *sadhus* (renunciants). Righteous conduct was not exactly religious (or belief, as in England). The question of intention that British law imposed on donation did not fit religious gifts, which straddled the boundary between public and private benefit from the gift. The new colonial legal mode of a trust contract was imposed on relational webs of affiliation that had historically supported social welfare through extended family networks, family temples, family deities, and merchant castes.[43] Much of this legislation was an effort by the British to control financial capital they considered to be out of circulation, within the Hindu Undivided Family (HUF). The HUF was a threat to British colonial capitalism, particularly the extensive kinship networks and clan associations that facilitated merchant business by groups such as the Marwaris in north and eastern India. Mortmain law was used in this instance to establish a rule against perpetual holdings except in the case of charitable gifts. The distinction between public and private charitable trusts "recoded customary social welfare" as belonging to a domain of religion and culture in relation to taxation. This pattern is also seen in the British colonial state response to famine relief, and the privileging of institutional forms of charity.[44]

British notions of charity not only distinguished public from private welfare, they legally distinguished public welfare from religion through the Societies Registration Action (1860), which governed literary, scientific, and charitable societies; and the Religious Endowments Act (1863), which resulted from disputes surrounding temple complexes and governed Hindu and Muslim religious institutions of a public nature. This spate of legislation in the 1860s clarified the distinction between social welfare of members of an organization that reaped benefits (such as a religious group) and social welfare of an abstract public. The Indian Tax and Companies Acts that were passed later (in the 1880s) further reinforced notions of charity as gifts to an abstract public and provided incentives of tax exemption with charitable status. This series of legislative initiatives—known as the British laws of charitable trusts, societies, and endowments—focused on the intention of the gift by the donor, which also fit the British trust paradigm. Religion remained outside of circulation in personal and customary law. In the British legislation of charity and philanthropy, the ethics of welfare was one of public utility, distinct from religious values, custom, and institutions focused on religious teaching or worship. The distinction was also between "modern" methods of social welfare and "traditional" or customary ones. Although support of an abstract civic public was deemed a humanitarian good, Indian giving practices that fluidly straddled boundaries between public and private welfare—through family temples, for example—could not adequately be conscripted into binary distinctions.

In the 1920s, during the struggle for independence, the Gandhian concept of trusteeship appropriated the British legal concept of trust for nationalist purposes. The Charitable Religious Trusts Act (1920) identified religious trusts for public good and classified them as charitable trusts, tax-exempt. The legislation elaborated the governance of finances and accounts of charitable religious trusts, enforced an "ethics of public accountability," and was concerned with mismanagement of large temples and mosques. This era marked a *shift in the legislation of gifts toward the protection of rights*, codifying rights-based benevolence and reinforcing the notion of *the trustee as someone in service of an abstract public*.[45] The trust contract in British law mirrored the model of the rights-based joint-stock shareholder. Public discourse in Britain and India began to associate beneficiaries' rights with procedures used to protect shareholders, linked to public accounts and audits. Religious gifts as well fell into this legislation and were divided into those that were public (Charitable Religious Trusts) and those that were private (Religious Endowments). The language of rights and beneficiaries, and the notion of trust, became contractual in relation to the charitable gift governed through colonial capitalism. The discursive shift from charity to rights fit into a modernist narrative of scientific philanthropy, distinguished from charity, which was also taking place in Britain and the United States.[46] Some British colonial laws governing charitable donations, which included the Societies Registration Act, the Charitable Trusts Acts, and the Tax Acts instituted between 1870 and 1920, although amended, are still part of the Indian constitution today. NGOs in social welfare provision engage with this legal legacy on a daily basis. That these laws were intended for colonial rule, and their disjuncture with the cultural practices they set out to govern, are issues that those working in the NGO sector in India are forced to reckon with—if not directly, then by proxy, and at times by going around the law completely.

Secularism and Social Reform

A year after India's independence, in 1948, a first attempt was made to introduce and develop a uniform civil code to replace colonial law. The Hindu
Code Bill, led by India's law magistrate and the architect of India's constitution, B. R. Ambedkar, sought to codify regional Hindu customs and laws and
provide minority rights to untouchables.[47] There was extensive Hindu opposition to the bill, and in 1951 it was set aside without passage.[48] In the 1950s,
aspects of the bill were introduced again, but this time piecemeal, in laws including the Hindu Marriage Act (1955), the Hindu Succession Act (1956), the
Hindu Minority and Guardianship Act (1956), and the Hindu Adoptions
and Maintenance Act (1956). Although at first this legislation may not seem
immediately relevant to our discussion of the regulation of religious charity, it
represents legislative continuity regarding secularism and spheres of law in
India. In contrast to other secular states such as the United States—where
there is an understanding of individual rights, equality before the law, equal
opportunity, and individual freedom of religion—*India's secularism focuses on
the legitimacy and autonomy of cultural and religious (group-based) identities.*
This is an important distinction that we must keep in mind for the remainder
of this chapter.[49]

The British process of governance was one of supposed "religious neutrality" via indirect rule in the eighteenth and nineteenth centuries. The concept of neutrality toward religion was an attempt to avoid the perception of
promoting Christianity in its rule, and at first the colonial state did not intervene directly in religious doctrine and practice. Yet, as we have seen, it was
also deeply involved in religion by way of attempts to codify customary practice. The Indian National Congress (founded 1885) also relied on principles of
Victorian liberalism. The Congress Party, which fought for independence
and was led by Gandhi along with Nehru, was influenced by ideas of so-
cialism, Hinduism, and Western secularism, in an intersection that produced
an Indian secular nationalism for an independent Indian state.[50] The constitution of independent India today is radically secular. Article 25 addresses
freedom of religion by referring to state interference regarding exclusions of
caste, marriage practices, and personal laws; and Article 27 articulates that
"no person shall be compelled to pay taxes for the support of any particular
religion." Although the state advocates freedom of religion, it has also historically interfered with religion for social reform.

In the 1920s and 1930s, Hindu reformers forced open the doors of temples
to Harijans (untouchables), and outlawed child marriage and sati (widow

immolation). By legislating the social reform of religion, the state attempted to assert control over Hindu religious institutions.[51] It was the nineteenth century modernizing efforts of the Indian social reformers that solicited legal intervention by the colonial state. What resulted was legislation on Hindu religious and social matters immediately after Independence, including the Madras Devadasis (Prevention of Dedication) Act (1947), which outlawed dedicating young girls to temple deities (temple prostitutes); the Madras Temple Entry Authorization Act (1947), which made it a punishable offense to prevent any person on grounds of untouchability from entering or worshipping in a Hindu Temple (later, temple-entry provisions were added to the Constitution of India); and the Madras Animal and Bird Sacrifices Abolition Act (1950), which addressed animal sacrifice as an undesirable and "primitive form of worship." In these reform acts, the legislative arm of the state became the instrument for "purifying" Hindu religion.[52] The Indian nationalist movement post-Independence saw greater involvement in state administration and management of Hindu temples. In the Madras Hindu Religious and Charitable Endowments Act (1951), a department of government was set up to administer and oversee Hindu endowments, whereby a religious denomination still managed its own affairs while secular matters such as the management of property became the realm of the state. Here we see how, as the state sought to intervene in the realm of custom through regulation, the religious and secular legislative divide was reinforced through personal law and its distinction from territorial law.

Because of this initiative to use state legislation to reform Hinduism in a nationalist project, Partha Chaterjee suggests that the dangerous communalism of the Hindu right in India is a product not of colonialism but of nationalist modernity. He argues that a limitation of liberal political theory is that it cannot recognize the collective rights of cultural groups:

> Liberalism must hold as a fundamental principle the idea that the state, and all public institutions, will treat all citizens equally, regardless of race, sex, religion, or other cultural particularities. It is only when everyone is treated equally, liberals will argue, that the basic needs of people, shared universally by all, can be adequately and fairly satisfied.[53]

The locus of rights in liberal political theory is the individual citizen, who is the bearer of individual needs that include livelihood, health care, education, and cultural goods such as religious freedom, free speech, and free association.

As an alternative, Chaterjee suggests Foucault's concept of strategic politics and governmentality in relation to the rights of collective groups, and he makes a provocative statement: "What is asserted in a collective cultural right *is in fact the right not to offer a reason for being different.*"[54] With this perspective, one assumes there are such radical differences in worldviews and understanding that one group cannot possibly attempt to understand the other. When this strategic contestation is articulated in a language of rights, when "autonomy" and "freedom" are invoked, it presents an impasse of cultural relativism. Chaterjee suggests an alternate perspective useful for understanding how religious donations are treated by the state in personal law. He suggests *we look where governmentality is not successful*: where it cannot "encompass sovereignty." Assertions of minority cultural rights appear in such sites, and the rights being asserted are against governmentality. He says: "In a situation like this, the only way to resist submitting to the powers of sovereignty is literally to declare oneself unreasonable." He argues for "toleration" as a model for strategic politics and as a rubric for diversity in India. He does not see a uniform civil code as the solution. Instead, he asks, how can state involvement in minority religious groups be seen as legitimate and fair? A strategic politics of toleration might include the resistance of homogenization from the outside while pushing for democratization from within.[55]

As Arjun Appadurai has pointed out, minority politics are not merely issues of representation; they are issues of inclusion.[56] Religious and secular charitable organizations are at the forefront of addressing the social welfare and rights of those who have been excluded from society, whether by poverty or circumstance, or religious or cultural identity. Charitable organizations provide for citizens where the state does not. Religious and secular NGOs provide emergency medical treatment, refugee resettlement, and care of abandoned children, and they address issues of social and political advocacy. Many NGOs are activist organizations that struggle for social change in the distinct spheres that personal law engages with: women's rights, children's rights, and minority rights. As actors in the field of social welfare provision, NGOs and religious charities are required to engage with the state via legal registration for incorporation and tax law, which is an issue I visit in the following section of the chapter. As the statistics on giving mentioned earlier can document, religious charity is significant in terms of financial and social scope. It is also relatively ungoverned. Yet again, this is not an informal economy (as in the dual economy of economic theorists) but an underground, formal sphere of religious finance untouched by the secular state. It remains an arena of strategic politics, a semiautonomous field. One result of this is that much of the work of NGOs is considered "black money," and recent legislation aims to control money laundering by shady nonprofits. Ongoing attempts to regulate the work of charitable NGOs—religious and secular—through contemporary tax law are efforts by the state to intervene in flows of capital and to make claims on the social welfare provision of its citizens. This is a trajectory we have seen before: in British Trust law, in the laws of charitable endowments, and in secular personal law. Alongside this effort by the state to intervene for purposes of social reform and fiscal control is the struggle for autonomy on the part of religious and cultural groups.

Regulating Giving via Tax Law for NGOs

Attempts to make NGOs accountable have been at the forefront of efforts to regulate them, and the history of regulation and debates surrounding it affects the work of contemporary humanitarian NGOs. In order to understand this in the present, we must look at one more era of legislation regulating charitable donations, passed postindependence: the Income Tax Act of 1961. Like the Constitution of India, which does not define religion, the Income Tax Act does not define religious purpose (that which is excluded from garnering tax benefits). The Income Tax Act defines charitable purpose as: "Relief of the Poor, Formal Education, Medical Relief, and Any other object of general public utility (including social welfare and humanitarianism, advocacy, social justice and empowerment organizations)." Though many NGOs combine charitable and religious purpose in their activities, in terms of tax benefits for donors charitable purpose excludes anything that relates exclusively to religious teaching or worship. Religious Trusts, for example, are treated like Public Charitable Trusts in that they are tax-exempt (they do not have to pay taxes to the government of India). However, they differ from charitable trusts in that donations to religious trusts offer no tax benefits to donors. This is partly due to the history of colonial law, personal law, and regulation of religious activities in independent secular India.

Religious social welfare schemes are not the only places to donate funds for humanitarian efforts. There are government-sponsored public welfare programs, such as earthquake relief or the Prime Minister's National Relief Fund, that offer a 100 percent tax deduction for donors.[57] In addition, donations to secular charities listed in section 80(g) of the Income Tax Code permit a 50 percent tax deduction for donors, provided certain conditions are met: the institution was created for "charitable purposes in India," the institution or fund is tax-exempt, the institution's governing documents do not permit use of income or assets for any purpose other than charitable, *the institution or fund is not expressed to be for the benefit of any particular religious community or caste*, and the institution or fund maintains regular accounts of its receipts and expenditure. Here again we see the distinction, based on the "intent" of the donor's gift, whether it is for public or private benefit, and charitable or religious purpose. This artifact of British colonial trust law does not follow the logic of contemporary religious donation as it is practiced in India because, as I noted earlier, religious donation may also be intended for what are considered secular aspects of social welfare. Section 80(g) status of the Income Tax Code is sought by NGOs because it supplies an incentive to donors by offering a greater tax deduction. Religious NGOs do not qualify for 80(g) status if their activities serve specific populations.[58] Perhaps religious NGOs do not need 80(g) status as an incentive because religious dān is to be given without any expectation of a return, anonymously and without a tax receipt.[59]

But tax laws are changing. In 2006 the government imposed a 30 percent tax on anonymous donations, which it later revoked; it is still under debate.[60] Recently, a new set of tax laws called the Direct Tax Code Bill were introduced and debated in Parliament. NGOs have organized to try to stop the legislation. The new bill, which is scheduled to take effect in 2012, replaces "charitable purpose" with "permitted welfare activities" and regulates it more narrowly than charitable purpose. For example, NGOs with any businesslike activities may, in the future, be taxed.[61] Religious organizations are excluded from much of the new tax code bill in India, but secular organizations are increasingly being regulated. In a newsletter published by an NGO called AccountAid, an item appeared with the title "Direct Taxes Code 2010: Charity as Usual." It stated: "The revised Direct Taxes Code Bill, tabled in Lok Sabha on 30th August is fortunately like old wine, mellowed and rich, though with a new smart label. A quick glance shows that it generally retains the existing structure, though some critical changes are still there, including compulsory accounting on cash basis and a tax of 15 percent on unspent income." After describing the detailed measures that the government was taking to amend the tax code, it explained that the proposed requirement to spend 100 percent of receipts in the same year had been dropped, including limiting balances to be carried over between fiscal years. The newsletter stated: "Tax on anonymous donations is back on the books. The bureaucratic phrase 'permitted welfare activity,' which saw furious reactions from the sector has been replaced with the more acceptable 'charitable activity.'"[62]

The remainder of the chapter presents two ethnographic examples demonstrating how increased regulation of secular charity affects the workings of contemporary humanitarian NGOs. In practice, although the boundaries between religious and secular charity may not be easily distinguished, how they are treated by the state reinforces their division into two separate realms. Recently, the state, in dialogue with the NGO community lobbying for changes in the tax code, sought to increase regulation of NGO funds. NGOs (primarily secular ones) balked at the bureaucratic gestures of governance, while religious NGOs were notably absent from the new regulation, for reasons I have explained earlier: they exist in a separate, semiautonomous social field. In January 2009, I met with the directors of two nonreligious NGOs. One managed a charity shop that marketed handicrafts produced by cooperatives of disabled and leprosy-affected peoples. She was concerned with increasing financial oversight being levied on secular NGOs. Although religious organizations had charitable wings that fed the poor, provided medical care, and even offered humanitarian assistance in times of emergency, religious NGOs were exempt from a new aspect of the changing tax code that would require all NGOs to spend their funds by the end of every fiscal year. The proposed new tax code specified that any overage would be taxed as income and that all business aspects of charity would also be considered taxable. This was a potential problem for her donors.[63] She explained:

> If you don't use the project budget in the year, it is classified as income. You end up with an excess of income. [Both] two lakhs or 10 lakhs rupees [equivalent to USD $4,500 or $22,500] will make you taxable. With this new law, surplus is taxed. No funding organization will agree to that. They want to maximize the use of the money for the goals you put it towards. With the new tax laws, the donor is giving to the state and doesn't have control over the state. The state can use the funds for nuclear weapons.

Governments were accountable to each other, not to donors. She was worried that donors would not give if they thought they were giving to the government. This was an issue for her NGO because most of the money that funded it was given through individual donations. "I love India, that is why people give," she said.

> The old ladies in England, all these [Christian] scriptural texts that tell you people are going to fall through the net, charity catches them. If

[nations] can't afford social welfare in countries like Britain where
local giving supplements state social welfare programs, how can we
expect the Indian state to do this? We all need to learn how to budget
and monitor our budgets better, but they are talking about surpluses,
and taxing surpluses.

She told a Swedish donor not to send the next installment of his gift because
she did not want to end up with a surplus:

> Rather than asking too much and spending too little, rather than just
> spending for spending sake (which is what I am doing now) with a
> project I can't carry over [the surplus]. But with savings I can't use it
> because I will be taxed on it. We are being penalized for being prudent.

She offered an example of how this new tax code would affect donations for
humanitarian work. After the Indian Ocean tsunami, donations for relief in
India were phenomenal. This same Swedish donor phoned her to find some-
where to spend his money. "Sometimes donors are putting you under pressure
to spend money," she said:

> The south of India was rocking in money. It was wonderful, people
> gave, but organizations made disaster relief tents. People didn't need
> tents. They found other places to stay. But they couldn't find images for
> the donors and the donors were asking to show us what I have done.
> How have people's lives been changed? A lot of that money was given
> in the form of donations that could not have been used in that year.[64]

Later, I spoke with the director of another NGO that coordinated humanitarian efforts in India. Having heard about my research on giving, he wanted
to know how his membership organization could access the rich resources of
religious donations for social welfare, which he considered a new and
untapped reserve. His NGO, in the absence of national governmental oversight of humanitarian organizations, sought to coordinate between, and provide generalized standards for, humanitarian efforts. The necessity of this
NGO became apparent after the Indian Ocean tsunami, when some beneficiaries received aid from many organizations while others received no aid at
all. The NGO aimed to coordinate between organizations, develop a collective plan of action, and allocate geographical and thematic areas of intervention.[65] The director articulated a sentiment I had heard from other NGO

activists in Delhi: that there may be enough funds within India to solve India's problems with poverty and social inequality. Corporate India was booming—something visually apparent in the fancy new shopping malls in urban India and the streams of consumers who frequented them. Meanwhile, the stark contrast between the ultrarich and the ultrapoor was exponentially exaggerated. The director wondered if Indian entities could mobilize Indian resources, and if there could be a potential for social change. The NGO wanted to "tap into" this primarily Hindu, "local type of giving" and help it shift into the language of "best practices" and standards. I admired his initiative but doubted the prospect of its success. Religious donation existed in the unreasonable and incalculable social field of dān; it was against governmentality.

Conclusion

We have seen repeated attempts to regulate religious donation. The British colonial approach to "custom" left religious giving relatively ungoverned, as the state sought to understand its practice and codify it. In British trust law, the distinction of giving for the welfare of an abstract public contrasted giving for the welfare of known others. Because religious giving was for the benefit of a specific community (often a specific deity was being worshiped), this set it apart from secular charitable practice that benefited strangers or causes. This colonial distinction was overlaid on Indian practices of giving that straddled the divide between public and private benefit and between religious and secular donation. In the reform efforts of the Indian national struggle for independence and later, in the writing of the radically secular constitution that exists today, the realm of custom experienced intervention and social reform through personal law. During this period, attempts were made to regulate religious giving in a semiautonomous field. This era reflects the high political stakes involved in India's secularism and why some groups may endeavor to keep their customs out of state regulation. I have shown how, for some, being outside of secular regulation may constitute a strategic politics that reinforces the divide between religious and secular charitable practice. This may contribute to why the divide persists today, and why religious organizations are not clamoring to rewrite the legislation regulating charitable organizations. In contemporary India, the tax laws that regulate the work of humanitarian organizations are much stricter for secular organizations than for religious ones. The exception that religious organizations enjoy is both an artifact of historical regulatory processes and a direct engagement with India's secular state.

Attempts to regulate the sector of religious donation may be an impossibility, particularly given the sacred nature of gupt dān (anonymous donation) and the spontaneity with which most religious giving in India takes place, whether to individuals or to religious institutions.[66] Religious donation exists in a semiautonomous social field of legislation, in a social space outside of account books. In order to understand religious donation in India, within the context of charitable and humanitarian activity more broadly, I suggest we look at the history of secularity, the legislation of charitable trusts, and tax law. With neither a uniform civil code nor national laws governing this realm of welfare and relief, tax law becomes one of the only forms of state intervention. Alternatively, organizations such as NGOs form suprainstitutional regulatory bodies that advocate for the interests of the charitable sector. If we consider this realm of religious donation as one of strategic politics, only then might we understand why, for some, it best remains outside secular law in its own semiautonomous social field.

NOTES

1. Sundar (2002), 11.
2. Regulation of donations in India is situated in the wider context of increased scrutiny of donations to religious NGOs (Islamic NGOs in particular) since September 11, 2001. See Sidel (2010); the ACLU (2009) report regarding Islamic charities; and Benthall (2011), 99–121.
3. Sampradaan Indian Centre for Philanthropy (2001).
4. Agarwal and Dadrawala (2004).
5. Sundar (2002), 9; attendance at major shrines and their income.
6. Thanks to Michael Barnett and Janice Gross Stein for inviting me to participate in such a thoughtful and stimulating workshop, and to A. Aneesh, Meena Khandelwal, Marie Juul Petersen, and Mark Sidel, who offered helpful comments on early drafts.
7. Moore (1978).
8. See Appadurai (2006); Needham and Rajan (2007).
9. Chaterjee (1998).
10. See Shabnum Tejani, "Reflections on the Category of Secularism in India: Gandhi, Ambedkar, and the Ethics of Communal Representation, c, 1931." In Needham and Rajan (2007), 45–65.
11. In personal law, the category of Hindu is broadly defined to accommodate the majority population and includes atheists. The Adoptions and Maintenance Act (1956), for example, applies to Hindus, Buddhists, Jains, and Sikhs (by religion or conversion), any of their legitimate or illegitimate children, any abandoned children brought up by them, and any persons who are not Muslims, Christians, Parsis, or Jews.

12. Sampradaan Indian Centre for Philanthropy (2001).
13. Regarding these figures, 89 percent of the households surveyed gave money to individuals in need; 87 percent gave to religious organizations; 51 percent gave to secular, charitable organizations. Religious organizations received 30 percent of total volume of donations. Secular organizations received 21 percent of total share. The largest share, 50 percent (8.05 billion rupees), went directly to individuals in need. For a chart on how much each religious group gives to its religious organization, see Sundar (2002), 11.
14. Ibid., 12 (purpose of donation chart).
15. Ibid.
16. Ibid., 176.
17. Ibid.
18. Bornstein (2012).
19. See extensive historical scholarship on giving in India, including Anderson (1997); Heim (2004); Parry (1986, 453–473, and 1994); Raheja (1988); Laidlaw (1995, 2000).
20. Mauss (1990 [1950]).
21. Purity and the gift are dominant tropes in the anthropology of South Asia; see Parry (1994), in the context of Benares priests; and Raheja (1988), in the jajmani system of a rural north Indian village. Others have critiqued purity as an orienting frame: Appadurai (1988), 36–49; and Beteille (1979), 529–548.
22. *The Bhagavad-Gita* (1986).
23. Anderson (1997) and Heim (2004).
24. Publications by Sampradaan Indian Centre for Philanthropy: see Sundar (1997 and 2000); Kapoor and Sharma (2000). See also Bornstein (in press).
25. See Bornstein (2009, 622–651; 2011, 123–148; and 2012).
26. For detail, see Bornstein (2009).
27. Also known as the Shastras; see Larson (2001). For Islam, religious law is shari'ah.
28. See Chaterjee (1990); Mani (1990); Narayan (1997).
29. Larson (2001). For discussion of toleration in Islam, see Benthall (2005), 16–20. For historical discussion of Hindu-Muslim relations, see Gilmartin and Lawrence (2000). For documentation of how patterns of ancient temple desecration suggest religious conquest was a form of state-building and kingly rule, not religious rule, see Eaton (2000). For contemporary narratives of intersecting identity in village north India, see Gottschalk (2000).
30. Mani (1990); Narayan (1997).
31. Diwan (2007).
32. Cf. Fuller (1988), 225–248.
33. On the role of women, see Narayan (1997); Mani (1990); and Chaterjee (1990). On caste, see Dirks (2001).
34. Narayan (1997); Mani (1990); see also Fuller (1988), for more contemporary instances.
35. Cf. "customary law" in British colonial Africa; see Lugard (1965 [1926]).

36. Hastings was the first governor general of British India, from 1773 to 1785.

37. Van der Veer (2001).

38. Property held as corporation, in trust. Mortmain law is trust law.

39. For historical data on trusts as constituted in India, see Birla (2009). For F. W. Maitland's political philosophy of trusts, corporations, and the state in Britain, see McFarlane (2002), 83–107; and Runciman and Ryan (2003).

40. Birla (2009), 70; see also McFarlane (2002); and Runciman and Ryan (2003).

41. Birla (2009), 100.

42. See also Mansfield (2001).

43. Birla (2009), 68. Cf. Benthall, this volume, regarding *zakat* in Islam and debates over cultural proximity.

44. For examples, see Sharma (2001), 135–192; and Greenough (1982). Cf. parallel process regarding Muslim family endowments: Powers (1989), 535–571.

45. Birla (2009), 128.

46. See Gross (2003) and Friedman (2003).

47. Tejani (2007).

48. Larson (2001) and Williams (2006).

49. Although secularism in India is meant to deter persecution of religious minorities, its application has spurred heated political debate; see Bhargava (1998). Many consider secularism in India a crisis. For examples, see Needham and Rajan (2007). The term *secular* is a Christian one, articulating a required distance between the church and the world; see Asad (2003) and Taylor (1998). Early analysis of secularism in India (for example, see Smith, 1966) positioned traditional, religious Indian notions of religion and rule against Western, secular ones. However, the binary of a secular state that pits "tradition"—associated with religion and Asian cultures—against modern, Western, liberal, and democratic states has been contested, and I have explained why it is not a useful analytic; see van der Veer (2001) and Asad (2003).

50. Khilnani (2007).

51. Some scholars critique Indian secularism on the grounds that it has reinforced the Hindu right's ability to assert power through majority religious politics; see Chaterjee (1998) and Madan (1998).

52. Chaterjee (1998).

53. Ibid., 366.

54. Ibid., 371; emphasis added.

55. Debates surrounding Indian secularism are still alive and heated. See Zaheer Baber (2006), who sees secularism as the only political solution to prevent violence. Secular politics arouses critical questions of political membership, tolerance, and peace. Baber argues that (what he calls) antisecularists are in fact Hindu-centric, and he considers it a mistake, following Louis Dumont, to equate Indian society with Hindu society. According to Baber: "In the case of India, the problem was not that the actions of a secular state hell bent on purging religious values from

public life led to a religious reaction. Quite the contrary, the state was never sufficiently secular and made frequent concessions to religious forces for electoral gains" (ibid., 60).

56. Appadurai (2006).

57. Governmental charities include the Prime Minister's National Relief Fund, the Prime Minister's Armenia Earthquake Relief Fund, the Africa (Public Contributions- India) Fund, and the National Foundation for Communal Harmony.

58. The Income Tax Act specifies: "Donations to institutions or funds for the benefit of any particular religious community or caste are not tax deductible. A non-for-profit [sic] organization created exclusively for the benefit of a particular religious community or caste may, however, create a separate fund for the benefit of 'scheduled castes, backward classes, scheduled tribes, or women and children.' Donations to these funds may qualify for deduction under section 80(g) even though the organization as a whole may be for the exclusive benefit of only a particular religious community or caste. The organization must maintain a separate account of the monies received and disbursed through such a fund."

59. In-kind donations are not tax-deductible in India, unlike in the United States. In India, the Foreign Contributions Regulation Act (FCRA, 1976) regulates foreign donations. Although this may be seen as a separate issue, the FCRA reflects a similar concern regarding national control over resources. It was passed in 1976 amid fear of international political interference through the growing sector of humanitarian NGOs that entered India following natural disasters in the mid-1970s. See Puri (2008). The FCRA has recently been revised. For debates surrounding it, see Sundar (2010).

60. "Taxing NPOs—The Proposed Tax Code," *Accountable* 144 (February–March 2009), released August 2009.

61. Many activities that NGOs engage in, such as strengthening local *panchayats*, will no longer be applicable. Additional changes are that 100 percent of income during a year has to be used for permitted welfare activities; if an NGO spends 85 percent of the funds it receives in a year, the remaining 15 percent will be taxed; a trust can no longer be created from business assets; all receipts of an NGO except loans and advances will be treated as "income" (including grants); and restricted funds—grants given by donors for specific funds—will be treated as income.

62. "On Direct Taxes Code Bill 2010," *AccountAid Capsule* 299 (August 31, 2010).

63. Her NGO, although charitable and funded by donations, had never been able to get the 80(g) charitable exemption that allows donors in India to deduct their charitable gifts because it was involved with trade and was classified as a business. This distinction would not apply to foreign donors who paid taxes and deducted charitable donations in their home country.

64. See also Brauman (2009) for an analysis of the overflow of donations in response to the tsunami and MSF's controversial decision not to accept them.

65. It operates at the national level and as an interagency group at the state level (most laws for nonprofit organizations operated at the state level), integrating twelve states with member organizations paying a small membership fee. At the time of our interview, the NGO had forty-eight member organizations.
66. Bornstein (2009).

BIBLIOGRAPHY

AccountAid. *AccountAid Capsule 299. On Direct Taxes Code Bill 2010*. 2010 (retrieved August 31, 2010).

Agarwal, Sanjay, and Noshir Dadrawala. "Philanthropy and Law in India." In *Philanthropy and Law in South Asia*, edited by M. Sidel and I. Zaman. Manila: Asia Pacific Philanthropy Consortium, 2004.

American Civil Liberties Union (ACLU). *Blocking Faith, Freezing Charity: Chilling Muslim Charitable Giving in the "War on Terror Financing."* New York: ACLU, 2009.

Anderson, Leona. "Generosity Among Saints, Generosity Among Kings: Situating Philanthropy in South Asia." In *Philanthropy in Cultural Context: Western Philanthropy in South, East and Southeast Asia in the 20th Century*, edited by S. Hewa and P. Hove. Lanham, MD: University Press of America, 1997.

Appadurai, Arjun. "Putting Hierarchy in Its Place." *Cultural Anthropology* 3, 1 (1988): 36–49.

———. *Fear of Small Numbers: An Essay on the Geography of Anger*. (Public Planet Books.) Durham, NC: Duke University Press 2006.

Asad, Talal. *Formations of the Secular: Christianity, Islam, Modernity, Cultural memory in the Present*. Stanford, CA: Stanford University Press, 2003.

Baber, Zaheer. *Secularism, Communalism, and the Intellectuals*. 1st ed. Gurgaon: Three Essays Collective, 2006.

Benthall, Jonathan. "Financial Worship: The Quranic Injunction to Almsgiving." *Journal of the Royal Anthropological Institute* 5, 1 (1999): 27.

———. "Confessional Cousins and the Rest: The Structure of Islamic Toleration." *Anthropology Today*. 21, 1 (February 2005): 16–20.

———. 2011. Islamic Humanitarianism in Adversarial Context. In *Forces of Compassion: Humanitarianism Between Ethics and Politics*, edited by E. Bornstein and P. Redfield. Santa Fe, NM: School for Advanced Research Press.

Beteille, Andre. "Homo Hierarchicus, Homo Equalis." *Modern Asian Studies* 13, 4 (1979): 529–548.

The Bhagavad Gita: Krishna's Counsel in Time of War. Translated by B. S. Miller. New York: Bantam, 1986.

Bhargava, Rajeev. *Secularism and Its Critics*. Themes in Politics Series. Delhi, New York: Oxford University Press, 1998.

Birla, Ritu. *Stages of Capital: Law, Culture, and Market Governance in Late Colonial India*. Durham, NC: Duke University Press, 2009.

Bornstein, Erica. "The Impulse of Philanthropy." *Cultural Anthropology* 24, 4 (2009): 622–651.

———. "The Value of Orphans." In *Forces of Compassion: Humanitarianism Between Ethics and Politics*, edited by E. Bornstein and P. Redfield. Santa Fe, NM: School for Advanced Research Press, 2011.

———. *Disquieting Gifts: Humanitarianism in New Delhi*. Stanford Series in Human Rights. Palo Alto, CA: Stanford University Press, 2012.

Brauman, Rony. "Global Media and the Myths of Humanitarian Relief: The Case of the 2004 Tsunami." In *Humanitarianism and Suffering: The Mobilization of Empathy*, edited by R. A. Wilson and R. D. Brown. Cambridge: Cambridge University Press, 2009.

Chaterjee, Partha. "The Nationalist Resolution of the Women's Question." In *Recasting Women: Essays in Colonial History*, edited by K. Sangari and S. Vaid. Brunswick, NJ: Rutgers University Press, 1990.

———. "Secularism and Tolerance." In *Secularism and Its Critics*, edited by R. Bhargava. New Delhi: Oxford University Press, 1998.

Dirks, Nicholas. *Castes of Mind: Colonialism and the Making of Modern India*. Princeton, NJ: Princeton University Press, 2001.

Diwan, Paras. *Modern Hindu Law*. Delhi, India: Allahabad Law Agency, 2007.

Eaton, Richard M. "Temple Desecration and Indo-Muslim States." In *Beyond Turk and Hindu: Rethinking Religious Identities in Islamicate South Asia*, edited by D. Gilmartin and B. B. Lawrence. Gainesville: University Press of Florida, 2000.

Fuller, C. J. "Hinduism and Scriptural Authority in Modern Indian Law." *Comparative Studies in Society and History*, 30, 2 (April 1988): 225–248.

Friedman, Lawrence. "Philanthropy in America: Historicism and Its Discontents." In *Charity, Philanthropy, and American Civility in American History*, edited by L. Friedman and M. D. McGarvie. Cambridge: Cambridge University Press, 2003.

Gilmartin, David, and Bruce B. Lawrence. *Beyond Turk and Hindu: Rethinking Religious Identities in Islamicate South Asia*. Gainesville: University Press of Florida, 2000.

Gottschalk, Peter. *Beyond Hindu and Muslim: Multiple Identity in Narratives from Village India*. Oxford, New York: Oxford University Press, 2000.

Greenough, Paul R. *Prosperity and Misery in Modern Bengal: The Famine of 1943–1944*. Oxford; New York: Oxford University Press, 1982.

Gross, Robert A. "Giving in America: From Charity to Philanthropy." In *Charity, Philanthropy, and Civility in American History*, edited by L. Friedman and M. D. McGarvie. Cambridge: Cambridge University Press, 2003.

Heim, Maria. *Theories of the Gift in South Asia: Hindu, Buddhist, and Jain Reflections on Dana, Religion in History, Society, and Culture*. New York, London: Routledge, 2004.

Kapoor, Rakesh, and Amit Kumar Sharma. *Religious Philanthropy and Organised Social Development Efforts in India*. Occasional Papers No. 3. New Delhi: Indian Centre for Philanthropy, 2000.

Khilnani, Sunil. "Nehru's Faith." In *The Crisis of Secularism in India*, edited by A. D. Needham and R. S. Rajan. Durham, NC: Duke University Press, 2007, 89–106.

Laidlaw, James. *Riches and Renunciation: Religion, Economy, and Society Among the Jains*, Oxford Studies in Social and Cultural Anthropology. Oxford University Press, 1995.

———. "A Free Gift Makes No Friends (Anthropological Analysis of the 'Pure' or 'Free' Gift)." *Journal of the Royal Anthropological Institute*, 6, 4 (December 2000): 617–634.

Larson, Gerald James. *Religion and Personal Law in Secular India: A Call to Judgment*. Bloomington: Indiana University Press, 2001.

Lugard, Lord Fredrick. *The Dual Mandate in British Tropical Africa*. London and New York: Routledge, 1965 [1926].

Madan, T. N. "Secularism in Its Place." In *Secularism and Its Critics*, edited by R. Bhargava. New Delhi: Oxford University Press, 1998.

Mani, Lata. "Contentious Traditions: The Debate on Sati in Colonial India." In *Recasting Women: Essays in Indian Colonial History*, edited by K. Sangari and S. Vaid. Brunswick, NJ: Rutgers University Press, 1990.

Mansfield, John H. "Religious and Charitable Endowments and a Uniform Civil Code." In *Religion and Personal Law in Secular India: A Call to Judgment*, edited by G. J. Larson. Bloomington and Indianapolis: Indiana University Press, 2001.

Mauss, Marcel. *The Gift*. New York and London: Norton, 1990 [1950].

McFarlane, Alan. "Fellowship and Trust." In *The Making of the Modern World: Visions from the West and East*. New York: Palgrave, 2002.

Moore, Sally Falk. *Law as Process: An Anthropological Approach*. London; Boston: Routledge & K. Paul, 1978.

Narayan, Uma. "Restoring History and Politics to 'Third World Traditions': Contrasting the Colonialist Stance and Contemporary Contestations of Sati." In *Dislocating Cultures: Identities, Traditions, and Third World Feminism*. New York and London: Routledge, 1997.

Needham, Anuradha Dingwaney, and Rajeswari Sunder Rajan, eds. *The Crisis of Secularism in India*. Durham, NC: Duke University Press, 2007.

Parry, Jonathan. "The Gift, the Indian Gift and the 'Indian Gift.'" *Man (N.S.)* 21 (1986): 453–473.

———. *Death in Banaras: The Lewis Henry Morgan Lectures 1988*. Cambridge; New York: Cambridge University Press, 1994.

Powers, David S. "Orientalism, Colonialism, and Legal History: The Attack on Muslim Family Endowments in Algeria and India." *Comparative Studies in Society and History*, 31, 3 (July 1989): 535–571.

Puri, V. K. *FCRA Guide—Law Practice and Procedure*. New Delhi, India: JBA Publishers Jain Book Agency, 2008.

Raheja, Gloria Goodwin. *The Poison in the Gift: Ritual, Prestation, and the Dominant Caste in a North Indian Village*. Chicago: University of Chicago Press, 1988.

Runciman, David, and Magnus Ryan, eds. *F.W. Maitland: State, Trust and Corporation*. Cambridge Texts in the History of Political Thought. Cambridge: Cambridge University Press, 2003.

Sampradaan Indian Centre for Philanthropy. 2001. *Investing in Ourselves: Giving and Fundraising in India*. New Delhi: Sampradaan Indian Centre for Philanthropy.

Sharma, Sanjay. *Famine, Philanthropy, and the Colonial State: North India in the Early Nineteenth Century*. SOAS Studies on South Asia. New Delhi: Oxford University Press, 2001.

Sidel, Mark. 2010. *Regulation of the Voluntary Sector: Freedom and Security in an Era of Uncertainty, Critical Approaches to Law*. New York: Routledge.

Sidel, Mark, and Iftekhar Zaman, eds. *Philanthropy and Law in South Asia*. Manila: Asia Pacific Philanthropy Consortium, 2004.

Smith, Donald Eugene, and Council on Religion and International Affairs. *South Asian Politics and Religion*. Princeton, NJ: Princeton University Press, 1966.

Sundar, Pushpa. "Charity for Social Change and Development: Essays on Indian Philanthropy." In *Occasional Papers*. New Delhi: Indian Centre for Philanthropy, 1997.

——. *Beyond Business: From Merchant Charity to Corporate Citizenship*. New Delhi: Tata McGraw-Hill, 2000.

——. 2002. *For God's Sake: Religious Charity and Social Development in India*. New Delhi: Sampradaan Indian Centre for Philanthropy.

——. *Foreign Aid for Indian NGOs: Problem or Solution?* New Delhi: Routledge India, 2010.

Taylor, Charles. "Modes of Secularism." In *Secularism and Its Critics*, edited by R. Bhargava. New Delhi: Oxford University Press, 1998.

Tejani, Shabnum. "Reflections on the Category of Secularism in India." In *The Crisis of Secularism in India*, edited by A. D. Needham and R. S. Rajan. Durham, NC: Duke University Press, 2007.

Veer, Peter van der. *Imperial Encounters: Religion and Modernity in India and Britain*. Princeton, NJ: Princeton University Press, 2001.

Williams, Rina Verma. *Postcolonial Politics and Personal Laws: Colonial Legal Legacies and the Indian State*. New Delhi, New York: Oxford University Press, 2006.

7

Pyrrhic Victories? French Catholic Missionaries, Modern Expertise, and Secularizing Technologies

Bertrand Taithe

SINCE THE PIONEERING work of Jean and John Comaroff, historians have paid considerably more attention to the material conditions of missions and missionaries. Modern technologies and relief practices have been particularly highlighted as key tools for the purpose of a "colonization of consciousness," and much of the debate focuses on the development of a "missionary modernity."[1] Within the historiography of Protestant missionaries, demonstration of technical skills, deployment of relief work, and the close enmeshing of the two with more strictly religious activities were singled out as constituting the specific features of Protestant modernity fit for global export. From the colonial era to the postcolonial present, the transition from missionary work to faith-based organizations (FBO) or nongovernmental organizations (NGO) seems almost seamless, as witness the continuities of staff between these organizations.[2] It seems clear that development NGOs maintain and further many of the concerns with modernity that featured in Protestant missionary work. Though often competing with similar methods in appearance, Catholic missionaries were set in a different theological context, and their work had to confront modernity rather than embrace it. Catholic engagement with medical relief work, for instance, presented genuine theological difficulties by often dissociating physical and spiritual work. As this chapter shows, the manner in which Catholic missionaries attempted to combine efficient work and spiritual integrity was fraught with tensions, which revealed clearly the fundamental differences between missionary and secular NGO work in a manner that is perhaps less obvious in a Protestant context.[3]

Insofar as one can define clearly a genealogy of humanitarianism, it is clear that missionaries have long played an important part.[4] One could even argue that, over the long run, missionaries have overstayed their explicitly nonconfessional competitors, and that in their engagement with the locality missionaries often win in the competition for hearts and minds against modern international nongovernmental organizations (INGOs). Despite considerable experience of their field, their spiritual DNA often presents unique challenges when confronting the need to be competitive in efficiency terms. Engaging with the materialistic logic of efficiency was never value-free, and missionaries have had to contend with its profound ethical implications. As Jennifer Karnes Alexander shows, efficiency is often presented as the product of rational free agents fulfilling their role through their own free choice—something that Catholics would have found difficult to accept in those terms.[5] This is not to state that efficiency necessarily denotes a spiritual vacuum, but its measure remains a material affair that, in France at least, explicitly excluded spiritual considerations and associated measurable progress with a godless universe. In relation to secular modernity, the Catholic Church had clearly set its opposition through the *Syllabus of Errors* of 1864. The papacy of Pius IX openly challenged its enemies, among whom featured liberalism and much of what is now constitutive of "civil society."[6] This particular stance bore within itself seeds of self-contradiction, as churchmen and followers attempted to grapple with the complexities of a fast-changing scientific, economic, and political environment.[7] In some countries, such as France, this Catholic engagement with modernity was an open political debate from the 1880s, arguably until the 1980s.[8] Within the Catholic Church, in relation to theories of development and later the "Third World," the debate was on the primacy of faith over effective action, on religiosity in relation to interiorized faith. The gradual shift toward a discourse of rights and redistribution, predicated on more effective relief work and less open proselytizing, was a profound attempt at challenging secular modernity by proposing religiously meaningful "engagement."[9] The Church grappled with these concerns during the great upheaval of the Vatican II council of 1962–1965 and in many ways ensured that its dogma caught up with the work undertaken by Catholic missionaries.[10]

To explore this general theme, this chapter concentrates on French Catholic interventions in the colonial and postcolonial era, at a period when the humanitarian work done by the missionaries had to be uncoupled from the work done by the colonial rulers—a period of deep transformation in the Catholic Church itself, which, after a brief heyday in the 1950s, began to engage profoundly with a changing world in the 1960s.[11] The Protestant frame of reference[12] was always present and this competition was both a domestic one (French and franco-phone Protestant missionaries) and an international one (with the increasing presence of American missionaries in Africa after 1918).[13] The fundraising capabilities of Protestant missions were often noted and resented, while their presence contributed notably to the mollifying of anticlericalism from colonial administrations.[14] The French republicans preferred "their" missionaries to unknown groups who might be regarded as agents of foreign powers.[15] This competition nevertheless led to pragmatic decisions to compete in terms of delivery and to initiate relief practices less traditional in Catholic missionary work but crucial in Evangelical circles.[16] As this chapter shows, the missionaries had to enlist the support of less-clerical structures, faith-based organizations in the strictest meaning of the word, such as Ad Lucem in Cameroon.

In contrast to Ad Lucem, a specialist relief organization initiated by Catholics to respond to the Protestant challenge in a contested territory, the final section of the chapter considers the potentially damaging impact of technosecular imperatives that refer explicitly to the interaction between missionary work and the demands of relief work in an era of modern bureaucracies. The relevance of this historical question is clear in the sense that if expertise was constructed and established at the boundaries between the secular and the religious, the "vested interests" in maintaining these boundaries became vital. The chapter explores how technical know-how and faith could be combined—with faith informing logistical and ethical choices going well beyond identification strategies—when missionaries engaged with this challenge on their own terms, but also how NGO demands could prove overwhelming. If, as the introduction (Chapter 1) to this volume makes clear, my pithy statement "missionaries win" raised debates in the workshops leading to this volume, it was also perhaps that some of the statement could be ambiguous and that there is such a thing as a pyrrhic victory—something Catholics faced when they confronted a world of traceability and accountability that measured effectiveness entirely in material terms. Yet despite these challenges and in a century dominated by a secularization narrative for Western Europe, religious organizations maintained a stranglehold on humanitarian interventionism both at home and abroad, if the manifold small and parochial forms of humanitarian aid are included in our account of humanitarianism.[17]

Efficient Missionaries

Catholic missionaries often portrayed themselves as "less modern" or more indifferent to progress than their Protestant rivals, but much of this discourse was a pose. Even without the threat of more effective competitors, Catholic missionaries were pioneers in transforming sentimentalism into efficient processes that were nevertheless consistent with spiritual demands.[18] The technologies of fundraising they either created or transplanted from the home market are still with us. An example is that of the letter and photographic picture for Christmas in return for a yearly donation in order to support an orphan. When Msgr. Lavigerie, bishop of Algiers, developed this fundraising technique in 1869 after the great famine of Algeria, he probably did not anticipate that the method would still be used today.[19] It had many advantages from a fundraising point of view: it anchored the donor to a pattern of recurrent gift giving and made the income stream perennial, it enabled a faceless crisis to become more personal, and it permitted a sentimental response to become an effective act of relief. But it also carried with it the transformative implication (or perhaps even purpose) of orphanage relief work, namely that an Arab and Muslim child was proposed for conversion. This was a redemptive necessity in the missionary's eye, with the possibility for the donor to take part in the naming of that child. The purpose of the relief work was subordinate to this higher religious imperative.

Some donors followed the career of the orphans for extensive periods. Furthermore, in these relatively early days of the French colonial establishment in Algeria, this fostering by proxy also established the identity of children who had often ended up lost during mass population displacements. Affecting both identity and the flow of cash, this relatively minor innovation left a deep imprint. This idea that giving could turn into appropriating also leaves a dubious heritage today.[20] The technology of giving *enabled* religious processes as much as it was the product of established religious giving processes (for example, specific weekly campaigns in Catholic churches). A manner through which these organizations established a lengthy commitment was by the reiterative quality of funding campaigns. In missiological texts, provision of traditional forms of charitable relief (food, clothing, and shelter) could and would naturally be associated with spiritual activities. These might be the activities of the giver; they might invite sharing and joining in from the recipients, or they might be quite abstract—the giving being a religious obligation that entailed spiritual "profit" for the giver, this could be shared among the fundraisers and distant benefactors equally. In this sense, the missionary community extended itself, rhizomelike, throughout the society from which missionaries originated.[21] To support Livingstone enriched the Scottish and British community of faith rather than the African community since the explorer and medical missionary singularly failed to convert on a grand scale. Yet no one would have branded Livingstone a failure since his self-image and sacrifice embodied the values of his religion.

In the same literal vein, some of this charitable interaction could bring new life to the scriptures. The great fundraising in favor of lepers in the twentieth century picked up a Biblical suffering in our times and made it part of the Catholic religious year.[22] The Biblical nature of the disease was highlighted, as was its alterity, forgetting along the way that the disease had been common in Greece or Scandinavia until the nineteenth century.[23] The grounding of gift giving in scriptural evidence was not only the preserve of religious organizations; it went well beyond familiar religious spheres of influence. The famous broadcast from Ethiopia by Michael Buerk in 1984 similarly relied on scriptural language and borrowed its terminology from Biblical lessons deeply imprinted in the journalist's mind; in a recent interview on BBC Radio 4 (September 4, 2009) he related how the vivid illustration of his school Bible had come to mind when looking for terms that might further the message of his film. The addition of feelings—he asked the nurse of the feeding station "how she felt" about the mass starvation of children around her—stirred a powerful mix of sentimentalism and religious cultural stock imagery.[24] The rest of the story is well known and became a media phenomenon in its own right; yet in the analysis of Band Aid, too many people stressed the "new" role of the media in shaping the representation of the Ethiopian crisis at the expense of recognizing its imagery. The actual novelty was not one at all, and one could find many worldwide instances of similar confusion between the messenger and his or her message, of crisis news breaker becoming the answer to the crisis.

Missionaries and religious organizations of the nineteenth and twentieth centuries have, at times, acted in this way. In some instances historians even talk of conscious strategies of care, which developed relief practices specifically designed to support the missions' role.[25] The portrayal of medical need and spiritual want undertaken by missionaries in China or Africa, from the 1880s to the era of independence or even afterward, blended a description of multiple needs as well as a solution: continued giving.[26] Some of these organizations are still in place; they have evolved over time and shifted. The mix of religion and relief obvious in the work of Henry Dunant (Nobel Prize 1901), Dr. Albert Schweitzer (Nobel Prize 1952), or in the work of the Friends ambulance service (Nobel Prize 1947[27]), could evolve dramatically. The medical role of missionaries might have changed, but some major FBOs such as Ad Lucem (on which more later) in Cameroon retained a religious ethos not necessarily dominant in the public discourse about these organizations.[28] A number of new NGOs have, on the other hand, made their religious identity central (e.g., Islamic Aid, Christian Aid, Buddhist Aid, etc.) and retain their label, ethos, and often almost exclusive staffing policies.

Although a blatant religious identity can seem a hindrance or a limit to market appeal, which only careful editing can mitigate in a Western context, the connection to the religious can also open doors in the global south. Religious values—clearly expressed—explain a great deal that more secular organizations find difficult to express. Missionaries and religious organizations of the past made no bones about what they stood for. The proselytizing intent and their usually limpid correlation between relief work and conversion were clear to the givers and also the societies that received them. Conversely, relief work was often less successful than anticipated in producing effective and lasting conversions. Resistance to religious conversion could also undermine the effectiveness of this work, to the point that in some contexts it had to be distanced from proselytizing. In the Ottoman Empire, for instance, the considerable presence of Catholic and Protestant hospitals and dispensaries was explicitly dissociated from active proselytizing outside the Christian communities.[29] Nevertheless, nuns' motives were explicitly to obey a religious obligation of compassion and charity. That was clear to all. There was no need for abstraction, such as "humanity," or to call on any political philosophy to justify the organization—in its daily dealings there was a rule and a discipline that suffered no deviance. Of course, this was not entirely truthful. Religious organizations were not necessarily that distinct from imperial views; explicit references to the civilization and culture of their originating country flavored and connoted them in specific terms. The Jesuits in the Middle East between 1860 and 1939 regularly served specific French colonial interests.[30] In spite of an obvious tendency to favor one's own, a free market for missionaries appeared after 1919, and the colonial empires were open to a diversity of missionary activities (under considerable surveillance). This opening to missionaries frequently brought unwanted publicity, and in the earlier period of the twentieth century the great colonial scandals were often made public by missionaries.[31] Most famously Protestant missionaries documented the overexploitation of the people of the Free State of Congo by Leopold II's agents.[32] Missionaries bore witness, quite literally, and often to its most literal form of martyrdom. Catholic missionaries never shied away from danger and used martyrdom to great effect.

Yet there were limits to bearing witness, and being part of a large organization limited expression of individual criticisms. As a result, Catholics were often slower in distancing themselves from the excesses of imperial rule, and one has to wait for the 1920s to see missionaries voicing publicly the concerns they had since at least the 1870s. The core debate in the historiography centered on their role in the shaping of the postcolonial order. Their core duty, proselytizing, could be disconnected from any political role; yet this split has not necessarily been accepted—far from it. The immediate postwar witnessed the eviction of missionaries from their considerable welfare and missionary activities in Vietnam and China.[33] Nationalist regimes such as that of the Young Turks in the 1910s had also evicted most missionaries, despite their obvious and considerable input in the health care infrastructure of the country. Despite these setbacks, missionaries have multiplied and prospered as well as the multiplicity of small FBOs that support the extraordinary range of their activities.[34] The transparent role of the missionaries remains: conversion. The motive of the volunteers remains the same: faith and religious obligation. And their behavior remains codified according to straight and narrow rules. This omnipresence does not mean universal acceptance and it is a legacy of empires and missions that NGOs confront daily.

Compare this omnipresence and clarity of purpose with that of overtly secular NGOs. The rationale of a humanist intervention is not always clear to societies that either ignore or find the concept of secular anathema. The motives of NGO workers vary at the individual level, sometimes religious and often not. Behavior also varies and muddies the waters—though a conversion mission statement may be offensive, it is at least clear. Some common (religious) ground may be found: a humanist mission statement is unclear and seems, by default, purely political. Worse even, it could be proselytizing in disguise. This image is made more confused by the frequent developments of hagiography in popular accounts of humanitarian work.[35] These texts recall the hagiography devoted to the great missionaries of the past. Since the technologies of humanitarian aid borrow so much from that of their rivals and predecessors (the missionaries), one should not be surprised that confusion arises and that NGOs that are not confessional should find themselves confused or assimilated to them.

From Mission to FBO: Ad Lucem in Cameroon

Nevertheless, NGOs have singular advantages too. They emerged relatively late in the history of missionary work, but nevertheless they commonly arrived more fully focused on a single mandate and goal. The emphasis they presented on action speaking louder than words also challenged the priorities traditionally abided by missionaries. There is an element of technological determinism that needs to be fully understood in its entire range of consequences; humanitarian technologies carry baggage and entail far more moral loading than one perceives at first glance. Missionaries embraced relief with different sets of values and sometimes with considerable apprehension. In particular, the division line between labor and spirituality was always something potentially self-destructive. Focusing on the Catholic Church, which undoubtedly presented the more holistic and unified viewpoint on modernity and its dangers, is revealing of some of the deep tensions that sometimes recur.[36] If a latrine has no deep spiritual significance, one could query whether the same applies to more complex interventions (which may include providing latrines in specific locations). When one stretches the analysis to more complex physical encounters such as medical intervention, the interaction of the spiritual and bodily assumed greater significance still.

Some of the most violent debates on French secularization took place in hospitals. Medicine standing as a symbol of modernization invited contest, and medical training was a battlefield of secularization in France.[37] In nineteenth-century France, hospital work was predominantly staffed by religious orders until a campaign in the 1880s, led by secular doctors, drove the nuns away from most public-funded wards in order to replace them with qualified secular nurses.[38] At a fundamental level, the state attempted to oppose expertise and religion. In spite of extreme tensions between state and church leading to the end of the concordat in 1905, religious orders continued their work in the colonial empire and often provided the nursing staff of all but a few military hospitals. Beyond the control of hospital wards, the heart of the debate was the philosophy of medicine and its moral values. This was so significant that the Church attempted to create its own independent medical school in Lille to counter the materialist and atheistic teaching of French universities.[39] In the 1890s, the new psychiatry, led by Charcot, openly questioned faith, miracles, and stigmata as the expression of deranged mental functions.[40] Furthermore, some perceived biomedicine as incompatible with the existence of God. Correspondingly, this later nineteenth-century period is also one during which "faith that heals" was revived, often with considerable clerical anxieties, in large-scale expressions of popular faith, the most famous being Lourdes.[41] On the one hand, medicine took a largely antivitalistic turn and segregated somatic and psychosomatic events in such a way that religion ceased to apply directly to the body; on the other, faith (sometimes defined in psychiatric terms) proved time and again its healing potential.[42] By extension, colonial medicine and its "humanitarian agenda" was the continuation of this struggle and of debates taking place in metropolitan and other colonial spaces.[43]

The practice of medicine by Catholic missionaries might seem to have been contradictory, since the medical missionary would have to preach and practice contradictory dogma. This tension remained, and in most instances in French missions the sympathetic but autonomous practitioners worked for Church dispensaries. In this sense, the mission merely provided the platform and logistical support for medical relief, but the relief itself could not be said to have been profoundly religious in its practices. A Catholic bandage resembled a Protestant or a secular one. Yet this tension between spiritual relief and physical relief belied the fundamentals of religion, since Christ himself was a physical healer of men. It took a papal letter that chimed with the missionary world exhibition at the Vatican in 1925 to clarify the matter.[44] The letter made it clear that Catholic missionary medicine might exist after all and that its values could embrace the technical trappings of modernity and give them a spiritual context, which would benefit missions, and presumably patients. This clarification did not create *ab initio* medical relief in the missionary world, but it certainly supplied a new impetus and new training institutions, such as missionary medical training provided at Würzburg in Germany.[45] It also recast medical relief as part of a more important campaign for hearts and minds.

In France the impetus echoed internal politics. The increasingly divided political landscape of the interwar led some of the more socially minded clergy to new initiatives that would at last implement the social turn of the Catholic church dating from Pope Leo XIII. These initiatives included *la mission de France*, which applied missiological principles to a *reconquista* of French society; youth working-class movements Jeunesse Ouvrière Chrétienne (JOC) and spiritual groups aimed to block and counter the progress of the French communist party and its social work.[46] The focus of the church became more explicitly social and emphasized the need to engage vigorously colonial and metropolitan problems of society in order to transcend the binaries of colonizers and colonized.[47] One of these movements arose among the students of the Catholic university in Lille. It was inspired by Msgr. Lienart, who is widely credited with the urgent reformist tone of Vatican II.[48] Backed by the French high clergy, including the archbishop of Paris, Msgr. Suhard, the new organization, Ad Lucem, was led by medical students enthused with the possibilities of combining spiritual work and medical practice. At a crucial theological juncture the clergy sought to expand its influence in the elite of educated youth by inviting them to join a new associative form, a faith-based organization, which would exist within the church but further its Evangelical aims through direct action.

In its early days, the Algerian-born Louis-Paul Aujoulat was the dominant figure of the group. While some of his peers focused on Indochina, where the

French had developed extensive medical and educational institutions, he concentrated his attention on Cameroon, a territory under League of Nations mandate where Protestants, including American medical missions, were already well settled. Following exploratory travel in 1935, Aujoulat produced a report that casts an interesting light on the relationship between spirituality and relief.[49]

The critical dimensions of the report are the most interesting. Aujoulat had paid the usual visit to Lambaréné, by then the most famous missionary hospital in the world, where the most famous living missionary humanitarian, Dr. Schweitzer, exercised. Schweitzer had set up a hospital that ran on adapted Western principles, including a native village, and that created a missionary community around its building. Aujoulat commended the work done in medical terms, but he was critical of the sustainability of the model.[50] In particular, he judged Lambaréné far too reliant on its founder. In Cameroon itself he roundly criticized the range and centrality of French colonial provisions and those of the Protestant competition. The volume of help was far from impressive, and the quality was in his opinion extremely variable. He examined particularly the competing Protestant and administrative structures. In particular he despised the confusion between preaching and medical treatment and singled out the dispensary of Metet, where the pastor was also the chief medical practitioner.[51] This confusion was, in his view, deleterious and threatening to the medical *and* the spiritual integrity of the mission. In response to this Protestant confusion, Aujoulat proposed to support the existing Catholic missionaries with a new organization, but not to supplant them. Yet if the spiritual and the treatment of diseases would be segregated, the medical practitioners owed it to their faith to serve in quasi-monastic units. The value of their example would be enhanced by their medical results.

> [The medical] foundation would be the creation of the mission. We need to be doctors who appear only as instruments: of course we will lead [medical care] and we will work. But we will be doing so only because of the mission. For the blacks it is the mission which has brought us in, and we are its servants.[52]

In this sense, the Catholic bandage would be explicitly conditional on the existence of the mission, but medical acts and religious ones would appear intimately linked in the eye of the patient. Medicine would provide scientific legitimacy to the missionary presence; Christianity would provide a holistic home for medical acts and behavior. For Aujoulat and those inspired by the missiology studies led from Leuven Catholic University, Catholic Christianity had to become all-encompassing and total:

> While so many of our compatriots are only Christians at certain times, we need the lay missionaries to show how one can be Christian in every gesture throughout the day. Not a nurse and then a Christian but a Christian nurse, not a Christian in the morning and then a spouse but a Christian spouse; not a churchgoer on Sunday and unfair chief the rest of the time but a Christian Chief.[53]

In his view, medical practice steeped in Christianity was only one aspect of a unified Christian culture that, Aujoulat and his peers argued, corresponded most precisely to African social and spiritual norms. In this sense, they argued against the modernist "colonization of consciousness" described by the Comaroffs, but only to offer their own variant, which would limit the impact of modern science to a specific instrumental role. Their FBO would be separate from the missions themselves, though the initial intention was that it should be subservient. They perceived the physical and spiritual needs to be of equal importance and argued that the missionaries responded to a local demand as well as an urgent need. As a matter of fact, Cameroon experienced mass conversions in Béti territory, which made the territory a missionary priority.[54] At the same time, the territory became the flagship of innovative vertically integrated medicine. In particular, Cameroon was announcing spectacular results in the Jamot campaign against sleeping sickness.[55] From this early programmatic visit, Aujoulat led a mission that developed very successfully in the years preceding the war and during the war itself. From 1939, the medical mission demonstrated its efficiency. Medical technologies were then especially effective in a limited range of afflictions, such as the treatment of hernias.[56] Despite some obvious success in the field, from 1939 the medical and the missionary became a little more distant; from being a tool, the medical mission Ad Lucem became an agent and actively shaped its own priorities according to the needs of patients and relief priorities. In theological terms, this lay missionary work was potentially dissenting from the Church itself since the proselytizing could be meshed so intimately with medical training that it would not require extensive clerical presence:

> Our aim is to form integral nurses who are not only good technicians, our aim is to help young people understand their Christianity and integrate religion into their everyday life. Their technical training is

delivered by regular courses and practices with annual examination monitoring.[57]

The Second World War isolated French colonies from the metropolis, and Ad Lucem in Cameroon came out of the war in charge of a complex of dispensaries, laboratories, nursing training, and even primitive pharmaceutical production lines, while Ad Lucem France turned mystical and disengaged from social work. On his return to France, Aujoulat solved the dispute by having his mentor, father Prévost, sectioned as mentally unstable (a transparent victory of medical rationality over mysticism), which cannot be overstated as the victory of secularism nevertheless. More importantly in the context of the new imperial Union Française and rapid changes to the colonial governance,[58] Aujoulat had acquired the clout enabling him to represent the colony first in the "collège" of the colonizers and then as a representative of the Cameroonian people themselves. The humanitarian worker had become a politician in Africa and Paris. He also seized effective control of Ad Lucem, and the Catholic medical FBO grew under his guidance for the following twenty years.[59]

Although Ad Lucem began as a French Catholic FBO, it also developed university antennas in British and German universities in the 1950s and 1960s, holding international camps and disseminating its particular brand of applied Catholic activism. Some of the members of Ad Lucem UK, such as my informant "MBD," became medical practitioners and quasi-missionaries in their own terms. Although MBD, recruited in a British University and an Ad Lucem member throughout the 1960s, worked most of her life in Africa as a pediatrician, always within the spiritual rules of Ad Lucem, it was seldom in missionary hospitals—let alone Catholic ones. The Ad Lucem volunteerism points to another, more Protean dimension of religious activism: the presence of faith at the origin of contemporary humanitarian work, including its more "freelance versions." Much more difficult to document than the work of specific and concrete NGOs, which have institutional stories to tell, these individual lives shaped profoundly the humanitarian landscape of the 1960s and 1970s.[60]

The combining of politics, religion, and relief can be found in other corners of the French colonial empire, and even though it is perhaps too schematic to describe it as a pattern, there seem to have been a number of individuals such as Aujoulat who combined faith, mission, and technical expertise. Aujoulat served at the WHO as an expert, but he also had a ministerial career throughout the French fourth republic, showing considerable resilience to political changes.[61] He was arguably one of the architects of the famed Françafrique.[62] More fundamentally, his political career was undistinguishable from his medical and developmentalist career. One may ask, What happened to his religion?

On the face of it, we seem to return to the standard secularizing narrative according to which the certitudes of pre-Vatican II were shaken by the reform of the church, while the bipolar politics of the postcolonial era undermined spiritual values. The story proves rather more complex.[63] On the one hand, there is no doubt that Ad Lucem became more "third worldist" and may even have been influenced by liberation theology; neither was incompatible with the developments of the Catholic church in the 1960s. More importantly, the organization withered in France and across Europe while in Africa it grew considerably. Meanwhile, the European ex-members of Ad Lucem became central in other religious organizations such as the Union Fraternelle entre les Races (UFER, supported by UNESCO), Medicus Mundi (a Catholic medical FBO), and Union Catholique de Coopération Internationale, or they developed active and productive humanitarian careers abroad.[64] The success of Ad Lucem in Cameroon was owing to its local backing, the continuing faith of its members, and, increasingly through the 1960s, continued political support, rather than to its fragile associative framework. Yet even though the associative network in Europe seemed increasingly limited, the distribution of Ad Lucem members in various state and NGO operations, the UN, and French bodies seems to indicate a more diffuse propagation of its values. Ad Lucem presented an example of a missionary-FBO that followed two separate paths: Africanization of its structure and work in Cameroon, and privatization of its ethos to the point of ceasing to exist as an organization in the West.

In Cameroon the organization grew and is today the second largest provider of health care after the state. It is now run by the Cameroonians and is undoubtedly an African FBO whose director-general is a Cameroonian, Dr. Bidjogo Atangana, medically trained at the Catholic university of Lille (Aujoulat's alma mater).[65] In this sense, it is a considerable success story that mirrors the story of African churches. This acculturation was an explicit missionary aim with a direct impact on the delivery of aid. It was part of the organization. The major difference here from other INGOs of the same generation, arguably, is that the latrines are now provided by Cameroonians themselves.

Though acculturation is undoubtedly built into the programmed obsolescence of missionary work, it is not in itself a spiritual value but rather an operational one. Nevertheless, these organizations do not go native merely in the manner in which the missionaries wished. The core religious ethos may fade or become aggregated to indigenous belief systems, and there is business capital that can be cashed in from being associated with missionaries. As David Hardiman shows for India, the inheritance of missionary medicine became a multilayered hybrid science in a complex market through which various individuals competed to claim missionary cultural capital. Ultimately, the famed association of modernity and Christianity, central to missionary medicine, faded in the Indian region he studied, allowing modernity to become associated with Hinduism instead.[66] If missionary relief work may become acculturated to the point of losing both its scientific roots and its religious dimensions, arguably there are many more processes of "going native" than a simple rich-to-poor exchange.

The Challenges of Modernity

One of the most invidious forms of acculturation may indeed be that experienced by FBOs themselves when they encounter the demands of management and bureaucracy. The efficiency imperatives of the second half of the twentieth century and the need to compete for public funds also influenced the spiritual values of FBOs. Following Weber, one ought to query the philosophical and moral logic arising from double entry ledgers. Since at least the late seventeenth century, Catholic missionaries had to borrow "secular" accountability technologies, which ran in parallel with the conversion statistics overseen by the Propaganda Fide. Of the two sets of statistics, financial and spiritual, the latter was arguably the more important originally.

Yet from the mid-twentieth century, new lines of accountability and more strictly enacted demands on effective distribution of relief for its own sake emerged as part of a more materialistic humanitarian agenda. For instance, the arrival of massive American relief funds reordered the missionary world of North Africa in 1943. The religious orders in North Africa had often been the main providers of health care to the indigenous people on behalf of the colonial administration; the American relief ensured that this became their dominant task.[67] Building on the networks of Catholic charities of the interwar, notably the AMINA, which was devoted to the needs of indigenous people, the Americans used the White Fathers as their intermediaries to reorganize Catholic charities in North Africa. With a budget of $100,000 in 1943 and $135,000 for nine months in 1944, the American Bishops' fund subsidized twenty-one hospitals, thirty-three orphanages, thirty-two dispensaries, twenty-two care homes, eight hospices, thirty-seven professional schools, and forty-one youth groups.[68] Fourteen religious orders received funding according to their needs and ability to meet targets. The hospitals of Kabylia (eastern Algeria) alone declared having treated 127,315 patients in 1943. The American relief also forced the missionaries to conform to centralized distribution patterns that ignored ecclesiastical autonomy or diocesan boundaries and imposed sets of precise returns against named and identified objectives. The quasi-military nature of this ordering changed the relief landscape of Algeria and also *excluded* the colonists from the provisions made available by their own religious orders. The implicit message was clearly postcolonial, but it also forced relief to be given where it was most needed, going against the grain of a more traditional pastoral role.

From being the superstructure of relief, missionary work became the infrastructure. Becoming tools and reliant on foreign funds, Catholic charities profoundly altered their engagement with colonial society. The sudden surge of resources entailed a reordering of pastoral priorities. At a micro level, the human resources devoted to the war effort were resources distracted from proselytizing. The emphasis on deliverables and on clear material targets distracted from the less-tangible spiritual conquest. This immersion in the worldly was not negotiated but the product of a discourse of emergency and urgency that brought a relentless and breathless quality to this work. This led some missionaries to detach themselves from work that could distract from their pastoral role. The spiritually informed relief work would gradually become relief work. Later on, the politics of the Cold War altered the role of these relief operations, and some funds were used for anticommunist work, notably the JOC members. Many later developments of the Catholic FBOs were framed by this Cold War polarity, which replaced the conflict with the French secularizing state. In the 1950s and 1960s, the French communist party presented the particularity of having developed a humanitarian branch, arguably also a faith-based organization, le Secours Populaire, which opposed directly the French branch of Caritas, Secours Catholique.[69]

What this small example shows is that spiritual values themselves were reshaped by the priorities and the methods of accounting for progress against targets. At the practical level, medical and health care could also be stripped of explicit religious reference points. The Ad Lucem example showed a virtuous circle of expertise feeding into a mass conversion and mass politics development; other contingent circumstances would be less favorable. Expertise could become detached from the spiritual values; the missionary objectives, relegated to the background, could become an "ethos" statement rather than a driver. Yet arguably this ethos would in turn influence some essential aspects of technical expertise.[70] The rise of a discourse of relief and development expertise in the 1950s and 1960s presented the paradox of originating from the twin sources of missionary and colonial administration while reneging on both genealogies. The missionaries' Pyrrhic victory was to have been so successful at becoming experts and indispensable architects of the postcolonial world that their original role was weakened by the new one. The technicality of development and relief work created its own rules, which even if not antireligious left little room for spiritual maneuver or association. Surely one could argue that this forms a solid basis for a secularizing narrative.

Yet this would be a singularly impoverished understanding of secularization. Religious belief is a strong presence even in secular organizations today, as shown by Johanna Siméant; even if this belief does not explicitly shape the policies of NGOs it might have an impact on motives and practices.[71] Furthermore, theology and missiology matter to explanations of fundamental differences with secular NGOs. Notably, they mean that intent and timescale present fundamental differences. There is no such thing as "mission creep" in a proselytizing agenda. The entire point is to creep. Furthermore, in a competitive marketplace, missionaries have always played the long game, when they confronted the administrators of empire, they were known to remind the local people that administrators come and go and they remain.[72] Now the same discourse is implicit in the moving feast of UN and NGO workers descending onto one field or another; time poverty is a challenge to secular NGOs but not to missionaries and their associated FBOs and micro-FBOs. Unlike most Western NGOs until recently, missions have had a concrete and demonstrable record of "indigenation." By choice or as a reflection of their frugal resources, this led missionaries to live in modest circumstances and clothing, and speak the local language over decades of presence, with a depth of familiarity that invites comparison with anthropologists.[73] Compare this demanding self-discipline with the rigors of life for the users of air-conditioned SUVs. In many contexts, the NGO semiprofessional expats have taken over from the colonial administrators (often down to the same neighborhoods) and do not explicitly engage long-term with the locality. Over the duration and facing the vicissitudes of fast-moving geopolitics versus the almost geological timescale of religious political geographies, faith in mankind is harder to sustain than faith in God. In highly competitive humanitarian markets, this is their main advantage. In this sense, missionaries win—but at what cost?

NOTES

1. Jean Comaroff and John L. Comaroff, *Ethnography and the Historical Imagination* (Boulder: Westview Press, 1992), 235–260; Catherine Hall, *Civilising Subjects: Metropole and Colony in the English Imagination, 1830–1867* (Cambridge, UK: Polity, 2002).

2. Dana L. Robert, "The First Globalization? The Internationalization of the Protestant Missionary Movement Between the World Wars," *International Bulletin of Missionary Research* 26, 2 (2002): 50–67.

3. Bertrand Taithe is grateful to the colleagues of the workshops held in Geneva thanks to the generous support of the Luce Foundation, in particular to Stephen Hopgood, Michael Barnett, and Janice Gross Stein for their insightful comments as well as to colleagues from the Manchester Humanitarian and Conflict Response Institute (http://www.hcri.ac.uk), in particular Peter Gatrell and James Thompson, for their comments.

4. See Michael Barnett, *Empire of Humanity: A History of Humanitarianism* (Ithaca, NY: Cornell University Press, 2011), part 1.

5. Jennifer Karns Alexander, *The Mantra of Efficiency: From Waterwheel to Social Control* (Baltimore: Johns Hopkins University Press, 2008), 126–144, 146.

6. See Damien McElrath, *The Syllabus of Pius IX* (Leuven: Nauwelaerts, 1964); R. Scott Appleby, "History in the Fundamentalist Imagination," *Journal of American History* 89, 2 (2002): 498–551.

7. Massimo Mazzotti, "For Science and for the Pope-King: Writing the History of the Exact Sciences in Nineteenth-Century Rome," *British Journal for the History of Science* 33, 3 (2000): 257–282.

8. For a broader perspective of this relationship among charity, church, and state, see Adam J. Davis and Bertrand Taithe, "From the Purse and the Heart: Exploring Charity, Humanitarianism and Human Rights in France," *French Historical Studies* 34, 3 (2011): 413–432.

9. See, for instance, Charles-Édouard Harang, *Quand les jeunes Catholiques découvrent le monde: Les mouvements catholiques de jeunesse, de la colonisation à la coopération 1920–1991* (Paris: Cerf, 2010). This turn to rights fit broadly with the one mapped out by Samuel Moyn in *The Last Utopia: Human Rights in History* (Cambridge, MA: Harvard University Press, 2010), at least for its chronological turning point, which Harang dates from 1957.

10. John W. O'Malley, *What Happened at Vatican II* (Cambridge MA: Belknap University Press, 2008).

11. Michael Barnett, "Humanitarianism Transformed," *Perspectives on Politics* 3, 4 (2005): 723–740; Bertrand Taithe, "Reinventing (French) Universalism: Religion, Humanitarianism and the 'French Doctors,'" *Modern & Contemporary France* 12, 2 (2004): 147–158.

12. Jewish organizations were never perceived as competing with Catholic ones. Lisa Moses Leff, *The Rise of Jewish Internationalism in Nineteenth Century France* (Palo Alto, CA: Stanford University Press, 2006).

13. Jean Pirotte and Henri Derroitte, eds., *Église et santé dans le Tiers Monde, hier et aujourd'hui [Churches and Healthcare in the Third World, Past and Present]* (Leiden: Brill, 1991).

14. French inability to mass mobilize resources was partially linked to the so-called absence of civil society in France, noted by commentators ever since Tocqueville. Carol E. Harrison, "The Unsociable Frenchman: Associations and Democracy in Historical Perspective," *Tocqueville Review* 27 (1996): 37–56; Harrison, *The Bourgeois Citizen in Nineteenth-Century France: Gender, Sociability, and the Uses of Emulation* (Oxford: Oxford University Press, 1999).

15. J. P. Daughton, *An Empire Divided: Religion, Republicanism, and the Making of French Colonialism, 1880–1914* (New York: Oxford University Press, 2006).

16. Peter C. Williams, "Healing and Evangelicalism: The Place of Medicine in Later Victorian Protestant Missionary Thinking," in W. J. Sheils (ed.), *The Church and Healing: Studies in Church History* 19 (Oxford: Wiley, 1982), 271–284; David Hardiman (ed.), *Healing Bodies, Saving Souls: Medical Missions in Asia and Africa* (Amsterdam: Clio Medica, 2006); Charles M. Good, *The Steamer Parish: the Rise and Fall of Missionary Medicine on an African Frontier* (Chicago: University of Chicago Press, 2004); David Hardiman, *Missionaries and Their Medicine: A Christian Modernity for Tribal India* (Manchester: Manchester University Press, 2008); Megan Vaughan, *Curing Their Ills: Colonial Power and African Illness* (Cambridge, UK: Polity, 1991).

17. B. Duriez, F. Mabille, and K. Rousselet, *Religions et action internationale* (Paris: L'Harmattan, 2007); Claude Prudhomme, *Missions chrétiennes et colonisation: XVIe–XXe siècle* (Paris: Cerf, 2004); Denis Pelletier ed., special issue, "Mission et développement," *Le Mouvement Social* 177 (1996); Jean-François Chanet, Denis Pelletier, Guillaume Cuchet, and Jacqueline Lalouette, eds., special issue, "Laïcité, séparation, sécularisation 1905–2005," *Vingtième siècle*, 87 (2005).

18. On this precise theme, see Thomas Laqueur, "Bodies, Details and the Humanitarian Narrative," in Lynn Hunt (ed.), *The New Cultural History* (Berkeley: University of California Press, 1989), 176–204; Bertrand Taithe, "Horror, Abjection and Compassion: From Dunant to Compassion Fatigue," *New Formations* 62 (2007): 123–136; Carlo Ginzburg, "Killing a Chinese Mandarin: The Moral Implications of Distance," *Cultural Inquiry* 21 (1994): 46–60.

19. Bertrand Taithe, "'Algerian Orphans,' and Colonial Christianity in Algeria 1866–1939," *French History* 20, 3 (2006): 240–259.

20. One needs to refer to the French "Arche de Zoé" venture in Chad, convicted of abducting children, or recent events in Haiti following the earthquake of January 2010 to fully comprehend how this confusion of adoptive and relief work remains a live issue. Christian Troubé, *Les Forcenés de l'humanitaire, les leçons de l'arche de Zoé* (Paris: Autrement, 2008).

21. This is a process well explored in Catherine Hall and Sonya O. Rose (eds.), *At Home with the Empire: Metropolitan Culture and the Imperial World* (Cambridge: Cambridge University Press, 2007).

22. See the narrative of the leper foundation Raoul Follereau, which led this cause in France, in A. Récipon, *Combat pour la charité* (Paris: P. Téqui, 2000).

23. See Peter Richards, *The Medieval Leper and His Northern Heirs* (Lanham, MD: Rowman and Littlefield, 1977).

24. John Taylor, *Body Horror: Photojournalism, Catastrophe and War* (Manchester: Manchester University Press, 1998); Jonathan Benthall, *Disasters, Relief and the Media* (Wantage, S. Kingston, new edition, 2010); see also Terrence Wright, "The Refugees on Screen," http://www.rsc.ox.ac.uk/publications/working-papers-folder_contents/RSC-workingpaper5.pdf (accessed November 2010).

25. See, for instance, Rosemary Fitzgerald, "'Clinical Christianity': The Emergence of heroic Medical Work as a Missionary Strategy in Colonial India, 1800–1914," in Biswamoy Pati and Mark Harrison (eds.), *Health, Medicine and Empire: Perspectives on Colonial India* (New Delhi: Orient Longman, 2001), 88–136.

26. For the most famous instance: Paul Richard Bohr, *Famine in China and the Missionary: Timothy Richard as Relief Administrator and Advocate of National Reform* (Cambridge, MA: Harvard University Press, 1972); James Reed, *The Missionary Mind and American East Asia Policy 1911–1915* (Cambridge, MA: Harvard University Press, 1983).

27. This sequence is completed by the emergence of major INGOs in the Nobel pantheon such as MSF 1999 and ICRC 1917 and 1944, Amnesty International 1977, and the International Campaign to Ban Landmines 1997.

28. Florence Denis, "Entre mission et développement: une expérience de laïcat missionnaire, l'association Ad Lucem 1945–1957," *Le Mouvement Social* 177 (1996): 29–47; Florence Denis, "Entre Mission et développement, une expérience de laïcat missionnaire, l'association Ad Lucem de 1945 à 1957," (mémoire de maitrise, Université Lyon II, 1993).

29. This was primarily the work of nuns, a lesser studied subfield in missionary studies. Elisabeth Dufourcq, *Les Aventurières de Dieu* (Paris: Lattès, 1993), 326; J. Baeteman, *Les filles de la charité en mission à travers le monde*, 2 vols. (Paris: Poussin, 1936).

30. Mathew Burrows, "'Mission civilisatrice': French Cultural Policy in the Middle East, 1860–1914," *Historical Journal* 29, 1 (1986): 109–135.

31. Andrew Porter, *Religion Versus Empire? British Protestant Missionaries and Overseas Expansion, 1700–1914* (Manchester: Manchester University Press, 2004); Brian Stanley, *The Bible and the Flag: Protestant Missions and British Imperialism in the Nineteenth and Twentieth Centuries* (Leicester: Intervarsity Press, 1990).

32. The topic remains controversial today in Belgium; see Michel Dumoulin, *Léopold II de la controverse à l'histoire* (Brussels: Académie Royale, 2001).

33. Hospital work was considerable in the Far East between the wars; see J. M. Planchet, *Les Missions de Chine et du Japon* (Beijing: publisher unknown, 1933).

34. See, for instance, their role in Cameroon: Marc Éric Gruénais, "L'État à la conquête de son territoire national: l'exemple de la réforme du système de santé dans la province de l'extrême nord du Cameroon," in Gruénais (ed.), *Le système de santé en mutation, le cas du Cameroun*. APAD series, no. 21 (Paris: EHESS, 2001).

35. See, for instance, Olivier Veber, *French Doctors: les 25 ans d'épopée des hommes et des femmes qui ont inventé la médecine humanitaire* (Paris: Robert Laffont, 1995), 34–66; P.-E. Deldique and C. Ninin, *Globe Doctors: 20 ans d'aventure humanitaire* (Paris: Belfond, 1991); Jean de la Guérivière, *Les fous d'Afrique: histoire d'une passion française* (Paris: Le Seuil, 2001), 297–310.

36. Philippe Levillain, *Albert de Mun, Catholicisme Français et Catholicisme Romain, du Syllabus au Ralliement* (Rome: École Française de Rome, 1983).

37. Daughton, *An Empire Divided*.

38. Jacques Léonard, *La médecine entre les savoirs et les pouvoirs: histoire intellectuelle et politique de la médecine française au XIXe siècle* (Paris: Aubier-Montaigne, 1981).

39. Louis Dulieu, *La Médecine à Montpellier*, Tome IV, vol. 2 (Arles: Les Presses Universelles, 1990).

40. Mark Micale and Paul Lerner (eds.), *Traumatic Pasts* (Cambridge: Cambridge University Press, 2001), Introduction.

41. Ruth Harris, *Lourdes* (London: Allen Lane, 1999); Dr. Antoine Imbert-Gourbeyre, *La Stigmatisation, l'extase divine et les miracles de Lourdes. Réponse aux libres penseurs* (Grenoble: Jérôme Millon [1895], 1996).

42. Rhodri Hayward, *Resisting History: Religious Transcendance and the Invention of the Unconscious* (Manchester: Manchester University Press, 2007).

43. Shula Marks, "What Is Colonial About Colonial Medicine? And What Has Happened to Imperialism And Health?" *Social History of Medicine* 10, 2 (1997): 205–219; Warwick Anderson, "Where Is the Postcolonial History of Medicine?" *Bulletin of the History of Medicine* 72, 3 (1998): 522–530.

44. Ugo Bertini, *Pie XI et la médecine au service des missions* (Paris: librairie Bloud et Gay, 1930); Abbé Robert Prévost, *Pour une initiation aux problèmes internationaux et missionnaires* (Lille: Ad Lucem, 1932).

45. Archives des Œuvres Pontificales Missionnaires, Lyons (OPM), Abbé Prévost, Ad Lucem, Q14/I/38; Appel à la formation des missionnaires laïcs, 1932.

46. Susan B. Whitney, *Mobilizing Youth: Communists and Catholics in Interwar France* (Durham, NC: Duke University Press, 2009); Pierre Pierrard, Michel Launay, and Rolande Tempré, *La JOC regards d'historiens* (Paris: Éditions Ouvrières, 1984); Oscar Cole-Arnal, "Shaping Young Proletarians into Militant Christians: The Pioneer Phase of the JOC in France and Quebec," *Journal of Contemporary History* 32, 4 (1997): 509–526; Union Missionnaire du Clergé, *Le Service social dans les colonies françaises d'Afrique Noire* (Paris: Union Missionnaire, 1945).

47. E. Duthoit, "Pour préparer la semaine de Versailles: Quelques considérations sur le problème des rapports de civilisation," *Notes de Doctrine et d'Action* 22 (1935): 7–31; "Les Missions ont pratiqué l'assistance sociale avant la lettre' in Union Missionnaire du Clergé," *Le Service Social dans les colonies françaises d'Afrique Noire* (Paris: Union Missionnaire, 1945), 89–102.

48. The mission de France emerged in occupied France in 1941 under the leadership of Msgr. Suhard; Tangi Cavalin and Nathalie Viet-Depaule, *Une histoire de la Mission*

de France. La riposte missionnaire 1941–2002 (Paris: Karthala, 2007); Jean Vinatier, *Le cardinal Suhard. L'évêque du renouveau missionnaire en France* (Paris: Centurion, 1983); Jean Vinatier, *Le cardinal Liénart et la Mission de France* (Paris: Centurion, 1978).

49. OPM, Ad Lucem, Q/17/0171 and Q17 "Rapport de Louis-Paul Aujoulat à Mgr André Boucher directeur de la propagation de la foi," (1935): 18–19.

50. Louis-Paul Aujoulat, "Albert Schweitzer, médecin de brousse," in *Albert Schweitzer: conférences du Congrès international des écrivains médecins* (Debrecen: publisher unknown, 1966).

51. Docteur J. Debarge, *La Mission médicale au Cameroun* (Paris: Société des Missions Évangéliques, 1934).

52. OPM, Ad Lucem, Q/17/0171 and Q17, "Rapport de Louis-Paul Aujoulat à Mgr André Boucher directeur de la propagation de la foi," 1935, p. 83.

53. Ibid.

54. P. Laburthe-Tolra, *Vers la lumière? ou, Le désir d'Ariel: à propos des Béti du Cameroun: sociologie de la conversion* (Paris: Karthala, 1999).

55. Guillaume Lachenal, "Le Médecin qui voulut être roi. Médecine coloniale et utopie au Cameroun," *Annales, Histoire, Sciences Sociales* 65, 1 (2010): 121–156; Guillaume Lachenal "Biomédecine et décolonisation au Cameroun, 1944–1994" (Doctoral thesis, Université Paris VII, 2006); Sonne Wang, "Eugène Jamot: son œuvre lui a survécu, il n'appartient plus qu'à l'histoire, à la science et à l'humanité," *Médecine d'Afrique Noire* 41, 2 (1994): 74–75; Léon Lapeyssonnie, *La Médecine coloniale* (Paris: Seghers, 1988); John McKelvey, *Man Against the Tsetse: Struggle for Africa* (Ithaca, NY: Cornell University Press, 1973); Jean-Paul Bado, *Médecine Coloniale et Grandes Endémies en Afrique* (Paris: Karthala, 1996).

56. OPM, Abbé Prévost, Ad Lucem, Q14/I/44.

57. OPM, Q/17/0171, *Lettre aux amis d' Ad Lucem, La fondation médicale Ad Lucem au Cameroun pour l'année 1939* (Lille: Ad Lucem, 1939).

58. Tony Chafer, *The End of Empire in French West Africa: France's Successful Decolonization?* (Oxford: Berghahn, 2002); Frederick Cooper, *Decolonization and African Society: The Labor Question in French and British Africa* (Cambridge: Cambridge University Press, 1996); Louis-Paul Aujoulat, *La Vie et l'avenir de l'Union Française* (Paris: S.E.R.P, 1947).

59. For a fuller discussion of this case study, see Guillaume Lachenal and Bertrand Taithe "Une généalogie missionnaire et coloniale de l'humanitaire: le cas Aujoulat au Cameroon, 1935–1973" *Le Mouvement Social* 227 (2009): 45–63.

60. This is the topic of a broader oral history project. Interview with MBD, June 16, 2010, Bolsterstone, Derbyshire.

61. Étienne Thévenin, "Louis-Paul Aujoulat un médecin chrétien au service de l'Afrique," in Jean Pirotte and Henri Derroitte, eds., *Église et santé dans le Tiers Monde, hier et aujourd'hui* (Brill, 1991), 57–73.

62. Ironically, French NGOs have been instrumental in attempting to dismantle Aujoulat's political inheritance. See Gordon D. Cumming, *French NGOs in the Global Era: A Distinctive Role in International Development* (Basingstoke: Palgrave Macmillan, 2009), 177–198.

63. Denis Pelletier, "De la mission au tiers mondisme: Crise ou mutation d'un modèle d'engagement Catholique?" *Le Mouvement Social* 177 (1996): 3–8.

64. The main federation of organizations was the FEDER, a "spiritual alliance" with 3,000 members in twenty-four countries, led by the man who ran Ad Lucem after Aujoulat retired from a managing role, Joseph Foray. Archives Nationales d'Outre Mer (ANOM), Papiers Foray, FP 132 APOM/2.

65. See http://fondationadlucem.tmp38.haisoft.net/ (accessed November 2010).

66. Hardiman, *Missionaries and Their Medicine*, 225–246.

67. Archives Générales des Missionnaires d'Afrique (AGMA), fond Birraux 315 053 War Relief Service à Birraux, March 15, 1944.

68. AGMA, Birraux, 314.030.

69. Axelle Brodiez, *Le Secours populaire français, 1945–2000: Du communisme à l'humanitaire* (Paris: Presses Universitaires de Sciences Pos, 2006); Luc Dubrulle, *Monseigneur Rodhain et le Secours Catholique: Une figure sociale de la charité* (Paris: Desclée de Brouwer, 2008); Axelle Brodiez-Dolino, *Emmaüs et l'abbé Pierre* (Paris: Presses Universitaires de Sciences Pos, 2009).

70. S. Litsios, "The Christian Medical Commission and the Development of the World Health Organization's Primary Health Care Approach," *American Journal of Public Health* 24, 11 (2004): 1884–1893.

71. Johanna Siméant, "Socialisation Catholique et biens de salut dans quatre ONG humanitaires françaises," *Le Mouvement Social* 227 (2009): 101–122.

72. See, for instance, Joseph-Roger de Benoist, *Église et pouvoir colonial au Soudan Français* (Paris: Karthala, 1987).

73. Sjaak van der Geest, "Anthropologists and Missionaries: Brothers Under the Skin," in *Man* (New Series), 25, 4 (1990): 588–601.

8

Faith in the Machine?

HUMANITARIANISM IN AN
AGE OF BUREAUCRATIZATION

Michael Barnett

FOR MOST OF its history, emergency relief was staffed by individuals either immune or opposed to planning, centralization, and coordination. Reflecting the stereotype that aid workers come in three types—missionaries, misfits, and mercenaries—humanitarians seemingly savored a lifestyle that relied more on instinct than on institutions. Following the nineteenth-century spirit of charity and social work, humanitarianism enshrined the principle of volunteerism, which could be a euphemism for amateurism. Embodying a humanitarian ethic that was more about the imperative to act than the utility of operating according to guidelines that integrate past experiences, it seemed as if each relief operation had equal parts enthusiasm and historical amnesia. Acting as if they were young children in a playground who could do little more than parallel-play, the accounts by aid workers of the period are remarkably free of any signs of human life except for their immediate colleagues, the victims, and those who are responsible for turning people into victims.

Those days are long gone, as the humanitarian sector has bureaucratized, rationalized, and professionalized with an unpredictable passion over the last two decades. Emergency workers might come in the same three types, but they have developed the capacity to attend coordination meetings, produce spreadsheets, create budgets, manage accounts, and graduate from training programs. Volunteerism still exists, but in name only. Although those who join aid organizations still see themselves as choosing an alternative career path, it *is* a career path, with mundane concerns for salary, benefits, promotion, and the like. Increasingly, those who want to break into the aid sector must have specialized training, receive certification in one of the growing number of master's programs, and accumulate credentials that certify their professionalism. Informality has been replaced by formality. What is true for the organization is true of an entire field that has become, well, a field, with a growing number of rules, standards, codes of conduct, systems of account-ability, and other attributes befitting a modern professional sector.

These developments coincided with, affected, and were fueled by another emergent feature of humanitarianism: a rethinking of the practical philos-ophy of humanitarianism, that is, the method of engagement for improving their interventions, how they can gain knowledge of the proper way to act, and how such methods relate to basic identity-defining questions such as who they are and the moral universe that either does or should exist. Beginning in the 1990s, humanitarian organizations were increasingly pressed to discover (better) methodologies for determining their effectiveness and for reconsid-ering the broad and narrow ends of humanitarianism. These matters relating to their tools of intervention and evaluation implicated not only their tech-nique but also their relationship to the objects of their compassion. Humani-tarianism, after all, was intended not only to improve human welfare according to material indicators such as caloric intake and body counts but also to give vulnerable populations more control over the lives as they define them, and to enact, sustain, and deepen their common, transcendental, values.

The humanitarian community's practical philosophy bears a striking resem-blance to American Pragmatism.[1] Pragmatism offers a skeptical view of knowledge, emphasizes the importance of experience and practice for devel-oping better knowledge and tools for human improvement, embraces a highly practical approach to deciding whether or not something represents a solution to a problem, is committed to scientific inquiry, and believes that a democratic ethos is both a means and the end of human inquiry. These basic commit-ments, principles, and values are now featured prominently on the websites of the leading aid agencies.

How has the spirit of rationalization and pragmatism affected the sacred within humanitarianism? As argued in the editors' Introduction (Chapter 1), a dominant view in the community is that humanitarianism operates in the world of the sacred and is distinguished from the everyday, that is, the pro-fane. Yet rationalization and pragmatism contain pronounced elements of the profane. Rationalization feeds off the belief that the world, in principle, can be reduced to calculations, means-end reasoning, and cost-benefit analysis, and thus, as suggested in the Introduction, integrates the profane into the sacred world of humanitarianism. Anchored in a community of individuals committed to a spirit of intelligence, tolerance, and democracy, pragmatism seemingly has less need for religion than it does for a critical community of inquirers.[2] Indeed, whether pragmatism either needs, tolerates, or benefits from religion and a religious attitude is a longstanding controversy among pragmatists and between them and their critics. There is a prophetic branch, closely associated with Cornel West, and, more importantly for my purposes, various confessions and commentary on the justification for religion from leading pragmatists, including by C. S. Peirce, William James, and John Dewey, and later interpreters such as Richard Rorty. Although pragmatists do recognize the need for individuals to believe they are part of something bigger than themselves, they have an easier time imagining options that do not rely explicitly on religion or God. Their measured attitude toward religion suggests that humanitarianism's practical philosophy decreases its reliance on the sacred.

This chapter explores the relationship between the sacred and the profane in the context of a rationalizing and increasingly pragmatic humanitarianism. Section one casts humanitarianism's growing rationalization and practical philosophy as partly a response to a crisis of faith in the humanitarian sector, and outlines the central tenets of pragmatism and its complicated relationship to the transcendental and the sacred. Section two points to a central paradox: the humanitarian sector turned to rationalization and pragmatism to restore its faith in humanitarian action, but this "solution" has opened the floodgates to the profane. Humanitarianism's practical philosophy emphasizes the immanent rather than the transcendental. These tendencies are amplified by rationalization, which is closely associated with disenchantment, bureaucratization and its soul-crushing properties, and professionalization, which relies on occupational and disciplinary codes of conduct. The conclusion of the chapter raises the question of whether faith and a sense of the sacred can survive a pragmatic humanitarianism, suggesting that American Pragmatism's complicated relationship to religion provides insight into whether religious or secular agencies are more or less likely to avoid a crisis of faith that is partly of their own making.

The Rational and Pragmatic Response to Crisis

Although the 1990s might be remembered as a string of defeats for humanity and humanitarianism, it was the genocide in Rwanda in 1994 that caused even the most die-hard optimist to lose faith. Specifically, the relief effort in the camps was feeding not only Hutu refugees but also the dreams of the genocidaire of another chance to finish the task. This was not the first time that aid had fueled conflict or benefited evildoers, but it was practically the first time that aid workers, collectively, publicly, and systematically wondered about whether they were doing more harm than good.[3] What might have been a conversation solely about how to improve their craft became more faith breaking, because the very acknowledgment that they might be doing harm forced aid workers to ask themselves what their contribution to war and suffering was—in other words, on the list of contributors to harm, where did they rank? Were they above or below the perpetrators?[4] Such concerns, as Rony Brauman noted, demoralized the humanitarian community and caused it to wonder about its own goodness.[5] There was a crisis of technique—what do we do?—but also a crisis of faith—what we have done?

If the world turns to humanitarianism at the very moment that it questions its own humanity, as I have argued elsewhere, where do the humanitarians turn when they encounter their own doubts?[6] The delivery of the Rwanda evaluation report in 1996—which was a summary indictment of the response by the aid community, capturing the growing disquiet regarding what the humanitarian community was becoming—catalyzed a cavalcade of meetings, initiatives, and seminars dedicated to improving the humanitarian sector.[7] Although there was some questioning of the motives of some of the humanitarian agencies (were they more concerned about their financial health than they were about the health of the victims?), the humanitarian community found solace and hope in the rationalization of humanitarianism. Simply put, maybe they could save themselves by getting their house in order. Agencies began to rationalize, aspiring to develop methodologies for calculating results, abstract rules to guide standardized responses, and procedures to improve efficiency and identify the best means to achieve specified ends. They began to bureaucratize, developing specialized knowledge, spheres of competence, and rules to standardize responses and to drive means-ends calculations. They began to professionalize, developing specific knowledge, fixed doctrine, and vocational qualifications that derive from specialized training. What is striking is that agencies of all shapes and sizes, and all secular and religious orientations, have embraced this rationalization process.[8] In general, over the last two decades humanitarian organizations have gravitated toward similar organizational characteristics, suggesting that there is not a religious or secular way to run an organization; instead, there is a modern way that is superior to the premodern way of doing things.

It is, of course, overly simplistic to reduce rationalization to one factor, and the crisis of faith became intertwined with three other developments that pushed in the same direction. First, many aid agencies were getting bigger and maturing, growing from a small cadre of like-minded volunteers into large,

complex, multinational, and multidimensional organizations. The consequence was that whereas once the organization could get away with a high
degree of informality, now it had to introduce more systematic, organized,
and predictable routines in order to regulate action across great distances.
Moreover, these growing organizations had to accommodate a growing diversity of views within the organization, which in turn often meant watering
down, or softening the sharp edges of, the organization's founding mission
and identity. This was the case of many organizations, but especially visible
among many of the larger religious agencies. As World Vision International
(WVI) grew, it incorporated diverse Evangelical traditions, which led to a
period of "internationalization" and the search for common religious values;
one of the effects of its cross-cultural deliberations was to downplay conversion in favor of expressing faith through other forms of social action. In addition to these internally driven forces, the very process of practicing
humanitarianism—giving aid to distant strangers—also contributed to a poly-
phonic worldview. As these aid organizations worked outside their cultural
comfort zone, they frequently emphasized more pluralistic values in order to
make themselves less threatening to the local population. Even the ICRC,
which generally assumes its universal character, was periodically forced to inter-
rogate whether its values were more Christian and European than universal.

Second, in addition to creating a more comprehensive identity that might
accommodate diverse peoples and values, many organizations also began to see
the benefits of bureaucratization for gaining acceptance by locals. One of the
virtues of bureaucratization, and rationalization more generally, is that it presents
the appearance of objectivity, neutrality, and impartiality. Appeal to rules and
rationality can be particularly powerful as aid agencies cross borders. Specifically, aid agencies that appeal to common rules can, theoretically, depoliticize
their actions and gain greater acceptance on the part of local populations.

Third, and related, because these agencies work in the same environment,
they are likely to respond in similar ways that leave them looking more and more
alike. The last few decades in particular have left a lasting impression. Working
in the same complex emergencies, they confront similar problems, entertain
joint action, and coordinate their activities. Confronting many of the same failures and shortcomings in the field, they increasingly share lessons learned and
develop programs designed to improve their services. In this view, there is no
Christian, secular humanist, Islamic, or Hindu way to properly space latrines in
a refugee camp. Technique takes precedence. There also is a funding environment that shaves off differences. Competing for the same funds from the same
donors, they adopt many of the same characteristics and symbols of legitimacy.

Attempting to increase or retain their status in an ever-more-crowded field of aid agencies, they adopt the same organizational principles, codes of conduct, result-based outcome evaluations, accountability systems, and standards of excellence.[9] Conspicuous consumption, humanitarian-style. In fact, the incentive to be seen as an industry leader might be particularly heightened for those agencies attempting to either work their way into the upper tier of aid agencies or try to put their audience at ease. For example, one reason Islamic Relief became keen to join and become a leader of many professional associations is the hope that by doing so it would appear less "Islamic" and more "professional."[10]

Pragmatism

The increasingly practical philosophy of humanitarianism, with its emphasis on using scientific methods and experience to find workable solutions to the most pressing problems of the day, is reminiscent of several fundamental tenets of American pragmatism. Indeed, the background causes that led humanitarianism to rethink its philosophy resemble the very historical forces that created the foundations for pragmatism. As chronicled by Louis Menand and others, the destruction and despair caused by the American Civil War shredded existing dogmas and unleashed an important period of experimentation in all areas of American life, including religion and philosophy.[11] Pragmatism emerged against this bloody and faith-destroying moment in American history, and rather than searching for new certainties many theologians and philosophers began to explore positions that could accommodate both progress and skepticism.

American pragmatism should be distinguished from the streetwise understanding of pragmatism: the attempt to identify what works, to steer clear of ideology, and to find compromise, recognizing that the perfect should never be the enemy of the good. In this view, to claim that humanitarianism has gravitated toward pragmatism is to suggest how it has surrendered some purity in favor of getting things done. It is all well and good to have principles, but if these principles do not help the vulnerable, then what good are they? To be a pragmatist is to be a problem solver first and an ideologue second. The lines separating pragmatism from purity are not only descriptive; they also are judgmental. Pragmatists, according to those who claim to have not forsaken their principles, have become "political" (or part of the profane), joined league with the powerful, and been co-opted into the prevailing order of things. Those who cling to their principles, according to the pragmatists, are high priests and fundamentalists who are blind to how the times have changed, making their vaunted principles dysfunctional for current circumstances, and favoring defense of principles over rescue of victims. Whether or not someone is a pragmatist or priest, of course, depends on the time and place; the high priest of today's humanitarian community, the ICRC, demonstrated incredible pragmatism at the time of its birth. Nearly everyone is a pragmatist in the broadest understanding. But to be a Pragmatist, in the American philosophical tradition, requires an antifoundationalist view of knowledge, the centrality of experience and practice, the importance of practical interventions, the value of science, the splendor of democracy, and the possibility of progress.[12] Each of these elements is quite present in much of modern humanitarian action, if not in fact then at least as an ideal.

Knowledge. Many Pragmatists do not deny that there is a world "out there"; they just doubt that we can ever know with certainty what it is. Why? Concepts and theories are essential for building knowledge, but they come from our culture, our experiences, our habits, our prejudices, and our past attempts at solving practical problems. Consequently, we can never be certain that our knowledge perfectly represents reality, and thus there is no basis for a correspondence theory of truth. This skepticism has several important implications. It means we live in a world of doubt and must accept the ever-present possibility that our knowledge is fallible. But, as Hilary Putnam famously added, our doubt must also be justified.[13] We have no more basis for saying that something exists than we do that something does not exist. For instance, many who argue that God does not exist have no more evidence than those who argue that God does exist.

Epistemological skepticism also means that all human knowledge is partial; our theories might improve explaining why and how things work and work out the way they do, but they will never be complete. Relatedly, we cannot reject any theory or hypothesis; this is an observation that can be either liberating, because it places a value on tolerance and pluralism, or frightening, because the ground turns into quicksand. Although some Pragmatists are accused of relativistic leanings (most notably Richard Rorty), the founding figures of Pragmatism and especially John Dewey remained committed to the scientific method as a way of providing grounds for acting and intervening in the world. In general, many Pragmatists hoped to offer a skeptical approach to knowledge that humbles without creating hopelessness, a position that certainly resembles those I have met in the humanitarian community.

Experience and practice. Although there is considerable debate regarding what is meant by experience, or rather what Dewey meant by experience, it is central to Pragmatist thought, and for reasons that map onto contemporary humanitarian thought. First, experience—direct experience and not mediated experience—is essential for theory development. Whether or not he and other pragmatists were barefooted empiricists, and whether or not they had room for the existence of things that cannot be seen or verified (such as God), is a matter for debate. But less debatable was the general belief that practice generates the kind of direct experience that is absolutely essential for creating more usable and sustainable theories. And because Dewey and others were committed to finding ways to make knowledge useful for helping society, the ultimate test of their beliefs and experiences was whether they worked. Second, experience incorporates the mind and the soul. It includes "all that human beings suffer and do. It is the product of our interactions with other people and the larger world of nature."[14]

Practice might not make perfect, but improvement is impossible without it. Pragmatism's emphasis on practice was itself a response to overly abstract theories of knowledge that have little or no practical value. The relationship between theory and practice, therefore, works along several levels. It is by practice, by engagement, that we develop our theories and are able to fine-tune them in ways that give them a practical value. But practice absent theory would be useless, if not potentially destructive. To dismiss the relevance of theory would be nothing short of giving a license to anyone and everyone to intervene in the world as the spirit moves them. Accordingly, intelligent practice, to use a term favored by Dewey, requires abstraction, prior theorization, and method.

Whatever works. If we are forced to be epistemologically skeptical, then how can we choose one path over another? The answer: whatever works. One of William James's most controversial statements was "'the true,' to put it very briefly, is only the expedient in the way of our thinking, just as 'the right' is only the expedient in the way of our behaving."[15] If we cannot draw from abstract knowledge or absolutist claims to determine whether or not something is true, our only real guide is whether something is effective. In short, if something is functional, then it must be true. To many critics, this is a dangerous assertion that makes virtually anything justifiable. Expediency becomes the name of the game, and Pragmatism is another name for selling out.[16]

These dangers certainly exist, but for Dewey and others a potentially greater danger was that philosophers would get caught up in truth games and fail to see how action itself can help produce its own truth, and in the process make the world a better place. As Hilary Putnam summarized with respect to William James (but might have been written about Pragmatism more generally):

The opposition between philosophy which is concerned with how to live and philosophy which is concerned with hard technical questions is a false opposition. We want ideals and we want a world view, and we want our ideals and our world view to support another. Philosophy which is all argument feeds no real hunger; while philosophy which is all vision feeds a real hunger, but it is Pablum. If there is one overriding reason for being concerned with James's thought, it is that he was a genius who was concerned with real hungers, and whose thought, whatever its shortcomings, provides substantial food for thought— and not just for thought, but for life.[17]

Scientific inquiry. Because there are no guarantees that what we believe is true or will necessarily work, we must rely on scientific inquiry, or what Dewey called a "method of intelligence," a

> willingness to hold belief in suspense, ability to doubt until evidence is obtained; willingness to go where evidence points instead of putting first a personally preferred conclusion; ability to hold ideas in solution and use them as hypotheses to be tested instead of dogmas to be asserted; and (possibly most distinctive of all), enjoyment of new fields of inquiry and of new problems.[18]

Dewey, and others before and after him, wanted to know if we are wrong because knowing if we are wrong matters for human existence. How do we know if we are wrong? Pragmatists offer various statements that are consistent with forms of trial-and-error, experimentation, verification, empirical analysis, and the sort of interpretive and cultural analysis associated with Max Weber. In other words, the commitment to skepticism does not preclude the possibility of getting some things right and does not mean that because we are right today we will be right tomorrow.

Democracy. Perhaps because these were quintessentially American political theorists, Pragmatists maintained a strong commitment to democracy and liberalism. This democratic and highly anti-authoritarian spirit served several functions. It was only by applying democratic principles to scientific inquiry that we can discover better ways of acting. If we are ruled by experts, then there will be no room for individual creativity, experimentation, and learning that might offer important contributions and advances. If there is no truth, then there is no reason to exclude anyone a priori from contributing to the body politic. At a moment when religious belief was perceived to be in decline, democracy could represent a secularized God, a place where people could create a community of believers. Because there is no preordained purpose, then many visions must be accommodated. Pragmatists might be accused of being so in love with tolerance and diversity that they are willing to allow a thousand flowers to bloom, including those that are poisonous; however, many insist on the sorts of limits suggested by John Stuart Mill and Isaiah Berlin, that is, your freedom to act as you want stops when it begins to interfere with and affect my liberty.

Progress. It should be no surprise that a political theory that is American in spirit embraces the possibility of progress. William James described himself as a Meliorist, who believes that improvement is at least possible, charting a middle ground between the pessimist, who believes that it is impossible to save the world, and the optimist, who believes that its salvation is inevitable.[19] Dewey, of course, operated within the progressive tradition. Yet, according to Sandra Rosenthal, pragmatism is progressive also because it hopes to "expand and harmonize interactive contexts. Growth of self is understood as a harmonizing expansion, for it involves sympathetic internationalizations of the standpoints of the 'other' into the very dynamics of selfhood. Growth cannot be reduced to mere accumulation; rather, it is best understood as an increase in the moral-aesthetic and . . . ultimately spiritual dimension of the richness of human existence."[20] Even the purported relativist Richard Rorty acknowledges that he too operates with a notion of progress, or what he calls "social hope," which revolves around the possibility that "unnecessary human suffering can be decreased, and human happiness thereby increased."[21]

Perhaps the most striking feature of pragmatism, at least from the vantage point of a humanitarian community that has been wrestling with its own demons, is the attempt to acknowledge skepticism without losing the ground for action or the basis for hope. We are right to doubt the world we see, and we should doubt whether we can ever see the world clearly. But such skepticism does not constitute a warrant for epistemic resignation. Although there is no safe haven for certainty, it is through experience and practice that we can begin to distinguish what makes sense and what is nonsense. Such provisional claims, in turn, provide the foundation for action, action that should be guided by the scientific method and should aim to make modest improvements in the world. Such methods and action, though, must be done with a democratic sensibility, genuine openness to working, thinking, acting, and experiencing jointly with others. By following these steps, Pragmatists hope to redirect skepticism in the direction of hope. Could this not pass for a mission statement by CARE or Oxfam?

Religion and Pragmatism

Given these central tenets it becomes clear why Pragmatism has a well-earned reputation for slighting religion. John Patrick Diggins argued that pragmatism serves up a spiritually empty world.[22] Richard Bernstein observes how pragmatism is frequently accused of relativizing religion and is often "demonized as the doctrine of 'secular humanism' that is abhorred as the enemy of Christianity and indeed, the enemy of all religion."[23] Whether or not these judgments are fair, the very fact that both Pragmatists and their critics are of several minds regarding the relationship between religion and Pragmatism suggests, at the very least, that this relationship is not natural but rather requires considerable work on the part of those who want to make the connection. I am not the person and this is not the place to enter into this debate on whether Pragmatists have or can make their peace with God. Instead, I want to consider three possible lines of connection offered by three founding figures of pragmatism.

One view is that religion, a religious attitude, and the transcendental help to ensure that individuals resist human idolatry and are oriented toward the existence and possibility of creating human connections that have a moral component. According to C. S. Peirce,

> The gospel of Christ says that progress comes from every individual merging his individuality in sympathy with his neighbors. On the other side, the conviction of the nineteenth century is that progress takes place by virtue of every individual's striving for himself with all his might and trampling his neighbor under foot wherever he gets a chance. This may be accurately called the Gospel of Greed. Much is to be said on both sides. I have not concealed, I could not conceal, my own passionate predilection. Such a confession will probably shock my scientific brethren.[24]

In other words, religion and a religious attitude rescue us from our worst traits.

Religion and a religious attitude, relatedly, might also "work," a position most closely associated with William James. If we cannot look to evidence to decide whether or not God exists, then what should we do? In *The Will to Believe*, James argued that although some insist that in the absence of evidence we should withhold belief, if we did then there would be no logical ground for acting. In fact, James argued it would merely create a self-fulfilling prophecy: we do not believe that God exists, so we act as if he does not exist, and so we have outcomes that confirm our belief that there is no God. In order for God to exist, he continues, we must act as if God exists. He

writes that "there are cases when a fact cannot come at all unless a preliminary faith exists in its coming."[25] James is not arguing that people should
chase after windmills or be captured by their fantasies. "The talk of believing
by our volition seems . . . from one point of view, simply silly. From another
point of view it is worse than silly, it is vile."[26] Instead, he is counseling that
until we have actual evidence to conclude that God does not exist, we are
better off assuming he does. And if we act on the belief of God's existence,
then we might very well produce evidence that confirms our initial faith. By
making room for faith, we make room for what otherwise would have been
impossible. There is always, of course, the chance that we will bet wrong. "For
my own part," James asserted, "I have also a horror of being duped; but I can
believe that worse things than being duped may happen to a man in this
world."[27]

The last approach is associated with John Dewey. He begins by distin-
guishing between religion and religious experience, permitting for the possibility that individuals might have a religious attitude without necessarily
believing in God. A religious attitude, he wrote,

> needs the sense of a connection of man, in the way of both dependence
> and support, with the enveloping world that the imagination feels is a
> universe. Use of the words "God" or "divine" to convey the union of
> actual with ideal may protect man from a sense of isolation and from
> consequent despair or defiance.[28]

Although this can sound patronizing—if you need the term to save you, go
ahead—Richard Bernstein defends the position by observing how many theologians reject the notion of God as a supreme being. In any event, Dewey's
view of religious experience suggests several important features that furnish a
generative view of the movement from the individual to the transcendental: it
begins with our awareness that we are dependent on and need the support of
others; such an awareness requires expansion of the self and the ability to
incorporate the perspectives of others; this kind of intelligent inquiry alters
not only one's perspective but also one's identity in such a manner that it
creates a connection to a broader moral universe. In general:

> To understand the world religiously is to relate one's self with the uni-
> verse as the totality of conditions with which the self is connected. . . .
> Such an experience brings about a change in consciousness, a deeply
> embedded change is one's orientation toward the world. . . . This

involves the entire universe, for their emphasis on continuity reveals that at no time can we separate our developing selves from any part of the universe and claim that it is irrelevant.[29]

In this way, Dewey imagined the distinct possibility that through experience, practice, and intelligence we can become connected to a moral universe.

This view of religion and religious experience delivers a different understanding of the sacred. Many pragmatists, at times, have reduced the sacred to those mysteries of the universe that we cannot (at the moment) hope to solve through rational, scientific inquiry. Yet once religious experience is understood to include one's evolving sense of self in relationship to others and in the context of a moral universe that is beyond anyone's control, then an alternative meaning of sacred evolves; in fact, it resembles the distinction between the sacred and profane. The sacred "relativizes the everyday aspect of our lives, that is, the prosaic, literal minded, utilitarian workaday world. This is accomplished by justifying a wider significance." Second, it gives the broader universe a sense of "wholeness" and *holiness*. And it compels individuals to resist the belief that they are separate and superior to others, thus minimizing the possibility of human idolatry. "The sacred is accepted when there is open admission of dependence coupled with a sense that humans must adjust themselves to some harmony that is not of their making."[30] The sacred is distinguished from the profane and serves the essential function of creating a common faith.

These thoughts of the sacred are fine in theory, but what about in practice—which, of course, is the ultimate test of a pragmatic view? What sort of institutional form might best further pragmatism's tenets of skepticism, intelligent inquiry, and tolerance, and create the foundations for a religious attitude and a common faith? For Dewey and many other pragmatists, the best bet rests with a liberal democracy that has an educated population and extensive civil society. Pragmatists, especially those following in the tradition of Dewey, have written extensively about those features of democratic governance and practice that are most essential to the cause. In doing so, they also identified those developments in modern governance that pose a threat to effective practice, including the rising importance of bureaucracy and technocracy. In other words, the growing rule by experts and bureaucrats might crush those very features that pragmatists have identified as central to a healthy, vibrant, and progressive society, and by extension the foundation of religious experience and the sacred. The implication is that humanitarianism's central philosophical tenets might help lift a religious experience and sense of faith, but rationalization, bureaucratization, and professionalization might have a gravitational pull.

One final comment regarding Pragmatism's sense of what a global common faith might look like. At this point it should not be a surprise that a pragmatism that leans heavily on skepticism, inquiry, and tolerance finds a common faith not in religious practice, as conventionally understood, but rather in global ethics that promote diversity, tolerance, and dialogue, alongside a sense of moral progress defined as alleviation of suffering. In other words, and concretely speaking, the answer to the question (What do a global ethics and a common faith look like?) is human rights and humanitarianism. When Stephen Rockefeller and Richard Rorty reveal their understanding of a common faith, social hope, and moral progress, they invariably turn to the desire to protect and preserve human life.[31]

Whither the Sacred?

Can humanitarianism find deliverance in Institutionalization and Pragmatism? Or, might these very responses to a crisis of faith produce their own form of disenchantment? Will the factors that are intended to rescue the sacred and steer skepticism toward hope also provide a return passage to doubt and the profane? The history of Institutionalization and Pragmatism suggests this possibility, and so too does humanitarianism's experiment with them. Here I want to consider briefly three interwoven ways in which a pragmatic and institutionalized humanitarianism might supply the seeds of a new crisis of faith and open the floodwaters of the profane into the sacred. As I do so, though, I also want to speculate whether religious organizations might be better able to resist the profane. Even if they are, it remains an open question whether a sacred that serves the compassionate is necessarily the best thing for the victims of the world.

Bureaucratization and domination. Bureaucratization includes development of hierarchy and lines of authority, and of a division of labor based on specialization and expert knowledge. Although such characteristics can improve the precision, efficiency, and speed of decision making and implementation, it also can come at the expense of other values that are near and dear to pragmatism and humanitarianism alike, namely a democratic spirit.

A classic dilemma of modern governance is the presumed trade-off between democracy and technocracy. In democracy (the rule of the people), there is deference to the "general will," the "majority," and the "will of the people" on various grounds, including autonomy, liberty, and the belief that the people know best. In technocracy (the rule of experts), there is deference to those who have the knowledge—that is, experts—to make the decisions. In modern society, experts are those who have generalized knowledge, that is, knowledge that can be extended to various situations, contexts, and places; such knowledge typically comes from advanced education and specialized training. Although there is recognition that not all knowledge is general or obtained through education—sometimes referred to as "local," "experiential," or "practical" knowledge—the general presumption is that in modern society expert knowledge trumps local and practical knowledge.[32]

The humanitarian sector has been headed toward the rule of experts over the last several decades, and there is no indication of any letting up. However, it is hardly moving from rule of the people to rule of the experts—because there never was a rule of the people. Historically, aid workers have consistently believed that they know best, but what has changed is the epistemic basis of their confidence. For much of its history, such confidence derived from cultural biases: we are Christian, we are civilized, we are Western, and so on. Today it increasingly derives from formalized knowledge and training. On the one hand, this shifting basis of expertise is more democratic because it is (theoretically) available to anyone regardless of identity. On the other hand, it is biased against those without such formal training and thus maintains, if not expands, the gap between those who govern and those who are governed, especially in the context of humanitarianism, where the "recipients" are "victims," and victims, by definition, are deemed too incapacitated to act in their best interest.

Bureaucratization arguably amplifies the distance between the aid worker and the recipient. A characteristic of the bureaucracy is that power emanates from the top down, and as aid agencies grow in size by necessity they create new lines of authority that run from headquarters to the field. Although those in the field retain considerable discretion and authority, anecdotal evidence suggests that other processes are maintaining the barriers between the aid workers in the field and the recipients. As professionals who relied on expert, objective, and generalized knowledge, they had less need to learn about nuances of the local conditions before they developed and implemented their policies. As one MSF worker reflected about the noticeable lack of informal interactions with local populations, "We have less time to drink tea. Most of us avoid interacting on a one-to-one basis with the people. We don't have time. We like being on the internet. We don't think that much can be gained that will help us do our job."[33] Another similarly worried, "Few people are really close and in touch with people. The possible exception is the medical examination, but this is still open to the critique of Illich and others as being a highly ritualized affair with power firmly on one side." At times, their professional training included methodologies that explicitly attempted to incorporate the views of local populations, but in the end expert knowledge nearly always trumped local knowledge. The pressure to professionalize and demonstrate technocratic prowess, at the expense of other kinds of commitments, such as witnessing, solidarity, or religious duty, is resonant.[34]

It is hardly ironic, and instead is quite understandable, that the discourse of partnership and participation has flowered in this context. Aid agencies *were* aware that they were becoming dangerously distant from the very people they wanted to help and, accordingly, introduced reforms to mandate contact. The key buzzword was "participation." In the 1980s, the development sector spearheaded the push, a reaction to the conclusion that one reason for the failures of development and the structural adjustment reforms of the 1980s was their neglect of the views of marginal populations. The revolutionary conclusion was that people should be the authors of their change.

Although the discourse of participation had radical roots—perhaps most closely associated with the liberation theology of Paulo Freire—soon it arguably became mainstreamed in every sense of the term. Everyone in the development sector was now talking about participation and empowerment. But unlike Freirean interpretations of participation that imagined a radical reworking of state-society relations, the general view of participation, especially in places such as the World Bank, was that individuals needed to be liberated from the state and be able to enter into markets (the ultimate empowering institution). Participation also was important for getting stakeholders to buy into programs they were expected to implement. It became part of the means and not part of the ends of politics.[35] According to some critics, participation did little more than legitimate projects falling on hard times.[36] In a similar spirit, MSF makes much of the importance of the principle of proximity, though several staff intimated that insistence on proximity is probably an indicator of its growing absence.[37] In any event, the evidence is that promises have overwhelmed practices.

Such considerations raise the issue of accountability. Many aid agencies developed accountability systems in order to improve the quality of their services, but the systems they have developed are rumored to encourage them to tune in what their donors have to say and tune out the recipients. In short, the overall sense is that the systems in place minimize what "consumers" want.[38]

Consequentialism. The emerging Institutionalization and Pragmatism are encouraging humanitarian agencies to shift from deontological or duty-based ethics to consequentialist ethics. This development is driven partly by a growing concern with the negative consequences of humanitarian action and the related desire to measure effectiveness and impact.[39] Previously, humanitarian organizations instinctively used deontological or duty-based ethics to guide their practices. Some actions are simply good in and of themselves regardless of their consequences. Ethical action consists of identifying these intrinsically good actions and then performing one's moral duty. For humanitarian actors (and perhaps felt most intensely by religious agencies), there is a moral duty to heal the wounds and reduce the suffering of distant strangers.

The growing concern with unintended consequences, however, has fed into an ethic of consequentialism. In this view, whether or not an action is ethical depends on the outcome. The issue for humanitarian organizations is not whether aid has negative and unintended consequences (this is almost always so) but whether, on balance, it does more harm than good. Knowing the consequences enables aid agencies to determine whether the proposed action is ethical; a consequentialist ethic demands that before saviors rush to the rescue they consider the unintended consequences of their well-meaning acts. Yet such consequentialist reasoning requires that agencies identify the outcomes of concern. This development interacts with another. Aid agencies are attempting to do more than ever. Whereas once they attended to symptoms, now they give equal attention to causes of suffering. Toward that end, they have taken on development, human rights, and peacebuilding, and in turn considered how these other goals interact with emergency relief. Among the various challenges such a development presents, it is no trivial matter that they are potentially harder to measure, especially when aid agencies proclaim the goal of removing the causes of suffering.

The quest to measure impact and effectiveness can also abrade a central element of the humanitarian ethic: to demonstrate solidarity with victims and restore their dignity. Relief workers, in Rony Brauman's words, aspire to "remain close to people in distress and to try and relieve their suffering."[40] They do so by providing not only relief but also compassion and caring. The ethic of humanitarianism, in this respect, includes both consequentialist and duty-based ethics—it desires to provide life-saving relief and holds that the motives matter for ensuring benevolence. Yet can such nonquantifiable values be operationalized when attempting to determine the effectiveness and impact of humanitarian action? If not, are they left outside of the model? Is it possible to quantify, for instance, reuniting of families, provision of burial shrouds, or simply reducing the fear and anxiety of individuals who are in desperate situations?[41] If they are omitted from the model, will the model redefine how humanitarian agencies think about impact, downgrading basic ethical motives in favor of measurable outcomes? If the measurable variables are no longer dependent on the subjective needs of the "beneficiaries," will they even be consulted? Some have suggested that the aid sector's growing concern with demonstrating effectiveness has made them less keen to help those who are in most "need," if the needy are located in difficult-to-reach places.

Yet another implication of this emerging consequentialism is that it reduces the distinction between humanitarian agencies and others that might be able to relieve suffering but have previously been excluded from such an honorific title. As humanitarian agencies go on shifting from an ethic of duty to an ethic of results, motives matter a lot less than consequences. If so, then when danger strikes, we should turn to whoever can save the most lives at the cheapest price. What if a private contractor, Walmart, or the U.S. military is the most effective?[42] The presumed difference between the Walmarts and the Worldvisions is that the former do not have moral authority while the latter do, but this moral authority is premised not on consequences but instead on motives, on a particular ethic of action. What happens, though, as humanitarian agencies base their legitimacy on their ability to measure up to standards set by modern, for-profit firms? Will such a development undermine what makes humanitarian action distinctive?

Technocrats of misery. Institutionalization and Pragmatism can have their charms, but they also possess the ability to invert values. Over the years, onlookers have developed a stream of concepts to capture these unsavory developments, including the irrationality of rationality, the iron cage, the banality of evil, and the organizational man. These concepts are answers to two important developmental questions.

Can bureaucratic logic take on a life of its own? In terms famously captured by Mary Shelley's *Frankenstein* and the beloved Disney story *The Sorcerer's Apprentice*, the fear is that the very tools used to control the world can develop a mind of their own and potentially threaten precisely the things they were created to protect. Staff who were motivated to join because of a sense of duty to others might become more interested in advancing their careers, protecting the interests of the organization, defending their turf, and cultivating good relations with donors. Staffers might begin to believe that the organization's survival is more important than the survival of those they are mandated to protect, on the grounds that if the first line of defense disappears then everyone will be vulnerable. Many aid agencies adopt their principles of neutrality and impartiality for the specific function of helping them gain access to populations in need, but over time these principles can become ends, to the point where they develop a banality of indifference, a possibility I used in order to explain the UN's indifference to the Rwandan genocide.[43] Although organizations first create means to help them accomplish their ends, over time the means might become ends in themselves.

The second question is, in many ways, more chilling: What happens to those who staff the bureaucracy? Might they unknowingly come to regard the bureaucracy as an end in itself and not a means to an end? The bureaucracy encourages individuals to shed their private morality in favor of morality as defined by the organization, to shift their loyalties from the broader community to the organization, and to see the organization's well-being and survival as the measure of progress. Will the aid sector, as Bernard Kouchner worried in the early 1980s about MSF, become "technocrats of misery"? The bureaucracy, alongside other modernizing processes, can develop instincts and interests that are faith-destroying. Being virtuous is no safeguard against these transfiguring processes; in fact, confidence in one's own virtue can be a dangerous narcotic.

The humanitarian sector's growing centralization and professionalization, acceptance of an ethics of consequences, and transformation into technocrats of misery all suggest that Institutionalization and Pragmatism can produce their own disenchantment. The humanitarian ethic, according to many, places a premium not only on relief of suffering but also on a philosophy of intimacy— that being present is critical to the act. Yet here are humanitarians building machinery that creates more barriers to this very kind of personal engagement. Humanitarians turned to empirical analysis to defend their actions, only to discover that it provided no immediate answer and opened the floodgates to heretics such as states and commercial agencies, which could just as easily claim the consequentialist ground. Although any appraisal of humanitarianism that omitted lives saved would be a disembodied humanitarianism, any appraisal that disregarded the character of the relationship between the giver and the receiver would be a spiritless humanitarianism. Recently I have encountered many veterans from the humanitarian field who acknowledge the necessity of building the machinery but who nevertheless worry that something has been lost in the process.

Conclusion

Can a more pragmatic and institutionalized humanitarianism preserve faith and a sense of the sacred? It partly depends on what we mean by faith. This essay has floated back and forth between two kinds of faith. There is the faith that depends on the ability of hope to survive skepticism, a position that resembles William James's defense of God. If humanitarians do not believe that it is possible to improve the humanitarian sector, if they dismiss the possibility of moral progress, then nothing will happen. Consider this comment by MSF's Rony Brauman: "I am not sure if progress exists, but it is good to act as if I believe it exists."[44] Progress cannot occur unless we believe it is possible and act on that belief. Because we do not have sufficient evidence that humanitarianism does harm, we should continue to act as if it does good. In the meantime, we will continue to search for evidence of progress; with any luck, acting as if it is possible will eventually produce evidence of its existence. And, for what it's worth, acting as if progress is possible is good for one's soul. If somehow I manage to produce moral progress, then we are all better off. But even if I fall short, I am still a better person because I have developed my moral character. I might as well bet that humanitarianism works, because there are few costs for betting wrong and lots of benefits for betting right. The costs of betting wrong include the lives of those who otherwise would have been saved and spared unnecessary suffering.

There is a second, related, way in which faith comes to the rescue, and this is when faith refers to religion or the belief that there exists something above, beyond, before, and outside ourselves. Humanitarianism, as we have seen, is supported by both secular and religious versions of faith. Although they differ in important respects, ultimately both rely on a sense of the divine, a conviction that cannot be either decisively supported or refuted by empirical evidence.

Along the same lines, which is more likely to retain a sense of the sacred and keep away the profane: religious organizations, or secular? It might very well be that religious organizations more closely monitor whether techniques are crowding out religious values. As one longtime staff member of WVI put it to me, WVI was "constantly taking its temperature," by which he meant the staff were always wondering about the relationship between their religious values and their mandates. In the case of WVI, after years of emphasizing development, it undertook a review regarding whether there is anything Christian about development, and the conclusion was an emphasis on "transformational development." In the case of Catholic Relief Services, after having successfully become one of the world's premier development agencies, many staff wondered what had happened to its religious values, and one of the effects was the "justice lens" that drew directly from Catholic social teaching. In the case of Islamic Relief, after years of pushing best practices in development, the agency began to have discussions about how such practices reflected basic Islamic values. Perhaps because religions, and those who have religious belief, are more collectively attentive to the rituals, texts, and ultimately practices that define their religion, they might more easily maintain a sense of the sacred and faith in the machine—and not allow the machine to extinguish either faith or the sacred.

But in the end, our concern should be less with whether religious or secular agencies are best able to retain a sense of the sacred, and more with whether their sense of the sacred is best able to protect the lives of the vulnerable and give them a sense of dignity. Arguably, the humanitarian sector was awash with the "sacred" during the good old days of humanitarianism, but this sacred and pure humanitarianism was vulnerable to a crisis of faith precisely because it was not doing enough to help the victims of the world. In other words, the sacred might have been good for the compassionate, but from the vantage point of the vulnerable, it left a lot to be desired. Perhaps a little profanity is just what the sacred needs.

NOTES

1. For good overviews and collections regarding pragmatism, see Morris Dickstein, ed., *The Revival of Pragmatism: New Essays on Social Thought, Law, and Culture* (Durham, NC: Duke University Press, 1998); Louis Menand, ed., *Pragmatism: A Reader* (New York: Vintage, 1997); and Stuart Rosenbaum, ed., *Pragmatism and Religion* (Urbana: University of Illinois, 2003).

2. Richard Bernstein, "Pragmatism's Common Faith," in Rosenbaum, *Pragmatism and Religion*, 134.

3. See Fiona Terry, *Condemned to Repeat?* (Ithaca, NY: Cornell University Press, 2002).

4. Mary Anderson, *Do No Harm: Supporting Local Capacities for Peace Through Aid* (Cambridge: Collaborative for Development Action, 1996).

5. "Interview with Rony Brauman (II): The Humanitarian Movement," *MSF Internal Newsletter* (September–October 2002): 72.

6. Michael Barnett, *Empire of Humanity: A History of Humanitarianism* (Ithaca, NY: Cornell University Press, 2011).

7. Joint Evaluation of Emergency Assistance to Rwanda.

8. I develop this argument in Michael Barnett, "Humanitarianism Transformed," *Perspectives on Politics* 3, 4 (2005): 723–740.

9. Ibid. An alternative possibility is that aid agencies begin to differentiate themselves, though this is more likely in terms of the services they offer, developing something of a niche.

10. Laura Thaut, Janice Stein, and Michael Barnett, "In Defense of Virtue: Credibility, Legitimacy Dilemmas, and the Case of Islamic Relief," in Peter Gourevitch, David Lake, and Janice Stein, eds., *The Credibility of Transnational NGOs: When Virtue is not Enough* (New York: Cambridge University Press, in press).

11. Louis Menand, *The Metaphysical Club: A Story of Ideas in America* (New York: Farrar, Straus, and Giroux, 2002).

12. Hereafter, I will capitalize Pragmatism whenever referring to the movement in philosophy and use the lower case pragmatism when using it in ways that are consistent with street-level meaning of compromise to get something done.

13. Hilary Putnam, *Pragmatism: An Open Question* (New York: Wiley-Blackwell, 2009).

14. Stephen Rockefeller, "Faith and Ethics in an Interdependent World," in Rosenbaum, *Pragmatism and Religion*, 307.

15. William James, *Pragmatism* (New York: Dover [1907], 1995).

16. For a terrific discussion of pragmatism that critiques its abandonment of fundamental values and purpose, see John Patrick Diggins, *The Promise of Pragmatism: Modernism and the Crisis of Knowledge and Authority* (Chicago: University of Chicago Press, 1994).

17. Hilary Putnam, *Pragmatism* (Cambridge, MA: Basil Blackwell, 1995), 22–23.

18. "Liberalism and Social Action," in James Gouinlock, ed., *Excellence in Public Discourse: John Stuart Mill, John Dewey, and Social Intelligence* (New York: Teacher's College Press, 1986). Cited in Patrick Deneen, "The Politics of Hope and Optimism: Rorty, Havel, and the Democratic Faith of John Dewey," *Social Research*, 66, 2 (Summer 1999), 590.

19. Richard Bernstein, *The Pragmatic Turn* (Malden, MA: Polity Press, 2010), 61.

20. Sandra Rosenthal, "Spirituality and American Pragmatism," in Rosenbaum, *Pragmatism and Religion*, 235.

21. Richard Rorty, "Hope and the Future," *Peace Review* 14, 2 (2002): 154. Cited in Nicholas Smith, "Rorty on Religion and Hope," *Inquiry* 48, 1 (February 2005): 94.

22. Diggins, *The Promise of Pragmatism*.

23. Bernstein, "Pragmatism's Common Faith," 129.

24. Charles Sanders Peirce, in ibid., 132.

25. William James, *The Will to Believe* (New York: Dover, 1956), 25.

26. Ibid., 7.

27. Ibid., 19. For another statement on religious skepticism, see J. L. Schellenberg, *The Will to Imagine: A Justification of Skeptical Religion* (Ithaca, NY: Cornell University Press, 2009).

28. Bernstein, "Pragmatism's Common Faith," 132–133.

29. Rosenthal, "Spirituality and American Pragmatism," 235.

30. Raymond Boisvert, "What Is Religion?" in Rosenbaum, *Pragmatism and Religion*, 225.

31. See Rockefeller, "Faith and Ethics in an Interdependent World," 308–309; and Rorty, "Hope and the Future."

32. For various statements on these issues, see Cass Sunstein, "Experts, Expertise, and Democrats," in his *Free Markets and Social Justice* (New York: Oxford University Press, 1997), 128–150; Robert Thaler and Cass Sunstein, "Liberal Paternalism Is Not an Oxymoron," *University of Chicago Law Journal* 70, 4 (Fall 2003): 1159–1172; Stephen Brint, *In an Age of Experts: The Changing Role of Professionals in Politics and Public Life* (Princeton: Princeton University Press, 1996); Michael Goldman, "The Birth of a Discipline: Producing Authoritative Green Knowledge, World Bank-Style," *Ethnography* 2, 2 (2001): 191–217.

33. Johanna Grombach-Wagner, "A L'art de boire du thé," In *My Sweet La Mancha* (Geneva: MSF International, 2005), 48–49.

34. Joanne Macrae and Adele Harmer, *Humanitarian Action and the "Global War on Terror": A Review of Trends and Issues*, HPG Report, 14, Overseas Development Institute, London, 9.

35. Pablo Alejandro Leal, "Participation: The Ascendancy of a Buzzword in the Neo-Liberal Era," *Development in Practice* 17, 4–5 (August 2007): 539–548; Georg Frerks and Dorothea Hilhorst, "Evaluation of Humanitarian Assistance in Emergency Situations," *New Issues in Refugee Research*, No. 56 (Geneva: UNHCR, 2002); Rita Abrahamson, "The Power of Partnerships in Global Governance," *Third World Quarterly* 25, 8 (2004): 1453–1467.

36. Andrea Cornwall and Karen Brock, "What Do Buzzwords Do for Development Policy? A Critical Look at 'Participation,' 'Empowerment,' and 'Poverty Reduction,'" *Third World Quarterly* 26, 7 (2005): 1043–1060.

37. Fabio Pompetti, "Proximity: A Lapsed Illusion or a Necessary Way of Behaving?" In *My Sweet La Mancha* (Geneva: MSF International, 2005).

38. Larry Minear and Ian Smillie, *Charity of Nations* (Bloomfield, CT: Kumarian Press, 2003), 215–224; Hugo Slim, "By What Authority? The Legitimacy and Accountability of Non-Governmental Organizations," *Journal of Humanitarian Assistance* (March 10, 2002), http://www.concordeurope.org/Files/media/0_internetdocumentsENG/3_Topics/Topics/17_Role_of_the_NGOs/2_CONCORD_documents_on_the_role_of_NGOs/Legitimacy_of_the_NGOs_Mr_Slim_2004.pdf; Janice Stein, "Humanitarian Organizations: Accountable—Why, to Whom, for What, and How?" in Michael Barnett and Tom Weiss (eds.), *Humanitarianism in Question: Politics, Power, and Ethics* (Ithaca, NY: Cornell University Press, 2008), 124–142.

39. There also were growing calls to measure "need," to replace subjective and emotional assessments with cooler and more objective criteria as a way to reinforce the impartiality principle and bring more attention to the forgotten emergencies. In short, objective indicators are the best way to reestablish values and principles. Marcus Oxley, "Measuring Humanitarian Need," *Humanitarian Exchange Magazine* 19 (London: Overseas Development Institute, September 1999).

40. Rony Brauman, "From Philanthropy to Humanitarianism: Remarks and an Interview," *South Atlantic Quarterly* 103, 2–3 (Spring/Summer 2004): 400.

41. James Darcy, "Acts of Faith? Thoughts on the Effectiveness of Humanitarian Action," paper presented to the SSRC seminar series "A Transformation of Humanitarian Action," New York City, (April 12, 2005): 8.

42. Stephen Hopgood, "Saying 'No' to Walmart? Money and Morality in Professional Humanitarianism," in Barnett and Weiss, *Humanitarianism in Question*, 98–123.

43. Michael Barnett, *Eyewitness to a Genocide: The United Nations and Rwanda* (Ithaca, NY: Cornell University Press, 2002). See also Tony Waters, *Bureaucratizing the Good Samaritan: The Limitations of Humanitarian Relief Operations* (Boulder, CO: Westview Press, 2001).

44. Interview with author, Paris, February 10, 2009.

9

Bridging the Sacred and the Profane in Humanitarian Life

Andrea Paras and Janice Gross Stein

SCHOLARS HAVE ARGUED recently that religious humanitarian organizations frame their purposes and their work fundamentally differently from their secular counterparts.[1] Religious organizations situate their relief and development work within a divinely inspired framework and claim a "higher purpose" for their work, embedded within a higher "moral authority."[2] For those within religious organizations, beliefs are powerful motivators for action and give profound and sustained meaning to the work they do within humanitarian space.[3] The authority and legitimacy that religious organizations enjoy, their leaders claim, enhance their performance and their effectiveness.[4] This claim is especially important in an age where authority and legitimacy are fragmented and contested.

These arguments about fundamental differences between "religious" and "secular" organizations nevertheless misread the place of the sacred in the modern world. They presume a strict and impermeable separation between the religious and the secular, and they limit the sacred to religious space. In this chapter, we advance two arguments.

First, we argue that the boundaries between secular and religious organizations are fuzzy rather than sharp. Humanitarian space and human rights embody the sacred for both secular and religious humanitarians and are sanctified by both. Constructions of the sacred influence how organizations understand the nature of humanitarian action and their own identities as humanitarian actors.

Second, we propose that religious humanitarians are better prepared to navigate the boundaries between the sacred and the profane than are secular humanitarians. Religious traditions bring to bear centuries of thought and experience in relating to problems "in the world." Even as they emphasize the sanctity of humanitarian space, religious organizations understand its multiple connections to the political. Secular humanitarians, less literate in the vocabulary of the sacred and the profane, take the sanctity of humanitarian space more literally. Less fluent with "the sacred," we argue, they are consequently less skilled at navigating its connections to the political in the world.

The chapter proceeds in several parts. The first looks at the construction of the layered and complex meanings of the sacred in the life of contemporary humanitarian organizations. The second examines how four large, professional humanitarian organizations—two religious and two secular—articulate and give meaning to the sacred: Caritas Internationalis, Islamic Relief, Médecins Sans Frontières, and Oxfam International. The first two are major humanitarian organizations from differing religious traditions, whereas the latter two represent the well-established professional secular humanitarian tradition. In this study, we exclude the smaller Christian Evangelical and missionary organizations and the Wahhabi Islamist organizations that work very differently from the large professional federated organizations that sit atop the pyramid of global humanitarian activity. Finally, we examine the consequences of the creation of the sacred for the way religious and secular organizations engage with the "profane," for how they engage with and in the world.

To set the scene for our examination of the construction of the sacred, we briefly recap here the central arguments of the opening chapter. The prevailing narrative of our secular age is developmental—what Barnett and Stein call "the secularization thesis"—where secularism gradually displaces religiosity in much the same way that adulthood displaces childhood. Secularism deepened as science developed and became more authoritative. Yet as the resurgence of religious organizations demonstrates, the argument is belied by the evidence. In the last two decades, religious organizations have grown rather than receded in contemporary global life more generally and within the humanitarian community.

It is not only that science and the secular have failed to vanquish religious identities, patterns of organizations, and forms of political and social life. We argue in this volume that the boundaries between the religious and the secular are increasingly permeable and porous, that the sharp dichotomies between the two no longer conform to lived experience, and that the attempt to distinguish them sharply and cleanly misses much of what is important in contemporary global life.[5] Especially within the humanitarian community, Barnett and Stein argue, we are seeing the sanctification of the secular and the secularization of religious life, to create new forms and meanings of the sacred. It is these new forms and meanings that we explore empirically in this chapter.

The Sacred in Humanitarian Life

The concept of "humanitarian space" is one of the two most important concepts—along with human rights—in the narratives and lived experiences of humanitarian organizations. First articulated in the 1990s by the former president of Médecins Sans Frontières (MSF), Rony Brauman, "humanitarian space" has come to represent humanitarianism's central values; it sanctifies humanitarianism as a meaningful and inviolable sphere of ethical action.[6] The core principles of neutrality, impartiality, independence, and universality, formulated first by the Red Cross but then adopted by humanitarian organizations formally as a code of conduct, constitute and bound humanitarian space[7]; they are the "foundations of humanitarian action."[8] It is these principles that differentiate humanitarian organizations from any other kind of actor purporting to "do" humanitarian work.[9] "Humanitarian space" is tightly connected with the core identities of these organizations, as it is the register for their expression of the human values of compassion for distant strangers. For humanitarian organizations, it symbolizes the sacred and the values of solidarity, compassion, dignity, and universality. The concept of "humanitarian space" is simultaneously a condition for humanitarian action and its defining core.[10]

We do not claim that this construction of humanitarian space, which is treated as sacred by humanitarians, is separate and distinct from the instrumental purposes it serves. It is not. Humanitarians have good reasons to ensure strict separation of humanitarian action from politics. The political neutrality of humanitarian space helps first and foremost to secure and maintain access to all populations in danger, whatever their political allegiance or affiliation. The capacity to come to the assistance of all who are suffering, no matter who they are, is the core ethic governing modern humanitarianism. And (no small matter) neutrality also diminishes the likelihood that humanitarians will become potential targets of violence.[11]

That these principles serve instrumental purposes does not diminish the element of the sacred. "Detachment anchored itself, over time, in something approximating sacredness," Hopgood argues, "a calling, a mission, a fundamental and transcendent truth born out of the fact of existential— innocent—suffering."[12] Closely related, the emphasis on independence—or purity—is intimately allied to the sacred. The purity of these principles vests humanitarians with an authority that transcends the particular and flows from the universal beyond time and space. In addition to having instrumental and functional value, "humanitarian space" symbolizes humanitarian organizations' core principles of human solidarity in the face of suffering. These principles are, as the ECHO website describes them, "sacrosanct."[13] Physical and legal violations of "humanitarian space" certainly affect humanitarians, insofar as they make it difficult or impossible for them to carry out their work. But far more important, they constitute a fundamental threat to these organizations because they threaten the sacred values that give meaning to their activities.

Why this turn to the sacred, to the transcendent, articulated at the core of a modern, universalist humanitarianism that is simultaneously everywhere and nowhere? Writing about Amnesty International, a human rights organization, Stephen Hopgood captures the essential paradox:

> But, and here is the key, it [Amnesty International] has found that far from efficacy coming through the force of the better argument, its real power has been in giving modernity symbolic—that is, *sacred*—form in precisely the way modernity's own logic resists. This is the critical move. Amnesty acquired authority by representing modern liberal principles in transcendent—sacred—terms. By creating a sense of something that went beyond "why" questions and anchored itself in *feelings* of righteous anger generated by tales of suffering. This is a kind of *faith* and faith is the thing that reason is supposed to eclipse.[14]

It is by invoking the sacred that humanitarians acquire the authority and legitimacy that distinguishes them from others who claim to speak in the name of humanity in a context of multiple modernities. By examining how humanitarian organizations defend "humanitarian space" or "human rights," we seek to understand how organizations consider their own principles as sacred. Diverse understandings of what is "sacred" have important implications for how secular and religious humanitarian organizations situate themselves in relation to political authority and assert themselves as humanitarian actors.

If this argument is correct, we should expect to see in the discourses of the secular as well as the religious humanitarians a language of transcendence. The sacred, we argue, pervades the conversation and the lived experience of both religious and universalist humanitarian organizations. In this modern lifeworld, it becomes difficult to see where the boundaries between the secular and the religious are drawn; they are increasingly blurred in the language of the sacred that defines contemporary humanitarianism.

We turn now to the search for the sacred in the worlds of four large humanitarian organizations—Caritas Internationalis, Islamic Relief (IR), Médecins

Sans Frontières (MSF), and Oxfam International (OI). The first two are explicitly religious in their identification while the third and fourth—though quite different—are avowedly secular. Yet, we argue, all four claim legitimacy from the sacred and the pure. All sanctify humanitarian space and human rights, although they do so with their own emphases, draw on contrasting forms of authority to do so, and all relate the profane to the sacred in unique ways.

Caritas Internationalis

Caritas Internationalis is a confederation of 165 national Catholic relief and development member organizations, headquartered in Vatican City. National Caritas branches have existed since the late nineteenth century, but Caritas Internationalis was founded in 1954 by the future Pope Paul VI, signifying the birth of a global network of Catholic relief organizations under the banner of Caritas. In the wake of Vatican II, Caritas Internationalis gave voice to a fundamental—and sacred—reverence for life. The federated network operates today under the principle of subsidiarity, whereby the national member organizations have overall responsibility for any given emergency response; Caritas Internationalis acts to support local and national initiatives, coordinates among national members, and, most important, creates consensus around guidelines and principles for the global movement.[15]

Under the aegis of Caritas Internationalis, the Caritas network is one of the largest providers of emergency relief, but it also engages in human rights advocacy, development, environmental protection, and caring for HIV/AIDS patients. The organization views its work as an expression of global solidarity, which is "inspired by the example of Christian faith and Catholic Social teaching."[16] Caritas leaders view their work as an enactment of religious faith and ground their professional activities in transcendent expressions of the sacred. Its president gave voice to its mission:

> Caritas Internationalis has the responsibility to be the hands and heart of God in many parts of the world, especially among the most disadvantaged. Its disinterested service, which is the fruit of acknowledging God's love, is a guarantee that life, every life, has value. Hence the first way to globalize solidarity is to globalize respect for life, and I repeat, every life.[17]

To trace the thread of the sacred through the work of Caritas, we examine first how the Catholic Church developed a more politically engaged conception of its charitable activities over the past fifty years, with Caritas Internationalis at the center. We then examine how its conception of "true human development" is rooted in an understanding of the sacred that is informed by Catholic principles.

Charity has always played an important role in the history of the Catholic Church, but in the latter half of the twentieth century a series of papal encyclicals proposed a more politically engaged, and specifically Catholic, approach to development. Published after the Second Vatican Council in 1967, Pope Paul VI's *Populorum Progressio* reflected on the challenges faced by newly decolonized states in the Third World and argued that underdevelopment is not simply an economic or social problem, but also an ethical problem that should be of direct concern to the Catholic Church.[18] It proposed the need for an "authentic development" that meets not only the material needs of impoverished peoples but also the spiritual needs of people by transforming them from "less than human conditions to truly human conditions."[19] As Pope John Paul II later recognized in his *Sollicitudo rei socialis*, published on the twentieth anniversary of *Populorum Progressio*, John VI's encyclical legitimized the direct intervention of the Church in matters that had previously been considered strictly secular political or economic problems, and it did so to affirm the sanctity of every human life.[20] "True development cannot consist only in the accumulation of wealth and in the greater availability of goods and services, if this comes at the expense of the development of the masses, and without due consideration for the social, cultural and spiritual dimensions of the human being." Furthermore, since the Church is an "expert in humanity," it has the responsibility—a "mandate received from the Lord"—of working toward the development of peoples.[21]

Since becoming pope in 2005, Benedict XVI has released two encyclicals that directly reflect on the centrality of charity for the work of the Church—perhaps an indicator of how seriously the Catholic Church views its humanitarian role in an age where globalization has decreased the distance between the needy and those who provide aid. Benedict argues that charity is an "indispensable expression of [the Church's] very being" that extends beyond the frontiers of the Church.[22] Building on the arguments of Paul VI and John Paul II, Benedict draws attention to a tension between charity and justice: though the Church has historically concerned itself with the former, it has considered the "just ordering of society" to fall under the purview of states.[23] Yet Benedict proposes a new way of understanding how the Church can promote justice through its works of charity:

[Since] it is also a most important human responsibility, the Church is duty-bound to offer, through the purification of reason and through ethical formation, her own specific contribution towards understanding the requirements of justice and achieving them politically. . . . Even if the specific expressions of ecclesial charity can never be confused with the activity of the State, it still remains true that charity must animate the entire lives of the lay faithful and therefore also their political activity, lived as "social charity."[24]

Benedict argues that charity has transformative potential because it is the expression and enactment of Christ's love or "Caritas." There is no opposition between charity and justice, since they are inseparable: "Not only is justice not extraneous to charity, not only is it not an alternative or parallel path to charity: justice is inseparable from charity, and intrinsic to it in integral human development."[25] The sacred is the expression of life as the Church works through charity to achieve a more just society.

The work of Caritas Internationalis, as the primary coordinator of the international Catholic relief network, is a direct extension of the work of the Church. Its ecclesiastical role was formally recognized in 2004 when Pope John Paul II granted it canonical legal status in acknowledgment of its central role within the Church's charitable activities.[26] Its existence is predicated on the centrality of charity and its principles are sacred values founded on the belief in the universal truth of Christ's love. At its 18th General Assembly held in Vatican City in June 2007, Benedict XVI encouraged Caritas to "focus on the deepest needs of the human person: human dignity, well being, and in the final analysis, eternal salvation."[27] Benedict claims universality for the practices of Caritas even though the Church seeks salvation for the faithful.

The religious and the universal join together in sacred space. In the organization's most recent statement of its "Emergency Guidelines," the first section on guiding values and principles makes references to the papal encyclicals and Caritas Internationalis statutes in tandem with the Red Cross-NGO Code of Conduct and SPHERE guidelines.[28] Although Caritas is committed to meet the professional standards required by all providers of humanitarian assistance, at the same time it identifies a unique role in ministering to a broader set of spiritual needs—and, in so doing, fulfilling the duties of charity required by Christian faith. Aid cannot be reduced to a "technical problem," since even delivery of material relief is fundamentally aimed toward "authentic development" of peoples in a broader, more spiritual sense.[29] In its commitment to professional standards of humanitarian action, the religious is secularized and professionalized, but that professionalization is situated within a deeply held sense of the sanctity of life.

As is the case with other humanitarian organizations, the principle of solidarity is foundational for Caritas. Unlike organizations that describe themselves as secular, in Caritas the concept of solidarity is explicitly rooted in Christian values:

> Solidarity is the value binding us together in the common vision of establishing a world where all human beings receive what rightly belongs to them as sons and daughters of God. Solidarity is a value inherent in Church organizations, but also shared by many beyond Church structures. This enables Caritas to be inclusive and truly Catholic by working with those who share this vision if perhaps not its Christian faith basis.[30]

The principle of solidarity provides a bridge for cooperation with other humanitarian organizations that value solidarity but do not share Caritas's religious commitments. As John Paul II writes: "[Solidarity] is not a feeling of vague compassion or shallow distress at the misfortunes of so many people, both near and far. On the contrary, it is a firm and persevering determination to commit oneself to the common good; that is to say, to the good of all and of each individual, because we are all really responsible for all."[31] Caritas's belief in solidarity draws its moral authority from sacred beliefs about the human good, and "authentic development" of all people.

Although leaders of Caritas view its activities as an expression of religious faith, they extend help to the needy and the suffering "without regard to race or religion."[32] Its practices can consequently be understood as universal, a "preferential option to the poor and most marginalized."[33] It meets the core professional standards that have been put in place by large professional humanitarian organizations and big institutional donors. Caritas represents sharing of humanitarian space and secularization of the religious, but its professional standards are deeply rooted in religious commitments, in a sense of mission and obligation. Here then, the secular is infused with an abiding sense of the sacred.

Islamic Relief

Islamic Relief is a humanitarian organization founded in Britain, with thirteen partner offices in North America, Europe, Africa, and Asia and twenty-one field offices, primarily in states where there are significant Muslim populations.

Islamic Relief anchors its mission in the Qur'an and the teachings of the Prophet and works largely among the faithful:

> The modern humanitarian principles of saving lives and alleviating poverty are divinely entrenched in the teachings of Islam; according to the Qur'an, saving a life is like saving the whole of humanity. Inspired by these teachings, acts of charity, concern for others and the provision of social welfare have played an integral in Muslim societies for the last 1400 years.[34]

The organization's mission is "inspired by Islamic values": "The concept of charity is central to social justice, which is a sacred value in Islam and a central tenet of the faith."[35] It identifies dignity, charity, accountability, empowerment, neutrality, and integrity among its core values and beliefs.[36] We begin by examining how the organization's religious identity influences a distinct approach to humanitarian relief, and then we explore how Islamic Relief has developed, partly by accident and partly by design, its approach to negotiating humanitarian space by bridging multiple cultures and communities. It too embodies the dynamic tension between secularization of the religious and sanctification of the secular that is the central theme of this volume.

The humanitarian work of Islamic Relief is strongly grounded in Islamic beliefs about charity and obligations toward the poor. The practice of *zakat*, which is the obligation to provide for the poor and marginalized, is the third pillar of Islam after the declaration of faith and the obligation to pray five times daily. In addition to this obligatory form of charity, there are also other forms of voluntary giving (*sadaqah*). This includes *waqf*, which is a charitable endowment that consists of hospitals, schools, land, food distribution, or money used to support charitable activities through the return from its investment.[37] Historically, *waqf* is a well-documented form of voluntary giving, since it usually involved donation of large gifts from well-known figures, but other informal practices of *sadaqah* include charitable donations after Friday prayers or during Ramadan.[38] Another example of voluntary giving is *Qurbani*, when faithful Muslims sacrifice an animal during the festival Eid-al-Adha and distribute a portion of the meat to the poor.[39]

These practices of charitable giving are firmly enshrined in Islamic teachings about compassion and social justice, and threaded through statements by the leaders of Islamic Relief. As Abuarqub and Phillips point out, Islamic teachings have a holistic understanding of charitable giving: "Humanitarianism in Islam . . . is not confined to the transfer of resources between the rich and the poor. The

Prophet Muhammad (peace be upon him) taught that any act of kindness towards or concern for other living things is also an act of charity."[40] Humanitarian action is not only the transfer of tangible material goods but also exemplified in deeds and actions. Moreover, charitable acts are sacred acts because they are ways of "receiving Allah's assistance, atoning for sin, escaping punishment, thanking Allah for his mercies and bringing a donor closer to paradise on the Day of Judgment."[41] Finally, *zakat* and *sadaqah* are not simply good deeds; they also serve a social function of redistributing wealth more equitably. Charity and social justice are closely linked in Islamic teachings, since it is a moral duty for Muslims to provide for the poor, and protect the weak against exploitation.[42] As Amy Singer has observed, both *zakat* and *sadaqah* are central to Muslims, and "without them faith is incomplete."[43]

Islamic beliefs about the importance of charity strongly influence not only Islamic Relief's beliefs and values but also its practices. Islamic Relief delivers conventional humanitarian and disaster relief, as large humanitarian organizations typically do, but it also introduced the idea of processing and canning the large amount of uneaten meat sacrificed for *Qurbani*, to reduce waste and facilitate distribution of meat to the poor throughout the Muslim world.[44] Islamic Relief runs *shari'ah*-compliant microfinance programs that specifically incorporate Islamic principles of finance, contracts, and debt.[45] The organization facilitates donations of *zakat*, *sadaqah*, and *Qurbani* on its website, and there is an online *zakat* calculator to help donors make sure that they have met their obligation.[46] Especially for Muslims who live in the West, where there is no social infrastructure for traditional forms of giving, Islamic Relief helps them fulfill their religious responsibilities for charitable giving. Fundraising around religious holidays, which are a traditional time for giving, and facilitating *zakat* contributions have become major channels for fundraising and advocacy for Islamic Relief and other Muslim organizations.[47]

Working for a Muslim humanitarian organization allows many of Islamic Relief's employees who are members of a religious minority group in Britain to express their religious identity. As one employee explains, "Working in a faith-based organization brings all aspects of my identity together. Everybody is driven by their beliefs. Every day, at prayer, we reiterate our values."[48] Another claims: "This is a calling, a mission. I do this because I am a British-born Muslim, and I want to preserve and promote our reputation. I want to be a role model for the British Muslims and I want to give back to my Pakistani community."[49] Employees affirmed that Islamic Relief's moral authority draws on sacred principles and is deeply embedded in religious identity.

As a religious humanitarian organization headquartered in Britain, one of Islamic Relief's largest challenges has been to preserve its unique religious identity while demonstrating that it meets the professional standards of the large secular humanitarian NGOs. More than other secular or even Christian organizations, Islamic Relief has walked a tightrope between being "different" and being "alike." As a Western-based Muslim organization, it exists within multiple worlds. One employee observes, "[The] fact that many of us are Muslims born and brought up in the West has meant that we have spent our lifetimes trying to bridge cultures and communities and no doubt this has assisted this process [of engaging with the international development community]."[50] At times, Islamic Relief's "difference" is a source of strength and legitimacy, since it enables a level of access to Muslim communities that are largely inaccessible to the other large humanitarian organizations. "Local community leaders trust us because we're Muslim, unlike CARE.... The West embodies professionalism and transparency. We are the best of both worlds."[51] Islamic Relief was able to work in Afghanistan under the Taliban, and it is one of the few humanitarian organizations that were not expelled from Darfur by the Sudanese government.[52] Other non-Muslim organizations are eager to develop partnerships with Islamic Relief, because of the legitimacy it enjoys within Muslim communities.[53]

But this religious identity also creates challenges. Islamic Relief has struggled to preserve a unique identity while meeting a growing body of professional standards. Especially after September 11, 2001, governments subjected all Muslim organizations to higher levels of scrutiny. One employee of Islamic Relief describes the particular challenges faced by Islamic Relief:

Islamic faith-based organizations had to "modernize" and identify how their values were in fact similar to those of the secular international humanitarian community. Many Muslim charities have of course had their assets frozen, financial transfers restricted and their activities have diminished or stopped altogether. We wanted to continue working and so we have had to adapt our fundraising and programme activities, adopt a particular language and deliberately engage more with the western international development community.[54]

Islamic Relief had little choice but to professionalize, to engage actively with the secular humanitarian community and its donors, practices, and standards. The religious and secular worlds collided, and the boundaries between the two shifted and faded as Islamic Relief worked with British authorities to develop meticulous standards of financial accountability and transparency.[55] From the perspective of its senior employees, Islamic Relief has had to work harder and more consistently than non-Muslim organizations to meet international standards.[56]

Islamic Relief displays a certain self-consciousness about its multiple layers of identity, a self-consciousness that reflects and articulates the simultaneous secularization of the religious and sanctification of the secular. It deliberately uses language familiar to the large humanitarian organizations and adopts the professional practices of well-established Christian and secular organizations.[57] Senior leaders are acutely sensitive to the professional image of a provider of impartial aid. As one observed:

> I hope that we will open an office soon in Latin America where we will work through local partners. One of the reasons for working there is because with a negligible Muslim population in the region we can more explicitly demonstrate that we assist all poor people regardless of religion.[58]

Some employees fear that Islamic Relief puts its core religious identity and values at risk when it pushes hard to meet international standards; they worry that Islamic Relief will look more and more like its counterparts—indeed, that it will become "an instrument of the West."[59] Within the organization, there have been ongoing debates and division about how to express the different layers of its identity. In part as a consequence of these continuing external and internal negotiations, Islamic Relief moves with facility between religious and professional principles and mediates between the sacred and the profane in its practices.

More so than any other large humanitarian organization, Islamic Relief lives in multiple worlds. Partly through circumstances and partly through design, it brings the sensibilities of both the sacred and the profane to the construction of humanitarian space. Like Caritas, at one level it is universalist in principles and practices; it gives help based on "solely on the needs of beneficiaries" without heed to "color, race or creed."[60] Islamic Relief, however, goes further. It explicitly acknowledges drawing from both religious and secular sources to form, shape, and reshape its values. It draws spiritual inspiration and sacred knowledge not only from Islamic teachers and texts but also from the "knowledge and practice gained over the years from dedicated and principled humanitarian workers, academics and professionals from all faiths and regions who have developed universally recognized good practice in this field."[61] Islamic Relief conceives of the sacred through Islamic values and practices and also articulates conceptions of the sacred through the principles and practices shared with others. Its values are sacred, yet commensurate with and translatable into other forms of humanitarian practice, both religious and secular.[62] Partly because of what it is and partly because of where it is, Islamic Relief bridges the religious and secular to give complex and textured meaning to the sacred. It sanctifies the secular and secularizes the religious to create a flexible concept of the sacred.

Médecins Sans Frontières

Médecins Sans Frontières (MSF) is one of the largest and most successful secular humanitarian organizations, providing emergency medical relief to populations in danger in more than seventy countries. Unlike the classical humanitarianism of the International Committee of the Red Cross (ICRC), MSF interprets neutrality differently than do Dunantist humanitarians.[63] Breaking from that tradition, MSF anchors its practices in the moral obligation to serve as witness for those who have no voice.[64] As a secular organization, its values are grounded not in religious faith but rather in its commitment to universalist concepts of human rights based on a reverence for life and on beliefs about the inherent dignity of every human being.

MSF was founded by a group of French doctors who broke away from the Red Cross movement during the Biafran crisis in the early 1970s. Its identity is intimately tied to its name: MSF's humanitarian space is borderless insofar as the organization is committed to "bringing medical assistance to people who are suffering regardless of geographical, political, ethnic, religious or social borders."[65] It is this universalist ethic that marks the "individual medical-humanitarian act," which is the emblem of solidarity with victims, and which constitutes MSF's unique model of humanitarian assistance.[66]

Médecins Sans Frontières has a special attachment to the concept of "humanitarian space," a concept that was developed by one of its early founders.[67] The source of moral legitimacy within MSF is a sanctified conception of "humanitarian space" that emphasizes three related elements: the humanitarian act as an emblem of solidarity with victims, the principle of *témoignage* (or witnessing), and strict separation of humanitarian from political action.

James Orbinski articulated this sense of the ineffable, the sacred, when he accepted the Nobel Peace Prize on behalf of Médecins Sans Frontières. Humanitarian action, he argued, is an "ethic framed in a morality" that is not reducible to "rules of right conduct and technical performance": "Humanitarian action is more than simple generosity, simple charity. . . . More than offering material assistance, we aim to enable individuals to regain their rights and dignity as human beings."[68]

Delivery of medical relief is the foundation of MSF's work, but like Caritas, the humanitarianism of MSF does not reduce to charity or medical competence. It is an ethical expression of solidarity with humanity: "We bear witness because it is part of our understanding of humanitarian responsibility and our desire not to reduce our acts to the merely charitable or logistical."[69] For MSF, humanitarian relief is delivery of medical aid and an expression as well of the fulfillment of a moral duty to act in human solidarity by taking care of suffering bodies.[70]

MSF shares its solidarity with suffering individuals with other humanitarian organizations—including Caritas and Oxfam—but what distinguishes this particular brand of solidarity is how it views the responsibility to bear witness, a term resonant with religious overtones. The principle of *témoignage*, which commits MSF to act as a witness and speak on behalf of populations in danger, is *how* it enacts solidarity with victims of violence as well as advocates for political responsibility.[71] *Témoignage* implies that "acting and speaking [are] two inseparable elements of providing relief to endangered people."[72]

The obligation to bear witness plays a central role in the organization's founding. French doctors broke away from the ICRC—which along with other humanitarian organizations remained silent to protect their principles of neutrality and impartiality—and made the decision to speak out against the Nigerian government as the crisis in Biafra deepened. The organization's La Mancha Agreement of 2006, the result of more than a year of internal discussion and debate, affirmed that *témoignage* was inseparable from the organization's other operations; its obligation to bear witness is what sets MSF apart from other humanitarian organizations.[73]

It is this sacred obligation to bear witness that renders humanitarianism a moral act. MSF creates and sanctifies humanitarian space by speaking out when it witnesses human suffering. "MSF's public statements should be seen not as moralizing rhetoric *per se*," argues D. Robert Dechaine, "but rather as characteristic of the responsibility that is endemic to humanitarian space itself."[74] There are ongoing debates within MSF about what constitutes *témoignage*, but even in the most minimalist form bearing witness remains an integral part of the organization's identity.[75]

It is the sanctity of "humanitarian space," a space that is almost walled off, separated, pure, inviolate, that distinguishes the humanitarian from the political sphere. One of the primary hallmarks of "the space for humanitarian aid," argued Rony Brauman, a founder of MSF, is "independence from all political powers."[76] MSF jealously guards its independence by raising funds largely from private donors—in 2008 it received 89.9 percent of its funding from private sources—and by resisting efforts by the United Nations, states and other NGOs to form an integrated approach to disaster relief.[77] Those who urge integration of humanitarian relief situate emergency assistance within the broader goals of nation building, peace, and development. In Afghanistan, for example, the United Nations and some of the contributing states put in place strong financial and operational incentives to encourage humanitarian organizations to work closely with provincial reconstruction teams (PRTs) and coalition partners.[78] MSF strongly denounced "the co-optation of the aid system by the international coalition" and stood firmly against efforts to integrate aid into long-term political objectives.[79] Xavier Crombé writes:

> The coordination agenda is presented in a manner that appears to be depoliticized and to comply with the challenge of effective international action.... It is understandable that the United Nations has the intention of reinforcing order among its very components. However, a situation whereby non-governmental organizations allow themselves to be coordinated is in reality an act of subordination.[80]

This strong emphasis on independence and on the purity of humanitarian space, on its inviolability, certainly serves instrumental purposes. If local communities see humanitarians acting in conjunction with Western militaries, their trust diminishes and humanitarian workers can easily become tactical targets.[81] But the commitment to independence cannot be understood solely, or even largely, as tactical. Loss of independence is "tantamount to the disintegration of its very humanitarian values," of the soul of the organization.[82] "MSF does more than pit humanitarian action against political action," Dechaine argues. "It also pits the borderlessness of humanitarian space against the power and force of political space."[83]

The barely concealed subtext is deep fear of the violation of sacred space, of corruption, of the impure, represented by states or even NGOs that have "crossed the line beyond humanitarian action while retaining that label.... Through a multi-mandate approach, the NGO community themselves have, unwittingly in some cases, allowed themselves to become the implementing partner of NATO's state-building efforts in Afghanistan, while calling themselves humanitarian."[84] Here, sanctification of the secular is clear. MSF stands as the rebel against a corrupted political order, as the defender of the "transcendent global civic religion" symbolized by humanitarian space, and at times as its martyr.[85]

Although MSF's values are not embedded within an explicitly religious framework, they are sacred, grounded in what Charles Taylor calls "intra-human sources of motivation for universal benevolence," a transcendence that is "horizontal, not vertical."[86] The act of providing medical assistance, an act infused with reverence for life, occurs within humanitarian space, which renders these acts sacred, beyond the profane and the political. As James Orbinski noted in his Nobel speech, "The time and space of the humanitarian are not those of the political."[87] It is within "humanitarian space" that human dignity and rights can be restored, where humanitarians can act as mediators between violence and victims, where they can give voice to those who have lost their own through suffering and indignity. And like Caritas and Islamic Relief, it is *because* MSF situates its activity beyond the profane and the political that it claims moral authority for action. Even though MSF's values are not grounded in religious beliefs, the humanitarian space it occupies is, nevertheless, sacred.

Oxfam International

The Oxford Committee for Famine Relief was founded in Britain in 1942 to deliver food to a starving population in Nazi-occupied Greece. Formed in 1995, Oxfam International (OI) is a confederation of fourteen national Oxfam organizations working in ninety-nine countries around the world on issues related to poverty and inequality.[88] Oxfam's work is informed by a rights-based approach that advocates solidarity with the poor and a commitment to fighting global injustice.[89] In its most recent strategic plan, Oxfam International identifies four broad areas of engagement: economic justice, essential services, rights in crisis, and gender justice.[90] It identifies "emergency response" and "peace and security" as only two of the fifteen major issue areas in which it works, which also include climate change, education, gender justice, indigenous rights, trade, and youth outreach.[91] The mission statement posted on its home page does not include the word "humanitarian."[92] Nevertheless, the largest proportion of its annual expenditures in 2008–09, nearly 32 percent, was spent on humanitarian activities directly related to life and security rather than advocacy or short- or long-term development.[93] Oxfam is present on the ground in many of the same emergencies and conflicts as other humanitarian organizations: the flooded areas in Pakistan, Haiti after the earthquake, Darfur, the Democratic Republic of Congo, and Afghanistan. In

practice if not in theory, Oxfam International is de facto a humanitarian organization; it engages in the traditional activities of disaster and conflict relief,
even though it also participates in long-term development activities.

Oxfam International is a secular organization, but it elevates and enshrines
the sanctity of human rights as a core principle: "We believe that respect for
human rights will help lift people out of poverty and injustice, allow them to
assert their dignity and guarantee sustainable development."[94] It is committed
to transforming the underlying structures that produce and reproduce poverty
and sees itself as playing an important moral as well as political role in fighting
against structures of inequality and injustice. This rights-based approach
informs its engagement on a wide variety of issues, from health care and education advocacy to defense of the poor against the negative effects of climate
change—and, not least of all, to humanitarian intervention.[95] In a 2009 report
on the challenges for humanitarianism in the twenty-first century, Oxfam
International proposes a rights-based framework for humanitarian action:

> A system is needed whose primary focus is to support states in their
> efforts to reduce risks and respond effectively in emergencies; a system
> that reinforces *both* states' responsibilities to provide assistance *and*
> citizens' capacity to claim it. This twenty first century humanitarianism
> must combine the best of the twentieth-century humanitarian system
> and its principles of humanity and impartiality with an approach rooted
> in the rights of those affected by emergencies.[96]

It is precisely this rights-based approach to humanitarianism that allows
Oxfam International to break down the traditional distinctions between
short-term relief and long-term development. The goal of relief work is to
reduce the factors that make people vulnerable to disasters.[97] This is a radically
different—and more politically engaged—conception of humanitarianism
than that of MSF, since it emphasizes a long-term project of empowerment
rather than relief delivered during the acute phase of a crisis. Human rights
have a sacred and transcendent quality.

Oxfam's twofold mission—humanitarian relief in crisis and reduction of
inequality enshrined in human rights—creates tension and at times contra-
diction for Oxfam leaders. It cannot sanctify humanitarian space—keep
it pure and inviolable as the others do—while simultaneously advocating
structural change to enhance the rights of the poor. Oxfam claims to be neutral in delivery of humanitarian relief but partial in advocacy for the poor;
this is a delicate and difficult balance to maintain.[98] Oxfam's commitment to

solidarity with the poor, to an emphasis on rights, is precisely what sanctifies its work. In this respect, Oxfam is hardly unique among rights-based
organizations.[99]

Oxfam subordinates other activities to its primary goal: reduction of "the
structural causes of poverty and related injustice."[100] As it does so, Oxfam more
fully and directly occupies the space of politics than do the other three humanitarian organizations that we examined and looks much more like many organizations in the human rights community. Oxfam International's rights-based
approach informs interactions with structures of authority in the everyday; it
is the bridge between the sacred and the profane, the quotidian political:
"Oxfam believes that citizens have a right to hold governments and institutions
accountable, to expect them to respect their rights and do what they say they
will do."[101] Oxfam's deep commitment to extensive standards of transparency
and accountability is shaped by this rights-based approach and is a central feature of its identity. In addition to publishing annual reports, which is standard
practice for humanitarian NGOs, Oxfam also publishes the results of internal
and external evaluations, as well as a response to the evaluations[102]: "Oxfam has
chosen to publish the evaluation externally, in the interests of transparency and
accountability. We think it is important to model openness and a learning
approach and we try to show here how the lessons are being incorporated into
future plans."[103] Oxfam International also publishes its accountability policies,
as well as detailed explanations of financial accounts for recent years.[104]

Does it matter that Oxfam International sanctifies "rights" far more than it
does "humanitarian space"? What organizations choose to sanctify does appear
to make a difference in their practices. Oxfam does not engage in the same
debates about humanitarian values and identity that occupy MSF, Caritas, or
Islamic Relief. It devotes far less energy to demarcating humanitarian space and
to defending its purity and inviolability. Debates about values such as neutrality
or impartiality are important only insofar as they have practical implications for
how Oxfam carries out humanitarian work. Sanctification of rights leads Oxfam
explicitly to the secular, as it engages most directly and actively with the political
and structural conditions that create poverty and injustice. Oxfam sees itself
explicitly as a political actor in ways that the other three organizations do not.

Conclusions: Sanctification of Humanitarian Space

Creation of the sacred is common to both religious and secular humanitarian
organizations. The attributes of "secular" and "religious" organizations, however, do not conform neatly to expectations; nor are they especially useful in

understanding what the large, professional humanitarian organizations do in practice. As Barnett and Stein emphasize in their introductory chapter, the lines between the religious and the secular are porous, as each organization navigates across these boundaries in its own way and builds elements of the sacred into its principles and practices. The religious organizations, both overtly preoccupied with the sacred, nevertheless make space to engage actively in the secular world, to work with "professional" standards and with the humanitarian community to share and improve practices in everyday life. They do so with considerable ease, fluency, and comfort with the need to engage the profane to protect and enhance the sacred. All four organizations, however, locate their authority in the language of the sacred, to give a deeper sense of purpose to their actions, promote global solidarities, and imbue their actions with a deep sense of moral worth. More unites these four large professional organizations than separates them.

Three broad implications emerge from this examination of the fuzzy boundaries between the religious and the secular. First, our argument suggests that we should not overstate the degree to which religious identity contributes to the success and legitimacy of humanitarian organizations. Creation of the sacred, Hopgood argues, provides authority and legitimacy in a modern life-world that systematically strips away authority. Sanctification reemerges as a critical wellspring of the authority and legitimatization of humanitarian activity. All four of these organizations insist that what they do goes far beyond technical or professional competence. Their delivery of humanitarian relief and rights-based engagement with the poor is both a demonstration of human solidarity and an enactment of sacred moral principles. Whether these principles are "religious" or "secular" has little bearing on their sacred value.

At the same time, however, three of these organizations—Caritas Internationalis, Oxfam International, and Islamic Relief—seek explicitly to meet professional standards of delivering humanitarian relief and combine their principles with internationally recognized professional codes, such as SPHERE or the Red Cross Code of Conduct. Appeals to the sacred may be necessary, but they are generally not sufficient for humanitarian organizations to achieve legitimacy and moral authority. Rather, they must do so by engaging and negotiating with political authority, and Médecins Sans Frontières does so in practice while it resists doing so in principle.[105] Even within the sacred space of humanitarian principles, organizations must negotiate with the political and the profane to legitimize their authority.

Second, what organizations sanctify matters. We have argued that sanctification of humanitarian space creates a refuge, a safe space that is inviolable and beyond challenge. Within this space, a discussion of accountability is at best irrelevant and at worst offensive. Humanitarians stand on sacred ground where discussions of the profane and the mundane, of principal-agent contradictions, of conflicts between donors and recipients, of humanitarian marketplaces, are divisive, intrusive, inappropriate, unwelcome, disrespectful, and in decidedly poor taste.[106] The hallowing of the space in which humanitarians work places much of what they do outside the boundaries of normal questioning and investigation. Once "humanitarian space" is sacred, it becomes much more difficult to problematize what humanitarians do in that space. At the same time, humanitarianism is also a living practice that is not static, and, similar to religious traditions, there is a constant process of reinterpretation of sacred principles.[107] Our discussions with Islamic Relief staff members revealed a division within the organization between those who want to prioritize preservation of religious values, and others who want to professionalize. For some staff members, the pressures to professionalize, to build in mechanisms for greater accountability and transparency, constitute an existential threat to the organization's religious identity and sacred principles.[108] For others who favor moving toward professionalization, these pressures represent an opportunity for the organization to have its values speak directly to politics, and thus increase the organization's legitimacy.

Finally, creation of the sacred foregrounds the challenge of navigating the political, of working with other forms of constituted authority. Differences in the approach to negotiation of the political among these four organizations flow in large part from what they have constituted as sacred. It may well be that religious organizations, habituated throughout the centuries to acknowledging the presence of institutional and political authority in this world, can more easily sanctify the work they do within humanitarian space, while acknowledging the explicitly political character and consequences of what they do. They are comfortable navigating the porous borders between the sacred and the profane.

This kind of sensibility is especially apparent among the leaders of Islamic Relief, who display more self-consciousness and sensitivity about the dilemmas of a religious nongovernmental organization in a professional field that is occupied by many types of organizations, all of whom work within the shadow of politically constituted authorities that can invoke different kinds of authority and legitimacy. The sensitivity of Islamic Relief to legal and political authority, and its openness to conversations about accountability, reflect its minority status as a Muslim organization based in a predominantly Western, Christian culture.[109] Leaders of Islamic Relief are experienced and practiced in explaining its mission and actions to multiple and quite diverse audiences. Caritas Internationalis, embedded deeply within Western traditions, is able to draw on a centuries-old discussion of the relationship between church and state, of rendering unto Caesar what is appropriately his. In contrast, Oxfam International is less able to articulate a clear vision of its humanitarian identity, but the sanctification of "rights," not "space," enables it to engage explicitly with politics and authority. And it is Médecins Sans Frontières, which articulates most strongly the sanctity, inviolability, and purity of humanitarian space, that lacks a vocabulary to structure this conversation. Its leaders argue that there are no humanitarian solutions to humanitarian problems but, at the same time, take its ethics and practices outside the boundaries of the political, the consequential, and the utilitarian. Interestingly, as it approaches its fortieth anniversary, MSF is now beginning to explore how humanitarian space, rather than being beyond politics, is "a space for negotiations, a balance of power and a convergence of interests between aid stakeholders and de facto authorities."[110]

Why does this discussion about sanctity of humanitarian space matter? It matters because the future success of humanitarian organizations—both religious and secular—depends on how they interpret the sacred, and whether they regard the sacred as beyond negotiation or find ways to negotiate the political within this space. To venture a metaphor: If sacred space is a door, is the door open or closed? We argue that negotiations over the sacred are inherently political conversations that require organizations to keep the door open, to view humanitarian space as contested rather than as an ethical realm of action that exists beyond the profane. The tension between the "sacred" and the "profane" is of far greater importance to the practices of humanitarians than the distinction between "religious" and "secular" organizations. We suggest that religious organizations may be more successful *not* by virtue of their religious identity, but because they may be better able to bridge the divide between the sacred and the profane, to renegotiate its contours, than their secular counterparts. In a world in which the search for meaning shapes legitimacy and authority, those humanitarian organizations that can draw on deeply embedded traditions—traditions that navigate the sacred and the profane—may be uniquely advantaged.

NOTES

1. Tara Hefferan, "Finding Faith in Development: Religious Non-Governmental Organizations in Argentina and Zimbabwe," *Anthropological Quarterly* (Summer 2007), 889.

2. Laurie Occhipinto, *Acting on Faith: Religious Development Organization in Northwestern Argentina* (Lanham, MD: Lexington Books, 2005); Hefferan, "Finding Faith in Development," 894.

3. Research indirectly supports these claims by documenting how religious organizations have access to larger networks and are therefore more successful in mobilizing resources and support. See "Faith-Based and Secular Humanitarian Organizations," *International Review of the Red Cross* 87, 858 (June 2005); Caritas Annual Report 2007 ("The potential of Caritas to help tackle poverty is enormous, but donors and governments do not use us enough. Caritas exists at every level, with an *unrivalled network of staff* working at the grassroots"; p. 8). See also the Caritas website: "The Church has *unprecedented access to people* with HIV and AIDS across the world and on a grassroots level. It has a global network of schools, churches, orphanages, hospices, organisations such as Caritas plus an army of faithful who offer their services" [our emphasis]. http://www.caritas.org/activities/hiv_aids/the_catholic_church_serving_people_with_hiv_and_aids.html (accessed August 24, 2009).

4. See Bruno De Cordier, "Faith-Based Aid, Globalization and the Humanitarian Frontline: An Analysis of Western-Based Muslim Aid Organizations," *Disasters* 33, 4 (2009): 608–628.

5. Charles Taylor, *A Secular Age* (Cambridge: Belknap Press, Harvard University Press, 2007), 600.

6. "A space of freedom in which we are free to evaluate needs, free to monitor the distribution and use of relief goods and have a dialogue with the people." Quoted in Inter-Agency Standing Committee 70th Working Group Meeting, "Background Document: Preserving Humanitarian Space, Protection and Security," http://www.unhcr.org/refworld/pdfid/48da506c2.pdf (accessed August 24, 2009).

7. The International Red Cross and Red Crescent Movement espouses seven fundamental principles: humanity, impartiality, neutrality, independence, voluntary service, unity, and universality. http://www.icrc.org/eng/resources/documents/red-cross-crescent-movement/fundamental-principles-movement-1986-10-31.htm (accessed December 17, 2011). See the Humanitarian Charter and Principles in the Sphere Handbook, http://www.sphereproject.org/content/view/27/84/lang.English/ (accessed May 17, 2010).

8. ECHO, "The humanitarian space under pressure," http://ec.europa.eu/echo/policies/humanitarian-space_en.htm (accessed December 17, 2011).

9. See Stephen Hopgood, "Saying 'No' to Wal-Mart? Money and Morality in Professional Humanitarianism," in Michael Barnett and Thomas G. Weiss (eds.), *Humanitarianism in Question: Politics, Power, Ethics* (Ithaca, NY, and London: Cornell University Press, 2008).

10. It is important to note that even though the language of "humanitarian space" originated within humanitarian NGOs, its wider use is not restricted to NGOs; nor does it have any formal definition. As Ulrike von Pilar observes, its use has become widespread, with various meanings that reflect various concerns or priorities. Ulrike

von Pilar, "Humanitarian Space Under Siege: Some Remarks from an Aid Agency's Perspective" (Background paper prepared for the Symposium "Europe and Humanitarian Aid—What Future? Learning from Crisis," April 22–23, 1999 in Bad Neuenahr). Whereas NGOs tend to view it as the symbol of their raison d'être, it also has both physical and legal connotations. For instance, "humanitarian space" can denote a physical, geographical area that is protected, such as "humanitarian corridors" or refugee camps. In this sense, the use of "humanitarian space" is closely connected to concerns about security, in the sense of providing protection for victims of conflict or calamity and the physical security of humanitarian actors. It is also a legal concept. The principle of neutrality was enshrined in the Geneva Conventions; the specific concept of "humanitarian space" was recognized by the European Parliament in December 2007 in the Statement on the European Consensus on Humanitarian Aid. Even while the idea of "humanitarian space" appears to be gaining greater currency, at the same time there seems to be wide-spread agreement that "humanitarian space" is under threat, which may somewhat explain attempts to further institutionalize humanitarian principles. Inter-Agency Standing Committee 70th Working Group Meeting, "Background Document: Preserving Humanitarian Space, Protection and Security," http://www.unhcr.org/refworld/pdfid/48da506c2.pdf (accessed August 24, 2009). But paradoxically, the use of "humanitarian space" by a wide array of actors—from development NGOs to militaries—seems to also be the main source of the threat to the humanitarian principles it represents. One of the main threats to humanitarian space, particu-larly in Iraq and Afghanistan, has been the convergence between state-building and democracy-promotion agendas on the one hand, and humanitarian efforts on the other. It goes beyond the scope of this chapter to explore these arguments in detail. See Antonio Donini, "Afghanistan: Humanitarianism Under Threat," Briefing Paper, March 2009, https://wikis.uit.tufts.edu/confluence/download/attachments/22520580/Donini-Afghanistan.pdf?version=1&modificationD atc=1237385488000 (accessed May 17, 2010); Nicolas de Torrente, "Challenges to Humanitarian Action," *Ethics and International Affairs* 16, 2 (October 2002).

11. See Hans Haug, "Neutrality as a Fundamental Principle of the Red Cross," *International Review of the Red Cross* 315 (1996): 627–630.

12. Stephen Hopgood, "Moral Authority, Modernity, and the Politics of the Sacred," *European Journal of International* Relations 15, 2 (2009): 242, 243.

13. ECHO, "The humanitarian space under pressure," http://ec.europa.eu/echo/policies/humanitarian-space_en.htm (accessed December 17, 2011).

14. Hopgood, "Moral Authority, Modernity, and the Politics of the Sacred," 229–255, 240.

15. See Caritas Internationalis, "Emergency Guidelines: Principles, Structures & Mechanisms," March 2007. http://www3.caritas.org/upload/eme/emergency-guideline.pdf (accessed May 27, 2010).

16. Caritas in Action, http://www3.caritas.org/about/waht_is_caritas.html (accessed August 24, 2009).

17. Cardinal Rodríguez Maradiaga, "The Catholic Church and the Globalization of Solidarity," speech delivered at Vatican City, July 7, 2003, http://www.caritas.org/upload/fth/fthecatholicchurchandtheglobalizationofsolidarity.pdf (accessed August 24, 2009).

18. *Populorum Progressio* was a response to an earlier series of papal encyclicals that addressed social issues, the first of which was *Rerum Novarum*, published by Leo XIII in 1891 on the topic of capital, labor, and the condition of the working class. *Populorum Progressio* was notable, however, because it was the first to offer an extensive analysis of the Catholic Church's response to underdevelopment in the Third World.

19. Paul VI, Encyclical Letter, *Populorum Progressio* (March 26, 1967): 20. http://www.vatican.va/holy_father/paul_vi/encyclicals/documents/hf_p-vi_enc_26031967_populorum_en.html (accessed May 26, 2010).

20. John Paul II, Encyclical Letter, *Sollicitudo rei socialis* (December 30, 1987): 8. http://www.vatican.va/holy_father/john_paul_ii/encyclicals/documents/hf_jp-ii_enc_30121987_sollicitudo-rei-socialis_en.html (accessed May 26, 2010).

21. Ibid., 7–8.

22. Benedict XVI, Encyclical Letter, *Deus Caritas Est* (December 25, 2005): 25(a,b). http://www.vatican.va/holy_father/benedict_xvi/encyclicals/documents/hf_ben-xvi_enc_20051225_deus-caritas-est_en.html (accessed May 26, 2010). See also Benedict XVI, Encyclical Letter, *Caritas in veritate* (June 29, 2009): 2: "Charity is at the heart of the Church's social doctrine."

23. Benedict XVI, *Deus Caritas Est*, 28(a).

24. Ibid., 28(a), 29.

25. Benedict XVI, *Caritas in veritate*, 6, 18.

26. "Caritas Internationalis, by its origin and nature, is closely linked to the Shepherds of the Church and, in particular, to Peter's Successor, who presides over universal charity (see Saint Ignatius of Antioch, Ep. ad Romanos, inscr.), and takes inspiration for its action from the Gospel and the tradition of the Church. . . . Therefore, in acknowledgement of the ecclesial role performed by this well-deserving Confederation, and in acceptance of the request specifically submitted in this regard, pursuant to apostolic authority and the Code of Canon Law, I hereby grant Caritas Internationalis public canonical legal status (see cann. 116–123 of the Code of Canon Law)." "Pope John Paul II Grants Canonical Legal Status to *Caritas Internationalis*," http://www.caritas.org/about/CanonicalLegalStatus.html?ts=200806261415 (accessed May 26, 2010).

27. Caritas General Assembly 2007 Special Bulletin, http://www3.caritas.org/upload/1in/1ing07.qxd;2ing062.pdf (accessed August 24, 2009).

28. Caritas Internationalis, "Emergency Guidelines: Principles, Structures & Mechanisms," March 2007. See also Caritas Internationalis, "Caritas Internationalis Relations with the Military." http://www3.caritas.org/upload/mil/military-ing1_11.pdf (accessed December 17, 2011).

29. John Paul II, "*Sollicitudo rei socialis,*" 41.

30. Caritas Internationalis, "A Caritas Internationalis Handbook for Reflection and Action," 52, http://www.caritas.org/upload/par/partnership.qxd1.pdf (accessed May 28, 2010).

31. Ibid.

32. Caritas General Assembly 2007 Special Bulletin.

33. Caritas Internationalis, "Emergency Guidelines: Principles, Structures & Mechanisms."

34. Mamoun Abuarqub and Isabel Phillips, "A Brief History of Humanitarianism in the Muslim World," July 2009, 3. Available at http://www.islamicrelief.com/Indepth/downloads/A Brief History of Humanitarianism in the Muslim World New Format.pdf (accessed August 24, 2009).

35. Abuarqub and Phillips, "Brief History," 3.

36. "IR Beliefs, Values and Code of Conduct," Birmingham: Islamic Relief Worldwide, 2008, http://www.islamic-relief.com/Indepth/downloads/IRs Beliefs, Values and Code of Conduct.pdf (accessed August 24, 2009).

37. Abuarqub and Phillips, "Brief History," 3.

38. Ibid., 5–8.

39. For a good overview on Islamic charitable practices, see Rianne C. ten Veen, "Charitable Giving in Islam," Birmingham: Islamic Relief Worldwide, 2009. http://www.islamic-relief.com/indepth/downloads/Translating faith into development.pdf (accessed June 6, 2010).

40. Abuarqub and Phillips, "Brief History," 3.

41. Khan, Tahmazov and Abuarqub, "Translating Faith into Development" (Birmingham: Islamic Relief Worldwide, 2009), 4; available at http://www.islamic-relief.com/indepth/downloads/Translating faith into development.pdf (accessed June 6, 2010).

42. Ten Veen, "Charitable Giving in Islam," 3. For a good overview of the relationship between charitable giving and social justice in Islam, see also Khan, Tahmazov, and Abuarqub, "Translating Faith into Development."

43. Amy Singer, *Charity in Islamic Societies* (Cambridge: Cambridge University Press, 2008), 218.

44. Islamic Relief, "When Sacrifice 'Meats' Hunger," May 19, 2010, http://www.islamic-relief.com/NewsRoom/4-289-when-sacrifice-meats-hunger.aspx (accessed June 6, 2010).

45. Email exchange with Ajaz Ahmed Khan, Islamic Relief Worldwide, Birmingham, October 19, 2009. See also Ajaz Ahmed Khan and Isabel Phillips, "The Influence of Faith on Islamic Microfinance Programs," Islamic Relief Worldwide, 2010, http://www.islamic-relief.com/Indepth/downloads/The influence of faith on Islamic microfinance programmes.pdf (accessed June 6, 2010).

46. See http://www.islamic-relief.com/Zakat/calculator.aspx (accessed December 17, 2011).

47. De Cordier, "Faith-Based Aid," 612.

48. Barnett and Stein, interview with Shagufta Yaqub, Islamic Relief, London, January 14, 2009.

49. Barnett and Stein, interview with Ajaz Ahmed Khan, Islamic Relief, London, January 14, 2009.

50. Email exchange with Ahmed Khan, October 19, 2009.

51. Barnett and Stein, interview with Ismayil Tahmazov, Islamic Relief, London, January 14, 2009.

52. Barnett and Stein, interview with Ahmed Khan.

53. Ibid.

54. Email exchange with Ahmed Khan.

55. Barnett and Stein, interview with Haroun Atallah, Islamic Relief, London, January 14, 2009.

56. Barnett and Stein, interview with Ahmed Khan.

57. De Cordier, "Faith-Based Aid," 610.

58. Email exchange with Ahmed Khan.

59. Barnett and Stein, interview with Ahmed Khan.

60. Islamic Relief Annual Report 2007, http://www.islamic-relief.com/WhoWeAre/Files/AnnualReportandFS2007_a.pdf (accessed August 24, 2009).

61. "IR Beliefs, Values and Code of Conduct," Birmingham: Islamic Relief Worldwide, 2008: 6, http://www.islamic-relief.com/Indepth/downloads/IRs%20Beliefs,%20Values%20and%20Code%20of%20Conduct.pdf (accessed August 24, 2009).

62. Bruno de Cordier observes: "[Islamic Relief combines] an Islamic identity, references and values with professional modes of operation, communication and fundraising that are traditionally associated with 'Western' aid agencies" ("Faith-Based Aid," 610).

63. See Thomas Weiss, "Principles, Politics, and Humanitarian Action," *Ethics and International Affairs* 13 (1999).

64. See "MSF: About US: History and Principles." http://www.doctorswithoutborders.org/aboutus/?ref=main-menu (accessed December 17, 2011); "Advocacy and témoignage." http://www.msf.org.uk/advocacy.aspx (accessed December 17, 2011).

65. "MSF's Principles and Identity—The Challenges Ahead." http://www.doctorswithoutborders.org/publications/ar/report.cfm?id=3251 (accessed December 17, 2011).

66. "It is plain that business interests or religious, ethnic and ideological solidarity cannot ever be called humanitarian." Jean François, ed. *Populations in Danger* (London: John Libbey, 1992), 7. See the 2005 La Mancha Agreement, http://www.msf.dk/OmMSF/Hvemervi/LaMancha-aftalen/ (accessed May 10, 2010).

67. See ECHO, "The Humanitarian Space Under Siege"; Jean François, ed. *Populations in Danger* (London: John Libbey, 1992), 7.

68. Nobel lecture by James Orbinski, http://nobelprize.org/nobel_prizes/peace/laureates/1999/msf-lecture.html (accessed August 24, 2009).

69. "MSF's Principles and Identity—The Challenges Ahead."

70. Rony Brauman, "Humanitarian Aid," October 1996, CRASH Papers; available online at http://www.msf-crash.org/drive/ad96-rb-1996-humanitarian-aid-_uk-p.10_.pdf

(accessed May 19, 2010). Stephen Hopgood has similarly observed, "It seems that humanitarianism is about solidarity with suffering, rather than a simple meeting of needs." "Saying 'No' to Wal-Mart?," 113.

71. See "MSF: About Us: History and Principles."

72. Françoise Bouchet-Saulnier, "Between Humanitarian Law and Principles: The Principles and Practice of 'Rebellious Humanitarianism,'" http://www.msf.fr/ sites/www.msf.fr/files/2000-06-01-SaulnierVA.pdf (accessed December 17, 2011).

73. See "MSF's Principles and Identity."

74. D. Robert Dechaine, "Humanitarian Space and the Social Imaginary: Médecins Sans Frontières/Doctors Without Borders and the Rhetoric of Global Community," *Journal of Communication Inquiry* (2002): 363.

75. There are those within the organization who believe that more public forms of *témoignage* are a distraction from the medical functions of the organization, or that it moves MSF too much in the direction of human rights advocacy organizations. Yet *témoignage* remains fundamental to even the minimalists within the organization, who believe that the individual act of providing medical assistance is an act of bearing witness and thus of human solidarity.

76. François, *Populations in Danger*, 7–8.

77. MSF Financial Report 2008, www.msf.org/source/financial/2008/MSF_Financial_Report_2008.pdf (accessed December 17, 2011).

78. See Antonio Donini, "Afghanistan: Humanitarianism Under Threat"; Tony Sheldon, "Bearing Witness," *BMJ*, Volume 328, February 20, 2004; Fabrice Weissman, "NATO and the NGOs: Honeymoon Over," Fondation CRASH, May 4, 2010, http://www.msf-crash.org/en/sur-le-vif/2010/05/04/355/nato-and-the-ngos-honeymoon-over/ (accessed July 6, 2010).

79. Michel Hoffman and Sophie Delaunay, "Afghanistan: A Return to Humanitarian Action," March 12, 2010, http://www.doctorswithoutborders.org/publications/ article.cfm?id=4311&cat=special-report (accessed December 17, 2011).

80. Xavier Crombé, "Independence and Security," CRASH website, December 2006, http://www.msf-crash.org/drive/db8f-xc-2006-independence-and-security-_ uk-transcript_-p.8.pdf (accessed May 20, 2010).

81. Hoffman and Delaunay, "Afghanistan: A Return to Humanitarian Action." See also Jerome Oberreit, "Speaking Notes for Presentation to CIMIC and Reconstruction Operations 2010, May 20th, London," internal MSF document.

82. Captier, "MSF's Principles and Identity."

83. Dechaine, "Humanitarian Space and the Social Imaginary," 362–363.

84. Oberreit, "Speaking Notes."

85. Dechaine, "Humanitarian Space and the Social Imaginary," 363.

86. Taylor, *Secular Age*, 678, 677.

87. Nobel lecture by Orbinski.

88. Oxfam International, "History of Oxfam International," http://www.oxfam.org/ en/about/history (accessed August 11, 2010).

89. Oxfam International, "Oxfam's Commitment to Human Rights," http://www.oxfam.org/en/about/why (accessed August 11, 2010).

90. Oxfam International, "Demanding Justice: Oxfam International Strategic Plan, 2007–2012," http://www.oxfam.org/en/about/accountability/strategic-plan (accessed August 11, 2010).

91. Oxfam International, "Issues We Work On," http://www.oxfam.org/en/about/issues (accessed August 11, 2010).

92. See Oxfam International, "Oxfam International's Mission Statement," http://www.oxfam.org/en/about/what/mission (accessed August 11, 2010).

93. This was also the case for the two years previous: approximately 37 percent was spent on issues related to "life and security" in 2007, and in 2006 the figure was roughly 44 percent of annual expenditure. See Oxfam's Annual Reports for 2006 and 2007, http://www.oxfam.org/en/about/annual-reports.

94. Oxfam International, "Oxfam's Commitment to Human Rights," http://www.oxfam.org/en/about/why (accessed August 11, 2010); see also Oxfam International, "Climate Wrongs and Human Rights: Putting People at the Heart of Climate-Change Policy," Oxfam Briefing Paper 117, September 8, 2008, http://www.oxfam.org/en/policy/bp117-climate-wrongs-and-human-rights (accessed November 24, 2010): "Oxfam International believes that realising human rights is essential to lift people out of poverty and injustice."

95. Oxfam International, "In the Public Interest: Health, Education, and Water and Sanitation for All," September 1, 2006, http://www.oxfam.org/en/policy/in-the-public-interest (accessed November 24, 2010); "Climate Wrongs and Human Rights."

96. Oxfam International, "The Right to Survive: The Humanitarian Challenge for the Twenty-First Century," April 20, 2009: 17, http://www.oxfam.org/en/policy/right-to-survive-report (accessed November 24, 2010).

97. Ibid., 77–79.

98. In their report, Oxfam's external evaluators questioned the organization's ability to be neutral in some circumstances and partial in others: "Can OI be partial in its development work and neutral in its emergency response?" Oxfam International "Promises to Keep," February 2006: 78, http://www.oxfam.org/en/about/accountability/promises (accessed November 22, 2010);

99. See Hopgood, "Moral Authority, Modernity, and the Politics of the Sacred."

100. "Oxfam International's Mission Statement."

101. Oxfam International, "Accountability," http://www.oxfam.org/en/about/accountability (accessed November 24, 2010).

102. "Promises to Keep," February 2006.

103. Oxfam International, "OI Response to Promises to Keep," December 2006, http://www.oxfam.org/en/about/accountability/promises (accessed November 24, 2010).

104. Oxfam International, "Oxfam International Board Accountability Policies," http://www.oxfam.org/en/about/accountability (accessed November 24, 2010). See financial reports at "Accountability." http://www.oxfam.org/en/about/accountability (accessed November 24, 2010).

105. MSF was a participant in the initial phase of the SPHERE Project but later withdrew from the project: "The Executive Committee of MSF, at a meeting on October 11, 2002, decided that MSF will not be involved with Sphere because MSF believes that that answer to the problem Sphere tries to tackle is political and not technical." Quoted in Jacqui Tong, "Questionable Accountability: MSF and Sphere in 2003," *Disasters* 28, 2 (2004): 186.

106. Janice Gross Stein, "Humanitarian Organizations: Accountable—Why, to Whom, for What, and How?" in Barnett and Weiss, *Humanitarianism in Question*.

107. We are grateful to Cecilia Lynch for this helpful point of clarification.

108. Barnett and Stein, interview with Willem van Eekelen, Islamic Relief, London, January 14, 2009.

109. Laura Thaut, Janice Gross Stein, and Michael Barnett, "In Defense of Virtue: Credibility, Legitimacy Dilemmas, and the Case of Islamic Relief," in Peter Gourevitch, David Lake, and Janice Gross Stein, eds., *Credibility and Non-Governmental Organizations in a Globalizing World* (Cambridge: Cambridge University Press, 2012).

110. "Our freedom of action . . . is the product of an on-going process of transactions with local authorities and the stakeholders that influence their decisions." Fabrice Weissman, "Book Proposal: Humanitarian Policies of Compromise," internal MSF document, January 22, 2010.

Contributors

Michael Barnett is University Professor of International Affairs and Political Science at the George Washington University. His most recent book is *Empire of Humanity: A History of Humanitarianism*.

Jonathan Benthall is Honorary Research Fellow in the Department of Anthropology, University College London. He has published widely in the fields of the sociology of religion and humanitarianism. His most recent books are *The Charitable Crescent: Politics of Aid in the Muslim World* (with J. Bellion-Jourdan) and *Returning to Religion: Why a Secular Age Is Haunted by Faith*.

Erica Bornstein is Associate Professor of Anthropology at the University of Wisconsin-Milwaukee. Her books include *Disquieting Gifts: Humanitarianism in New Delhi* and *The Spirit of Development: Protestant NGOs, Morality, and Economics in Zimbabwe*. She is co-editor (with Peter Redfield) of *Forces of Compassion: Humanitarianism Between Ethics and Politics* and has published articles in *American Ethnologist, Cultural Anthropology, Ethnos, Political and Legal Anthropology Review (PoLAR)*, and the *Journal of Religion in Africa*.

Stephen Hopgood is Reader in International Relations at the School of Oriental and African Studies, University of London, and Co-Director of the Centre for the International Politics of Conflict, Rights and Justice (CCRJ) at SOAS. His publications include *Keepers of the Flame: Understanding Amnesty International*; "Saying 'No' to Wal-Mart? Money and Morality in Professional Humanitarianism," a chapter in Michael Barnett and Thomas G Weiss (eds.), *Humanitarianism in Question: Politics, Power, Ethics*; and "Moral Authority, Modernity and the Politics of the Sacred," *European Journal of International Relations* 15(2) (2009). He is currently the holder of a Leverhulme Major Research Fellowship under the title "Empire of the International."

Ajaz Ahmed Khan is an agricultural economist and currently works as Microfinance Advisor with CARE International. He was previously with Islamic Relief. He spent many years living and working overseas in Latin America, Asia and Africa and has written about microfinance, Islamic microfinance in particular, as well as Muslim faith based organisations and Islamic perspectives on development.

Henry Louis, a former researcher at the Feinstein International Center, works in the areas of international development and humanitarianism.

Dyan Mazurana is Associate Research Professor at the Feinstein International Center at Tufts University.

Andrea Paras recently completed her Ph.D. at the University of Toronto and is now on the faculty at the Women's University of Bangladesh.

George Scarlett is a Senior Lecturer at the Eliot-Pearson Department of Child Development at Tufts University.

Janice Gross Stein is the Belzberg Professor of Conflict Management in the Department of Political Science and the Director of the Munk School for Global Affairs at the University of Toronto. She is the coauthor, with Eugene Lang, of the prize-winning *The Unexpected War: Canada in Kandahar*; and co-editor, with Peter Gourevitch and David Lake, of *Credibility and Non-Governmental Organizations in a Globalizing World*. Her most recent book is *Diplomacy in the Digital Age*.

Bertrand Taithe is Professor of Cultural History at the University of Manchester, where he also is a director of the Humanitarian and Conflict Response Institute (www.hcri.ac.uk) and edits the *European Review of History–Revue européenne d'histoire* and book series for Manchester University Press. He has published widely on war and medicine, humanitarianism and missionaries, including *Defeated Flesh*; *Citizenship and Wars*; *The Killer Trail*; and *Evil, Barbarism and Empire* (eds. T. Crook, R. Gill, B. Taithe). He is currently working on a monograph on the history of humanitarian technologies.

Leslie Vinjamuri teaches at the School of Oriental and African Studies, where she co-directs the Center for Conflict and the Centre for the International Politics of Conflict, Rights and Justice. Her articles have appeared in leading journals, including *International Security, Ethics and International Affairs, Survival*, and the *Annual Review of Political Science*.

Amy Warren is Research Associate at the Institute for Applied Research in Youth Development at Tufts University.

Peter Walker is Director of the Feinstein International Center, an institute of Tufts University's Friedman School of Nutrition Science and Policy. In addition to his ongoing consultation work, he previously worked for the International Federation of Red Cross and Red Crescent Societies and Oxfam International. He has published widely on humanitarianism, including, with David Maxwell, *The Shape of the Humanitarian System*.

Index